# The Rational Believer

# The Rational Believer

## Choices and Decisions in the Madrasas of Pakistan

**Masooda Bano**

CORNELL UNIVERSITY PRESS ITHACA AND LONDON

FOUNDATION® BOOKS

Delhi • Bengaluru • Mumbai • Kolkata • Chennai • Hyderabad
Pune • Thiruvananthapuram

Published by
**Cambridge University Press India Pvt. Ltd.**
under the imprint of Foundation Books
Cambridge House, 4381/4 Ansari Road, Daryaganj, **New Delhi** 110 002

**Cambridge University Press India Pvt. Ltd.**
C-22, C-Block, Brigade M.M., K.R. Road, Jayanagar, **Bengaluru** 560 070
Plot No. 80, Service Industries, Shirvane, Sector-1, Nerul, **Navi Mumbai** 400 706
10 Raja Subodh Mullick Square, 2nd Floor, **Kolkata** 700 013
21/1 (New No. 49), 1st Floor, Model School Road, Thousand Lights, **Chennai** 600 006
House No. 3-5-874/6/4, (Near Apollo Hospital), Hyderguda, **Hyderabad** 500 029
Agarwal Pride, 'A' Wing, 1308 Kasba Peth, Near Surya Hospital, **Pune** 411 011
T.C. 25/ 2731 Lukes Lane, Ambujavilasam Road, **Thiruvananthapuram** 695 001



This edition has been published by Cambridge University Press India Pvt. Ltd. by arrangement with Cornell University Press.

First South Asia Edition 2013

ISBN 978-93-82264-88-0

Published by Manas Saikia for Cambridge University Press India Pvt. Ltd.

Printed at Bhavish Graphics, Chennai

# Contents

*To Ammi for her remarkable strength and affection*

# Acknowledgments

There are many organizations and individuals to whom I have acquired an enormous debt during the process of preparing this manuscript. My first debt is to the Economic and Social Research Council (ESRC), which funded me generously over a period of five years. The Arts and Humanities Research Council (AHRC) and the UK Department of International Development (DFID) also supported different aspects of the research that informs this manuscript. My second debt is to Oxford University, which has been a home for the last ten years. Its charming surroundings have been a perfect base for pursuing my research undisturbed, while having the luxury to indulge in discussions with great minds when in the mood for an exchange of ideas.

My intellectual debts are many. For intellectual inspiration I owe most to the work of Douglass North. Only those who are convinced of the power of empirically led theory can appreciate the excitement of a researcher who finds patterns emerging from the field meeting with consistent support in the work of a theorist. I was fortunate to experience that excitement. At Oxford University, the seminar on sociological theory with Diego Gambetta at All Souls College engaged my interest in exploring the rationality of apparently irrational behavior. At Wolfson College, with which I have been associated since 2006, a number of past and present Fellows have given generously of their time by contributing advice. I would particularly like to note Nick Allen, Marcus Banks, Anne Deighton, Denis Galligan, David Gellner, and Marc Van De Mieroop. Over the years, they have given encouragement and invaluable advice on matters both professional and personal. At Oxford University's Department of International Development, Dawn Chatty, Xiaolan Fu, Raufu Mustapha, and Laura Rival have been very supportive colleagues and mentors. Above all, Adrian Wood always gave the wisest advice. A six-monthly review session with him always helped keep me on track. For those who enjoy chapter two, the idea for this comparative analysis was his—though any inadequacies of the analysis are mine.

Outside Oxford, I would in particular like to thank David Lewis and Mick Moore whose appreciation of my work has been most encouraging. I am also greatly indebted to two reviewers who provided extremely useful comments that helped refine the manuscript. I was also extremely fortunate to work with an editor who himself read the text: Roger Haydon read many versions of the chapters and every time could find something to improve—and the problem was that he was always right. This meant more work, but it definitely refined the final piece. Irina Burns, my copyeditor, and Karen Laun, senior production editor at Cornell University Press, both provided excellent support.

There are many people whose support was critical during my fieldwork. I would like to acknowledge Bushra Waseem, who accompanied me on most of the field visits. I am also greatly indebted to senior officials of the five madrasa boards in Pakistan whose support for the project was central to securing access to a large number of madrasas. In particular, I would like to acknowledge the late Dr. Sarfaraz Naeemi from the Barelvi school of thought, who at the time of my fieldwork was leading the coalition body formed by the five boards and played an instrumental role in securing me access. Yasin Zafar at Jamia Salafia (Ahl-i-Hadith), Mr. Shahani and Maulana Najfi at Jamia Al-Muntazir (Ahl-i-Shia), Maulana Hanif Jalandari from Wafaq ul Madaris Al-Arabia (Deobandi), and Maulana Abdul Malik from Jamaat-i-Islami were constant reference points during the course of the fieldwork. The project would not have been possible without the openness of families that allowed me into their homes to understand their complex choices, and the students, teachers, and ‘ulama in the male and female madrasas who entertained my never-ending questions with great patience.

And then there have been those dear friends and family members who have been a constant source of emotional, moral, and intellectual support. Abigail Barr, Leah Bassel, Pam Clemit, Radhika Gupta, Adeel Malik and his wife Farah, Professor Talib, Massimo Rosati, Emma Samman, and Devi Sridhar have provided wonderful company and support. Leah and Emma in particular have also been great sources of intellectual and moral support, not to mention their great editorial help at times of crisis. Massimo was the first one to read the whole draft and Devi was always the first one to call whenever I was back from a fieldtrip.

However, none of this would have been possible without the love and support of my family. To Ammi I owe the most important reassurance: a home to go back to. Bahi, Sadia Appa, Appi, Mona, their partners and their children bring that much-needed color to life, just as Amna adds so much to life by being that loving though equally demanding younger sister. She has also been a great companion on many of my field visits. And, Noreen Khala has always helped put things in perspective. This strong support base has been central to sustaining the energy demanded of a project as ambitious as this.

# A Note on Transliteration and Spelling

Because this book is likely to draw readership from different disciplines, transliteration of Arabic and Urdu words has been kept simple. With the exception of the ‘ to indicate the Arabic and Urdu letters ‘*ayn* and ’*hamza,* diacritical marks have not been used. Except for the word ‘ulama, the plural form of Arabic or Urdu words is indicated by addition of an s to the singular form. To avoid strain on the eyes and minimize disruptions while reading, words that are frequently repeated (e.g., madrasa) are not italicized. Other non-English words are italicized only at their first occurrence. Non-English words used only once in the text are not included in the glossary.

# Glossary

| | |
|---|---|
| Akhlaqiat | Moral behavior |
| 'Alim | Learned man, religious scholar; Senior Secondary degree in 'Aliya madrasas, Bangladesh |
| 'Aliya | Bachelor's degree in madrasas, Pakistan |
| 'Alimiya | Master's level religious education in madrasas in Pakistan. This is the final category in the teaching of Dars-i-Nizami. It is also called Daura-i-Hadith. It results in the degree of Shahadat-ul-'Alimiya Fil 'Uloom-il-'Arabia-wal-Islami, awarded by the five state-recognized wafaqs. It is equated with an MA in Arabic and Islamic Studies by the Higher Education Commission, Pakistan. The primary to bachelor degrees awarded by the wafaqs, however, are not equated with degrees awarded in the formal (secular) education system |
| 'Aliya madrasas | Reformed (state-supported) madrasas, Bangladesh |
| 'Asar | Afternoon prayer |
| Ashraf | Honorable, respectable people |
| Burqa | Long dress with facial covering used by Muslim women |
| Dakhil | Secondary (6–10 grades) in 'Aliya madrasas, Bangladesh |
| Dars | Lesson |
| Dars-i-Nizami | Islamic curriculum developed by Mullah Nizam-ud-Din of Farangi Mahall in the early eighteenth century and taught in Pakistani madrasas to date. |
| Du'a | Prayer |
| Fatwa | A legal opinion issued by a Mufti (jurisconsult) |
| Fazil | Bachelors (13–14 grades) in 'Aliya madrasas, Bangladesh |
| Fiqh | The technical term for the science of Islamic jurisprudence |
| Hadith | Sayings of Prophet Muhammad |
| Hafiz/Hafiz-i-Quran | One who has memorized the Quran |
| Hifz | Process of memorizing Quran |
| Hajj | The annual pilgrimage to Mecca |
| Hijab | Headscarf used by Muslim women |
| Ibtida'iya | Primary (1–5 grades) in 'Aliya and Qaumi madrasas in Bangladesh and also in madrasas in Pakistan |
| Ijaza | Certificate |
| Ijtihad | Systematic reflection on the foundational sources of the law to arrive at legal rulings on matters not already or explicitly determined by Islamic law |
| Imam | Leader or head of the community; prayer leader at the mosque |
| 'Isha' | Night prayer |
| 'Iqra' | Read |
| Istikhara | Special prayer to seek direction |
| Jihad | Struggle, including armed struggle against non-believers |
| Jihadist | One who joins jihad |

| | |
|---|---|
| Jilbab | Long dress worn by Muslim women |
| Kamil | Master's level (15–16 grades) in 'Aliya madrasa, Bangladesh |
| Kharzi madrasas | Generic name for traditional madrasas in West Bengal, India |
| Khasa | Senior secondary level of religious education in madrasas in Pakistan |
| Kheerat | Religious alms |
| Khutba | Sermon |
| Madrasa | Institution for higher Islamic learning |
| Manqulat | The "revealed" or "transmitted sciences" |
| Ma'qulat | The Islamic rational sciences |
| Maulvi/Maulvi Sahib | Generic term for Islamic scholar, prayer leader or preacher |
| Mujahedeen | Those waging jihad |
| Mujtahid | One qualified to undertake the effort to form an opinion in Islamic law |
| Maktab | Quranic schools |
| Nafs | Negative self; ego |
| Namaz | Daily five prayers |
| Neeyat | Intention |
| Niqab | Facial covering |
| Pardah | To cover; also refers to gender-based segregation |
| Qalb | Heart |
| Qasbat (Qasba singular) | Small towns |
| Qaumi madrasas | Generic name for traditional madrasas in Bangladesh |
| Qira'at | Vocalization of Quranic text |
| Radd | A process of scholarly refutation of arguments by 'ulama of different schools of Islamic thought |
| Ramadan | The month of fasting |
| Roza | Fast |
| Ruh | Spirit |
| Sadaqa | Religious alms |
| Sadaqa-i-Jariya | Permanent alms |
| Sakoon | Inner peace |
| Shari'a | The law of Islam based on Quran and Hadiths |
| Shirk | Associating partners with God |
| Sufi | Muslim mystic |
| Sunna | Practice of Prophet Mohammad |
| Tajweed | Pronunciation of Quran |
| Takhassus | Specialization |
| Takreeri | Debating |
| Taraweeh | Special night prayer in Ramadan |
| Tauheed | Belief in oneness of God |
| 'Ulama ('alim singular) | Religious scholars |
| 'Umrah | Optional pilgrimage to Mecca |
| Wafaq | Central madrasa board |
| Waqf | Religious endowment |
| Zakat | Islamic alms—tax paid annually on one's accumulated wealth |
| Zuhur | Mid-day prayer |

# THE RATIONAL BELIEVER

1

# RELIGION AND REASON

## A New Institutionalist Perspective

> **Economists usually assert that institutional dynamics reflect optimal responses of decision makers to current and expected conditions. Social scientists working in other disciplines and historians, however, assert that institutional dynamics reflect the shackles of history. Each side of this debate captures a potentially important aspect of reality, but neither is satisfactory by itself.**
>
> —Avner Greif, *Institutions and the Path to the Modern Economy* (2006: xv)

> **Untruth naturally afflicts historical information. There are various reasons that make this unavoidable. One of them is partisanship for opinions and schools. . . . Another reason is unfounded assumption as to the truth of a thing. This is frequent. It results mostly from reliance upon transmitters. Another reason is ignorance of how conditions conform with reality. Conditions are affected by ambiguities and artificial distortions. The informant reports the conditions as he saw them, but on account of artificial distortions he himself has no true picture of them.**
>
> —Ibn-Khaldun, *The Muqaddimah: An Introduction to History* (1967: 35)

For twenty-five years, the Red Mosque amiably carried out its routine religious functions in the densely populated neighborhood of Aabpara—with its congested residential area, thriving commercial market, and bustling central bus station. As the central mosque of Pakistan's capital city, Islamabad, its Friday prayers were heavily attended by local traders, travelers, and government officials; its Quranic education classes were crowded with local children; and its female madrasa (Islamic school) boasted a student population of some 3,000. The Red Mosque acquired national repute; its imam was nominated to many government committees; and, during those years, it epitomized all that it means to be a "good mosque."

Beginning in January 2007, however, priorities at the mosque underwent what looked like an almost complete reversal, with the ʿulama (Islamic scholars) and students abandoning religious education in favor of an armed struggle to impose Shariʿa (Islamic law). The students of Jamia Hafsa, the female madrasa attached to the mosque, took over a public library and later held a brothel-owner hostage while preaching at her to quit the profession; students from Jamia Fareedia, the male madrasa, visited movie rental stores in the neighborhood advising the owners to abandon their profession as it promoted vulgarity. A two-day national conference held at the mosque in April 2007 led to the establishment of a Shari'a Court, set up to rival the state judicial system and the two 'ulama leading the resistance repeatedly rebuffed government ultimatums threatening serious consequences. When the state finally initiated military action on 3 July 2007, the resistance, however, lasted for fewer than ten days during which well over a hundred students were killed, along with one of the 'ulama leading the resistance. The police took the surviving 'alim, his family, and some of the male students into custody.

To the outsider—not just to a secular Western observer but also to the largely believing Pakistani public—the behavior of the actors at the Red Mosque was so puzzling that many shrugged it off as cult-like behavior resulting from religious indoctrination: a process of religious exploitation where students from deprived socioeconomic backgrounds were misguided into laying down their lives for the promise of "seventy-two black-eyed virgins." Many members of the public also attributed vested interests to the 'ulama who led the resistance. A closer examination of the recent history of the Red Mosque, however, reveals the limitations of such quick judgments, and highlights the importance of addressing three critical questions if Islamic militancy is to be properly understood.

First, what made the 'ulama and the students adopt such apparently irrational preferences, advocating disengagement with modernity and calling for the replacement of civil law—designed to meet the needs of modern life, with Shari'a—crafted primarily between the eighth and eleventh centuries? Second, what factors led them to make such flawed "means–end" calculations? The 'alim and students were not on a suicide mission: they wanted to live, and they expressed this wish repeatedly while under siege. Yet they calculated that armed resistance was a feasible strategy despite clear signs that they could not match the state in numbers or resources. Third, and perhaps most important, how does one explain the dramatic reversal of preferences within the Red Mosque? The dominant assumption today—that the Red Mosque episode (like much militant Islam) was the result of religious indoctrination in the context of deprivation—seems flawed in the light of how suddenly the preferences of 'ulama and students shifted. For twenty-five years the 'ulama had exemplified good religious behavior; yet one day they rejected it in favor of an apparently futile armed struggle. Attributing this shift to religious indoctrination is too easy a way out of a complex puzzle that is worthy of deeper engagement. Even if the episode itself was the result of indoctrination, we still need a better explanation of the factors that make individuals susceptible to indoctrination.

Precisely the same sorts of questions and issues arise regarding acts of global Islamic militancy. The actions of militant Islamic groups not only contribute to insecurity of life, high economic costs, and the curtailment of civil liberties in the West (Doumani 2006); they also make life difficult for moderate Muslims, who now find their access to the Western world further restricted.[1] From a normative standard of efficiency, in their desire to impose an Islamic way of life on others, these groups manifest an irrational preference; moreover, their assumptions regarding the suitability of the means adopted to attain their ends appear to be faulty. What is it that convinces al-Qaida members to target civilians in the name of Islam? What convinces them of their leaders' predictions that the demise of the world's leading power, the United States of America, will be brought about through isolated acts of militancy? How is one able, moreover, to account for the dramatic transformation within Islam itself? At one time associated with the production of the finest scholarship and a steady source of inspiration for Western learning,[2] Islam is now widely identified with destructive militant tendencies. To answer these complex questions through reference to socioeconomic deprivation and religious indoctrination alone is unconvincing.

This volume proposes answers to these three critical questions by developing a detailed account of the decision-making processes of the religious actor, with a focus on the madrasas of Pakistan—often regarded as an important recruiting ground for Islamic militants.[3] I show that viewing the religious actor as primarily driven by irrational impulse—a position often adopted to account not only for extreme cases of religious fundamentalism but also for routine religious acts involving material sacrifice—represents a normative judgment, not actual reality. Rather than assume that the religious actor passively imbibes religious values, I develop a theory of the religious actor that accounts for why forward-looking, rational individuals opt to be believers. Such an approach no longer takes religious institutions as a given; rather, it explains their existence as the outcome of individual actors' strategies and choices (Coleman 1990). Based on an empirical study of the madrasas of Pakistan, this book attempts to elaborate why and how religion attracts followers, as well as how and why religion is shaped by the choices and strategies of these very followers.

1. Since 2001, male Muslims, including students admitted to prestigious Western universities, have faced increased difficulties in securing entry visas (Nasulgc and O'Briant 2002).

2. For a review of Islam's contribution to modern science, see Saliba (1994, 2007); for broader contributions to Western civilization, see Makdisi (1981) and Robinson (2001a).

3. Madrasas in the tribal belt of Pakistan have been the target of U.S. military strikes; and it is argued that two of the 7/7 bombers received training in Pakistani madrasas (Plett 2006).

## Madrasas and Jihad in Pakistan

The madrasa system gradually evolved in South Asia starting from the twelfth century, but came to international attention mainly after 11 September 2001. Many of the senior Taliban leaders who were providing protection to Osama bin Laden had been educated in the madrasas of Pakistan (Rashid 2001). Since then, many influential American and European think tanks have identified madrasas as bases for the recruitment of Islamic militants (ICG 2002; Singer 2001). In the popular media, madrasas are accused of promoting religious fanaticism and sectarian violence within Pakistan, and of "breeding terrorists" for international Islamic jihad.[4] However, prior to the Red Mosque incident, these claims drew primarily on anecdotal evidence and interviews with a few individuals related to the madrasa network (ICG 2002; Singer 2001).

The events at the Red Mosque were the first clear case of 'ulama and students within a Pakistani madrasa taking up arms in opposition to the state. The resistance movement—which lasted six months, from January to July 2007—emerged suddenly, expanded rapidly, and elicited divided reactions from the Pakistani public. Despite its apparent irrationality, the resistance was not universally condemned, and in fact many members of the public from the immediate neighborhood as well as from other cities came to support the besieged madrasa leadership. But not all Muslims supported it: liberal feminist and human rights groups within Pakistan, as well as political parties with a liberal orientation, staged nationwide rallies against the movement and called upon the state to take strong action. Once the state launched the military operation, public reaction was equally mixed.

Many liberals approved of the military operation, despite the deaths it caused. Ordinary members of the public, though refraining from any direct action themselves, found the operation too violent: media reports suggested that although only a minority defended the Red Mosque 'ulama, the majority found the use of force excessive. There was a third category, however: those who had lost sons, daughters, siblings, or friends in the operation and who promised to avenge the death of their loved ones. I experienced firsthand the Red Mosque resistance and the complex societal response it generated, because when the incident broke out I was seven months into fieldwork. The Red Mosque naturally became an important field site for me, and remained so in my follow-up visits in 2009 and 2010. By the time of my visit in March 2010, twenty-five new branches of Jamia Hafsa

4. Headlines of the two articles—"British Businesses Are Funding Schools That Breed Terror" (*Times*, 10 August 2002) and "Inside Jihad University: The Education of a Holy Warrior" (*New York Times Magazine*, 25 June 2000)—give a taste of such perceptions.

had opened across Pakistan, some of which I visited, and many more communities were asking Umme Hassan, the wife of the Imam of the Red Mosque, to open a branch in their area. In addition, the markets contained a rich collection of recordings of songs and speeches, as well as books and brochures valorizing the *shuhada* (martyrs) of the Red Mosque. The owner of one Islamic bookstore that I routinely visit in Rawalpindi to collect recent Islamic literature reported the availability of a hundred book titles related to the Red Mosque—almost all eulogizing the resistance fighters.

The crushing of the Red Mosque resistance gave rise to another madrasa-based armed resistance movement in the Swat Valley, where a local ʿalim, Maulana Fazlullah, raised an army of 2,000 *shaheen* (eagle) fighters allegedly to avenge the Red Mosque operation. This resistance quickly spilled out of the madrasa and took on a greater dynamic, spreading across the valley to involve nonmadrasa groups. Little information is available yet regarding the connection of this wider movement with the Red Mosque. Prolonged military interventions were required before the government secured Swat valley. These two cases thus raise legitimate concerns about possible links between madrasas and jihad; however, the cases alone do not prove the existence of a direct connection, as there are 16,000 registered madrasas in Pakistan, the vast majority of which show no tendencies toward militancy. Rather than demonstrate a link between madrasas and jihad, the Red Mosque incident forcefully presents a real analytical challenge: namely, why an educational tradition, which at one time was associated with reasoning and debate (Robinson 1997; 2001b), would in recent times gravitate toward militancy.

In the absence of a coherent answer to this puzzle, Western governments have encouraged Pakistani officials to pursue a carrot-and-stick policy—a selective use of funding and drone attacks. In 2006 a U.S. drone attack on a madrasa in Bajour in the tribal belt of Pakistan killed eighty children, generating public outcry; meanwhile, madrasas have been offered financial incentives to change the content of their curriculum. In 2002, the U.S. government committed US$225 million to madrasa reform (Bano 2007b) with a focus on integrating modern subjects such as mathematics, English, and social sciences into the madrasa curriculum. However, the reform program failed to win much cooperation: by 2007, only 250 of 16,000 madrasas had accepted the reforms (Bano 2007b). In a press briefing held in April 2009, the Minister of Education announced the formal closure of the program, noting that Rs 5,759 million (US$71 million) provided by the U.S. government for reform programs could not be utilized.

These facts raise critical questions about madrasas, as well as about our understanding of them. Without empirically grounded analysis we are unable to answer key questions such as: How legitimate are the claims that madrasas are linked with militancy? What are the forces that lead parents and students to gravitate toward madrasas, despite their apparent lack of this-worldly relevance? What factors guarantee the existence of enough patrons to sustain this system, which in the dominant discourse is viewed as a serious concern for Pakistani society? What are the forces of change internal to this system, such as those that have led to the emergence of female madrasas since the 1970s? Answers to these questions can in turn help to advance our understanding of the basis of religious behavior.

## The Working of Beliefs: The Limitations of Existing Frameworks

Recent scholarship within the sociology of religion and the field of political Islam recognizes the limits of purely structuralist and rationalist theories in explaining religious behavior—because both approaches end up reducing religious action to instrumental reason (Bruce 1999; Euben 1999, Furseth and Repstad 2006). Religious action is primarily explained as a response to socioeconomic deprivation or religious indoctrination; the possible appeal of religious ideas themselves in creating or sustaining a demand for religion is rarely explored. Further, attempts to explain religious behavior as a result of interaction between these two domains of motivation are even rarer.

The very foundation of sociology rests on a conception of religion as an irrational force: the position that the working of human societies must be explained by natural—as opposed to supernatural—factors initiated a process that shifted religion out of the realm of the rational (Furseth and Repstad 2006).[5] The "secularization thesis" expected all societies to secularize as a result of modernity. Challenging the assumptions of religion being an irrational force, in the 1970s, a prominent group of American sociologists started to undertake empirically grounded studies of religious behavior, borrowing methods of analysis from economics in a bid to recast the believer as a rational actor.[6] These studies take as their point of departure the idea that agents are utility-maximizing and reasonably well-informed—as opposed to the conception of a passive agent adopted within the structural-functionalist tradition. Religion was now explained as a result of conscious cost–benefit calculations rather than of childhood socialization. Here, individuals were thought to value religion because it provides certain rewards—in terms of security against existential concerns and the human

5. For a review of the treatment of religion by the founding fathers of sociology, see Furseth and Repstad (2006).

6. For a review of these studies, see Stark and Finke (2000).

search for the meaning of life—for which, it was argued, there was a general and inexhaustible demand (Stark and Finke 2000). In advancing this position, analysts were drawing on theoretical works that expand the material conception of "utility" to accommodate other motives, including other-regarding behavior (Becker 1993).

Applied to the behavior of actors within the Red Mosque, rational choice theory would explain the decision of the ʿalim and the students to fight to the death as a result of conscious choice rather than indoctrination, assuming that their utility set had a higher preference for religious rather than material rewards. In this model, the actors were willing to incur the necessary cost to attain these religious rewards. Such an explanation attributes rationality to the religious actor but leaves important questions about preference formation unaddressed.[7] First, why did the ʿulama and students develop this extreme preference for religious rewards? Considering that even the exercise of routine religious practices could have secured for them the reward of heaven, why did they resort to extreme measures in order to maximize their religious utility? Second, given that the rational actor is assumed to constantly make cost–benefit calculations, why would such an actor give up the tangible benefits of this world for other-worldly rewards whose reality can never be rationally verified? Although an increasing number of studies within the sociology and anthropology of religion adjusts for both structural and intentional reasons for the operation of religion, we still lack any comprehensive framework that explains why religion impacts individual choices, why and how religions rise and change, and to what extent the nature of religious beliefs plays a role in ensuring their popular appeal.

If the literature within the sociology of religion fails to adequately address these critical questions about preference formation and the religious actor's means–end calculations, the literature in the field of political Islam[8] fares no better. Studies in both the structural-functionalist and the rationalist traditions explain Islamic fundamentalism, on the one hand, as a reflex reaction to political or socioeconomic deprivation—a reaction of the absolute poor to poverty, and of educated middle-class youth to the failure of governments to deliver on the promises of modernity and, on the other hand, as a process of religious indoctrination whereby religious texts are assumed to be absorbed without question, paying no attention to the process of belief formation. As Roy (2002) and Varisco

7. Arguing that subjective states are not knowable, rational choice theory takes preferences as given and focuses on "revealed preferences"—i.e., what individuals choose to pursue. This leaves the study of the processes of preference formation untouched (Bowles 2004).

8. The literature on political Islam, like that on the sociology of religion, has expanded steadily. See, for example, Esposito (1992), Roy (1995), Eickelman and Piscatori (1996), Wickham (2002), Krueger (2007), Tessler and Robbins (2007), Shafiq and Sinno (2010).

(2005) argue, such an approach reduces Islam to a theological corpus rather than studying it through engaging with the actual discourses or practices of Muslims—that is, as a lived experience. The consequence is that these macro-level accounts, on the one hand, reduce Muslims' gravitation toward radical ideas to facts about their material conditions and, on the other hand, turn to the Qur'an and the writings of prominent Islamists to find out why Islamic radicals act as they do; there is no space left, as Euben (1999: 25) argues, "to begin [the analysis] by attending to the inherent power of the ideas themselves" and to explore how these ideas are absorbed and translated at the individual level.

Admittedly, the application of rational choice theory to Islamic fundamentalism does recognize the intrinsic appeal of religious ideas, whereby if fundamentalists conceive of martyrdom as the price of salvation, even self-sacrifice can be construed as an expression of rational, self-interested behavior.[9] Once again, however, such an appeal is understood not in terms of the moral power of fundamentalist worldviews but in terms of the material conditions in which fundamentalists operate. Thus, just as in the sociology of religion, even when religion is considered to be intrinsically appealing, this appeal is believed to exist because of dire material conditions, and not because religious ideas themselves can have meaning. The result is that neither within the sociology of religion nor within the political Islam do we have studies that develop an empirically driven and theoretically consistent account of how belief systems operate. What is left after the correlations are established between the macro-level variables of the socioeconomic and political conditions of Muslim societies is a caricature of an "irrational rational actor": an actor apparently rational enough to "gravitate toward an ideology that is an effective and therefore appealing vehicle for essentially pathological reactionary sentiment" (Euben 1999: 22).

This book's account of the madrasa network in Pakistan is intended as a corrective to the image of the "irrational-rational actor" that today dominates the study of militant Islam. It shows that religious ideals indeed can influence individual and collective choices, but that in order to command adherence the given belief system must have moral or practical appeal for the believer. The 'ulama, the students, the parents, the patrons, and the jihadists with whom I engaged justified their commitment to Islam by referring to the moral or logical appeal of Islamic principle. More important, an analysis of their decisions showed that material conditions often did play an important role in leading many of them

---

9. Following rational choice assumptions, for Azzi and Ehrenberg (1975) religious participation is related to an afterlife consumption motive; for Iannacone (1995) religion offers commodities that are in high demand, such as assurance and security; and for Hechter (1987) it provides certain communities with insurance against the vagaries of nature and human relations.

toward religion: however, conviction developed only when the prescribed beliefs were repeatedly seen to help address the everyday realities of life. A study of religious behavior has to map not just the context but also the content of a given belief system to understand why forward-looking and utility-maximizing individuals might choose to be believers.

## New Institutional Economics and Religious Behavior

The rational actor operates (theoretically) in a world free of all constraints except those imposed by the budget set.[10] Alternatively, within the structural-functionalist framework, the actor is so confined by constraints that zero weight is given to his preferences, expectations, and decision-making mechanisms (Gambetta 1987). If these frameworks were to be applied to the madrasas in Pakistan, the structuralist analysis would explain their existence purely through economic deprivation, the rationalist as a result of the search for other-worldly rewards. Scholarship within the two fields has made impressive progress in moving away from these basic positions. Within structuralist theories the idea of agency is now well-developed, and within economics—especially development and information economics—much progress has been made in recognizing the role of information constraints in restricting maximizing behavior.

However, the most systematic attempt to bridge the two positions in the past thirty years is manifest within the field of New Institutional Economics (NIE)—a field of inquiry initially chalked out by economists, but now increasingly drawing contributions from all social sciences including politics, sociology, anthropology, and applied fields such as organizational studies. This middle-road approach absorbs recent advances in information and behavioral economics by recognizing the limits of human decision-making processes while retaining a focus on the forward-looking and maximizing behavior of the rational actor. It also recognizes the role of power in restricting attainment of optimal institutional outcomes, as recognized in Marxist and anthropological studies (Ensminger 1992). Thus, studying madrasas in Pakistan using the NIE framework allows us to record the functionalist as well as the ideational forces underpinning their popularity, while recognizing the possible role of domestic and global politics in the rise of militancy within some of them.

---

10. The budget set is the set of bundles of goods an agent can afford. This set is a function of the prices of goods and the agents' endowment.

Each chapter of this volume discusses a specific empirical puzzle about madrasas using analytical tools developed within NIE, paving the way to answer the three critical questions posed by the Red Mosque resistance. It is important first, however, to set out the main analytical tools being used.

First, within NIE, institutions are seen as "the rules of the game in a society, or more formally, [they] are the humanly devised constraints that shape human interaction" (North 1990: 3). In this way, institutions are not given or static; they result from the forward-looking behavior of individual actors and persist through time because they serve a definite purpose. The result is a two-way analysis: on the one hand, research within NIE aims to understand the role of institutions in shaping economic and political outcomes; on the other hand, it is concerned with understanding those factors that give rise to institutions and shape their evolution over time. Thus, NIE lends itself naturally to addressing the questions that are of interest to this volume: how religious beliefs come to command strict adherence and restrict the choices of the believer, but also how the given religious beliefs at any point in time are also open to change.

Second, the NIE literature draws a useful distinction between formal and informal institutions. Formal institutions are defined as rules and procedures that are created, communicated, and enforced within officially sanctioned channels (Helmke and Levitsky 2004); they include political (and judicial) rules, economic rules, and contracts. Informal institutions are taken to be socially shared rules, usually unwritten, that are created, communicated, and enforced outside officially sanctioned channels (Helmke and Levitsky 2004). They include norms, taboos, and traditions. Although the two share many features, informal institutions are thought to be "stickier"—they have a tenacious survival ability because, unlike formal institutions, they often become part of habitual behavior (North 1990; Williamson 2000). Religious belief, by virtue of restricting individual choices in light of divinely ordained rules that operate even in the absence of formal authority, constitutes an informal institution.

Third, NIE theory differs from standard rational choice theory in two crucial ways. Standard rational choice theory does not recognize any limitations to the information-gathering capacity of humans: agents are assumed to choose the best means to realize stable desires, acting on beliefs that are well-grounded in information that is the outcome of an optimal research process (Elster 1986; Gambetta 1987). Further, standard rational choice theory does not study preference formation; it is concerned only with preference maximization. Drawing on recent advances in informational and behavioral economics, NIE counters these assumptions, allowing that the actor's cognitive systems do not provide true models of the world about which they make choices, nor that the actor necessarily receives full information required to make optimal decisions (Bowles

2004; North 1990). Individual actors make choices based on subjectively derived models that differ from person to person, and the information the actors receive is so incomplete that in most cases these divergent models show no tendency to converge. Further, authors within this tradition argue that the motivations of the actor are more complicated (and preferences less stable) than is assumed in standard rational choice theory, as it is not just self-interest maximization that determines individual action, but also concern for others (Greif 2006). In many contexts, this generates self-imposed codes of behavior that constrain wealth-maximizing behavior (Bowles 2004; Ensminger 1992).

In making these adjustments, NIE overcomes many of the objections that critics have raised to standard rational choice theory—that it cannot account for altruistic behavior, that it cannot deal with asymmetries of power or changing preferences, that it cannot explain suboptimal or economically inefficient behavior, and that it ignores the development of institutional constraints that restrict the options individuals have (Ensminger 1992). Thus, as Greif puts it:

> Extending the scope of analysis to include the cultural, social, and organizational implies that the perspective developed here is *socioeconomic.* [note text] As is now common in economics, the perspective adapted here accepts that preferences and rationality are socially constructed, that social structures and meaning are important, and that the economy is an integral part of the society. (2006: 22)

With these adjustments we are better placed to examine why institutional beliefs led to apparently irrational preferences, whereby the ʻulama and students of the Red Mosque pursued disengagement with modernity and reversion to archaic rules, and why their means–end calculations were so flawed. We also stand to gain greater insight into the causes of the dramatic reversal of preferences within the Red Mosque. The work on causes of institutional change as well as those of path dependence within the NIE literature further makes this framework relevant to an analysis of the shifts within the working of madrasas and Islam and the entrapment of many Muslim societies in an apparently low development equilibrium.

This book explains why the notion of transaction costs resulting from incomplete information is important for understanding the demand for religion; how the strategic maximizing behavior (driven by pursuit of material and ideal rewards) of individual actors and organizations is significant in determining the direction of institutional change; and how path dependence, as a product of conscious choice, is central in ensuring stability. I pay special attention to identifying the incentives that motivate the religious actor; it is here that my research pushes the existing theoretical boundaries of NIE, suggesting that the standard assumption of utility-maximizing behavior needs to be adjusted not for multiple motivations, as some have argued, but rather for dual notions of utility: material and ideal. The notion of material utility rests on the human need for material achievement; that of ideal utility, on the pursuit of ideas. The constant struggle between material and ideal utility is central to the rationality of religious behavior.

## Studying "Players in the Field" to Understand the "Rules of the Game"

A central feature of North's (1990, 1995) approach is the distinction he draws between institutions, which provide the "rules of the game," and organizations, which are "players in the field." Institutions are sets of constraints that are often just psychological constructs limiting our choices and actions; organizations are tangible entities. Although the boundaries between these two concepts are admittedly fluid, North's distinction is nevertheless critical to understanding how individuals influence institutions and how institutions influence individuals. In order to study religion as an institution (i.e., as humanly devised constraints that restrict individual choices), it is important to focus on the organizations that most closely regulate the public interpretation of religion. In the case of Islam these are the madrasas, where the 'ulama who traditionally have the authority to interpret Islamic texts are trained.

In the absence of a formal religious hierarchy, the madrasas have played a central role in shaping the public interpretation of Islam. Since the earliest times, the transmission of knowledge from teacher to disciple in the madrasa system created networks of religious leaders who—in the absence of a formal clergy and an institutionalized church as in the case of Christianity—came to exercise religious authority in the Muslim community (Hefner and Zaman 2007; Robinson 2007a). The role of South Asian madrasas as agents of religious change (e.g., by reforming local religious practices) has been the subject of serious scholarship on South Asian Islam (Metcalf 1982); and the decline of the madrasa system is an important theme in theories about the decline of Islam. This book focuses on the madrasa system (and the action of a diverse range of actors within it) in order to consider the role it has played in shaping the public interpretation of Islam (and especially in initiating Islamic militancy), and how the madrasas themselves have been shaped as times have changed. As opposed to most work on NIE, which mainly concerns macro-level historical analysis and mathematical and economic modeling, this book draws on ethnographic and qualitative data gathered during eighteen months of fieldwork in developing an understanding of people's choices and decisions. Traditional rational choice theory is inductive, driven by armchair theorizing, which is then tested through application to large-scale survey data (Friedman 1996; Green and Shapiro 1994). The application of rational choice theory in the sociology of religion has largely relied on this method, and as a consequence the intrinsic meaning that religion holds for people has been sidelined in favor of its instrumental functions. In an attempt to counter this tendency, I draw on in-depth interviews, aiming to uncover the subjective logic that lies behind actors' choices and decisions, and emphasize that it is crucial to take account of actors' subjective reality in understanding how this logic expresses itself in specific institutions and processes of change. People are always forward-looking and utility-maximizing, but they value different things in different contexts; this is because they have different propensities and historically shaped preferences. Unless the researcher engages with people's own explanations of why they act the way they do—combining this with field observations—she runs the risk of attributing an alien logic to any correlations she is able to establish; and the risk of error is high when one proceeds entirely based on pre-coded questionnaires.

In light of the need to combine a micro-level narrative with macro-level data, my fieldwork was spread across eight geographical districts, selected on the basis of regional diversity and a high density of madrasas (see Appendix A). The research was strengthened through fieldwork with five state-recognized *wafaqs* (madrasa boards), established and managed by the religious elite. These wafaqs maintain data on madrasas within their purview, set out the ideological and textual position of their particular school, and engage with external agencies, including the leaders of foreign states in the Gulf region, on behalf of the madrasas of their sect. Drawing on interviews with senior officials of the wafaqs and an analysis of the data held by them, I develop a macro-level account of the madrasa system in Pakistan. Districts with the highest concentration of madrasas are normally located in urban areas, with Southern Punjab and rural Khyber Pakhtunkhwa being the two exceptions. The eight districts selected as the focus of fieldwork covered the capitals of all four provinces, the federal capital, Rawalpindi, Southern Punjab, and rural Khyber Pakhtunkhwa.

The reason for focusing on a large number of madrasas across eight districts, rather than developing in-depth accounts of a few cases, was that in Pakistan inter-madrasa relations and comparisons are as important as those within a particular madrasa. I selected districts with large numbers of madrasas in order to develop meaningful criteria for analyzing regional differences—if any. This district-level focus helped me to develop a narrative of the macro-level working of madrasas in addition to the micro-level accounts of activities within them. I studied a total of 110 madrasas; this group represented all five wafaqs and covered the diversity in terms of size and gender composition within the madrasa network (see Appendix A). Through interviews with actors involved at all levels of the madrasas—'ulama, parents, students, and donors—I developed micro-level accounts of individuals' choices and their processes of decision making.

I interviewed 150 'ulama and teachers, 250 parents, and 150 donors; in addition, I held group discussions with 350 students; and the fieldwork also drew on interviews with 50 men and women who had been involved with jihad. I supplemented these interviews with self-administrated questionnaires, which were completed by 'ulama, teachers, and students in the 110 madrasas. The findings also draw on ethnographic fieldwork carried out in the Red Mosque during the six-month confrontation with the government. While in the field, I laid emphasis on understanding why actors desire what they pursue (i.e., what shapes their preferences) and how they set about attaining these desires (i.e., the decision-making processes that shape their actions). The former relates to "ends" and the latter deals with "means." I draw on substantial field data from Pakistan and also from briefer periods of fieldwork in India and Bangladesh, leading to a broad analysis of madrasa reform in all three countries.

## Making Sense of the Madrasas of Pakistan

The religious actor, I shall show, is indeed forward-looking, strategizing, and utility-maximizing; but his behavior differs in some respects from that of the rational actor concerned with wealth maximization. The religious elite strategize and adjust the interpretation of texts to make them more meaningful for believers in their given context; but they do not entirely abandon those beliefs when the external environment becomes hostile. The religious hierarchy is competitive; however, certain attributes of the religious elite succeed in converting competition into deference. Conviction in religious ideas rests on experiencing their practical benefits and logical appeal—yet, like trust, conviction in belief is transitive: once convinced of the core, the believer tends to accept the broader belief system even when not fully convinced of each and every precept. Part 3 of the book shows that these exceptions cannot be understood without disaggregating the notion of utility. In advancing toward this conclusion, each chapter develops a distinct theoretical argument, drawing on concepts from NIE and using empirical evidence on madrasas.

Chapter 2 opens the debate on the religious actor by questioning whether religion, like other institutions, is open to change. It explores the relative strength of strategic (North 1990) versus evolutionary (Bowles 2004) theories of institutional change in explaining the reversal in the fortunes of South Asian madrasas—once responsible for grooming the elite in Muslim India, in recent decades they have primarily come to be viewed as a refuge for the poor. To further enrich the analysis, the experience of South Asian madrasas is compared with that of the University of Oxford—an institution that also has its origin in religious education. These two traditions started out in the twelfth century with a similar initial resource endowment and comparable supply and demand pressures, and followed a similar pace of consolidation over several centuries. Yet from the seventeenth century on their paths diverged: Oxford (with its Christian underpinnings) engaged with modernity, while madrasas (and Islam) opted for disengagement.

Chapter 3 explores the factors contributing to the stability of religious ideas. Moving to the present day, I describe how South Asian ʻulama have resisted pressures for the reinterpretation of core Islamic precepts. I examine how religious ideas have persisted and thereby illuminate the factors shaping institutional stability through the study of state-led madrasa reform programs in Pakistan, India (Uttar Pradesh and West Bengal), and Bangladesh. Partly motivated by the desire to produce a new class of ʻulama capable of interpreting texts in line with the demands of modernity, starting as early as the 1950s the states in these three countries have offered financial incentives to encourage ʻulama to complement the teaching of religious texts with secular subjects. The reform programs have met with differing levels of acceptance, but a common outcome is that they have failed to displace the traditional religious elite; the power to interpret Islam remains in the hands of orthodox ʻulama. In attempting to explain the madrasas' ability to resist state-led reforms and to preserve a traditional interpretation of text, the chapter considers the importance of informal networks among the elites of formal and informal institutions, the scale of financial incentives involved, the nature of the institution (i.e., Islam), and path dependence.

Considering the significance of the elite in determining the direction of institutional change as well as ensuring institutional stability, chapter 4 develops a theory of religious hierarchy. Islam, unlike Christianity, does not provide for formal religious authority. The emphasis is on establishing a direct link to God. Yet closer examination of the madrasa system reveals the existence of a clear formal hierarchy, in which subsystems have some formal reporting requirements, as well as an informal hierarchy, in which they do not. There are over 16,000 registered madrasas spread across Pakistan, and many more unregistered ones. These vary in terms of sect, student numbers, level of education on offer, and reputation. How do actors within this complex network relate to each other? Does a clear hierarchy underpin this complexity? And if it does, what are its organizational features?

Chapter 4 draws on empirical data to provide a clear idea of the number of madrasas in Pakistan, their variations and geographical spread. In doing so, the chapter records the existence of both a formal and an informal religious hierarchy. The book describes how madrasas in Pakistan are formally organized via five wafaqs, which are three-tiered hierarchical structures in which the authority to make decisions depends on the tier to which any given madrasa belongs. Wafaq membership is voluntary, yet most madrasas choose to join. The chapter explores what motivates madrasas from all three tiers to join the hierarchical structure. This is especially interesting in the case of the smaller madrasas which, due to their low rank, bind themselves to the decisions of the few big madrasas that control the top tier of the wafaq.

Chapter 5 examines the factors shaping individual preference for religion. It addresses two key questions: (1) Why do parents choose to send children to madrasas? (2) How do parents select a particular madrasa for their child? The first question provides the means to explore factors shaping preference for religious education, and the second illuminates the decision-making processes that parents follow in executing their religious preference. Examining the socioeconomic profile of students from 110 madrasas, I reject the idea that demand for madrasa education is the result of poverty. Drawing on 250 interviews with parents and students, I illustrate how the notion of transaction costs emerging from high uncertainty and existential concern can help explain the demand for religion. Further, I show how such transaction costs are enhanced in societies with weak formal institutions, thus leading to a higher demand for religion.

Chapter 6 examines the basis of religious conviction, addressing the important question of the role that religious ideas play in sustaining the demand for religion. This question has not been adequately explored within the sociology of religion or the field of political Islam. I explore the basis of religious conviction through studying the rapidly developing phenomenon of female madrasas. Until the late 1970s, Pakistan—like most Muslim countries—had no provision for female madrasas; today, however, the growth of female madrasas is outpacing those for men, and they are also attracting more affluent groups. Based on interviews with parents and group discussions with students, the chapter explains the popularity of Islamic principles and the demand for female madrasas as resting on two features: their practical relevance (i.e., their usefulness for the believer in a day-to-day context), and their appeal to reason. Against a background of low quality secular education and weak links between education and formal employment, female madrasas are in high demand because they empower the students psychologically (boosting confidence), socially (students become influential by becoming prayer leaders within their communities), and economically (graduates can open their own madrasas). Further, my analysis shows that notions of well-being and modernity are relative ideas, such that rules that may appear confining to Western feminists can be seen as liberating and empowering by Muslim women. Preference formation cannot thus be understood without recognizing the influence of history and culture, and the subjective nature of individual preference.

These chapters are intended to establish that a believer can be seen as rational once we acknowledge the limits to human information-gathering abilities and the complexity of human motivation. Chapters 7 and 8 elaborate on the nature of the religious incentives that lead to economically irrational behavior. Chapter 7 investigates the ability of religion to check free-riding in the use of public goods. Madrasas and mosques produce public goods in the form of trained imams and the performance of religious rituals, which all believers utilize. It is impossible to monitor the contribution of each individual believer in the production and maintenance of this public good, yet enough believers choose to make a contribution rather than free-ride. This presents a puzzle, for theory suggests that rational individuals should prefer to free-ride, especially when no religious injunction makes their contribution mandatory. Based on discussions with individuals who regularly donate to the mosque and madrasas whose services they utilize, I develop a detailed theory of religious (as opposed to economic) reward, and find in this an answer to the quandary of the economically irrational behavior noted above—the willingness to donate, the conversion of competition into deference, and the transitive nature of religious beliefs. This chapter also draws on other studies to illustrate how the complexity of rewards is central to explaining not just religious behavior but also much altruistic and ideologically driven behavior.

Chapter 8 examines the incentives that can lead individuals to engage in another form of economically irrational behavior: sacrificing one's life for a collective end. It examines the motives and strategies of jihadists, illustrating the incentives that make individuals so constrain their choices under one institution that they crowd out all other possible affiliations. I first examine empirical evidence to test existing claims regarding the link between madrasa affiliation and jihad. After establishing that jihadists are drawn from across the socioeconomic spectrum (with madrasa students constituting a small fraction of the total pool), I examine the motives and decision-making processes of this diverse group. The chapter also explores the factors that win jihad mass public appeal. These questions are addressed through three main sources of data: interviews with fifty jihadists; ethnographic fieldwork within the Red Mosque during its six-month confrontation with the state; and systematic observation of the public response to the Red Mosque operation.

The concluding chapter summarizes the core arguments around the working of madrasas and Islam in Pakistan and notes the relevance of these findings for deepening our understanding of informal institutions in general. It then demonstrates their particular significance for students of both theory and practice of international development because they study societies where such institutions are prevalent, and also design interventions in form of development programs that aim to change their working.

Two methodological issues are central to the design of this project. First, it is a study that aims to understand what happens in the minds of the actors whose preferences and decisions collectively sustain the madrasa system—listening to their own rationales for their own actions is central to my method. Second, it is a study of the madrasa network in Pakistan, not an ethnography of one or two madrasas. The work is thus rooted in, and aims to contribute to, the analytical tradition aptly described by Avner Greif (2006: 7): "Understanding the impact, persistence, and change of nontechnological features requires examining the micro-mechanisms underpinning their emergence, stability, and dynamics at the level of the interacting individuals. This requires, in particular, considering the *motivation* (incentives) of these individuals to act in a manner leading to or manifesting itself in these particular nontechnological features." My eighteen months in the field between 2006 and 2008, and the follow-up visits in 2009 and 2010, enable me to offer data on the madrasa network in Pakistan, which are more complete than any presented in earlier studies. By focusing on the motivations and decision-making processes of the multiple actors involved in the madrasa network, the book helps us to refine existing theories explaining religious behavior.

# Part I
# INSTITUTIONAL CHANGE AND STABILITY

**Organizations and their entrepreneurs engage in purposive activity and in that role are the agents of, and shape the direction of, institutional change.**

—Douglass C. North, *Institutions, Institutional Change and Economic Performance* (1990: 73)

**In neoclassical economics, equilibrium is the reigning paradigm. Individual strategies are assumed to be optimal given expectations, and expectations are assumed to be justified given the evidence. We [evolutionary theorists], too, are interested in equilibrium, but we insist that equilibrium can be understood only within a dynamic framework that explains how it comes about (if in fact it does). Neoclassical economics describes the way the world looks once the dust has settled; we are interested in how the dust goes about settling. This is not an idle issue, since the business of settling may have considerable bearing on how things look afterwards.**

—H. Peyton Young, *Individual Strategy and Social Structure* (2001: 4)

# 2

# RELIGION AND CHANGE

## Oxford and the Madrasas of South Asia

**The University of Oxford was not created; it emerged. It emerged after a long period of discontinuous and fitful scholastic activity, which only gradually received the stamp of corporate identity in the first quarter of the thirteenth century. To understand how this came about it is necessary to start not at the time when the outlines of a corporate constitution appeared, but more than a hundred years earlier, when a school existed which has a shadowy connection with what was later to become the university.**

—R. W. Southern, *From Schools to University* (1984: 1)

**These summaries of the different emphases given to different aspects of knowledge in the region of the three empires at different times suggest that there may be connections to be made between these different emphases and changing political contexts. In a wantonly schematic and broad-brush fashion we suggest that the rational sciences . . . tended to flourish when Muslims were confidently in power . . . On the other hand, the transmitted sciences . . . tended to flourish when Muslims felt that Muslim state power, either because of compromises with non-Muslim forces within or because of compromises with non-Muslim forces from without, was threatened or destroyed as the upholder of Islamic society.**

—Francis Robinson, "Ottomans-Safavids-Mughals" (1997: 172–173)

At the dawn of the twelfth century, two migrations were taking place in pursuit of knowledge. Students aspiring to higher learning were traveling from England to Paris and Bologna to study Christian theology. Saints and scholars from Persia and Arabia were gravitating toward Hind (modern-day South Asia) to spread the teachings of Islam. The outflow of the young English students was a response to the growing domestic demand for higher ecclesiastical learning, and the inflow of Sufis and scholars into South Asia was creating a new demand for Islamic education through winning converts. Both were barren lands in terms of higher religious learning: Paris, not England, represented the heights of Christian theology, and Persia and Arabia, not Hind, enjoyed an international reputation for

Islamic learning.[1] Yet these migratory scholars led to the rise of organizations that, over time, acquired international repute for their expertise in interpreting the two religious traditions: by the fifteenth century the University of Oxford exercised considerable influence in the Christian world (Leff 1968). Three centuries later, Islamic scholars within the leading madrasas of South Asia were producing scholarship in a rationalist tradition that was being studied in Cairo and Damascus, prominent centers of Islamic scholarship (Robinson 2000).

This chapter studies the processes of the rise, consolidation, and change within Oxford[2] and the madrasas of South Asia in order to explain why, despite similarities in origin, the two pursued divergent trajectories in the twentieth century: Oxford and Christianity became synonymous with modernity and progress, and the madrasas and Islam with orthodoxy and regress. In tracing the divergent paths followed by these two organizations, the chapter highlights how the specific interpretations of Christianity and Islam prevalent at any point in time were a product of the developments within these organizations. For the purpose of such an analysis, the new institutional economics (NIE), which acknowledges that economic performance is not just an aggregate outcome of efficient transactions among free agents but is shaped by the socioeconomic and political institutions in which these transactions take place, provides some useful cues.

Broadly summarized, the NIE literature presents two main perspectives on institutional change: one places emphasis on the strategizing behavior of the dominant players in the field (North 1990), the other on evolutionary forces (Bowles 2004).[3] In the strategic or constitutional design approach prominently associated with the work of Douglass North (1990: 100), "the immediate instruments of institutional change are political or economic entrepreneurs who attempt to maximize at those margins that appear to offer the most profitable (short-run) alternatives." In this approach, relative price changes so alter the incentives provided by the existing set of institutional rules that it becomes more profitable for the dominant actors to work toward institutional change; the other source of such change is change in tastes.[4] In the evolutionary models of institutional

1. England was a slow developer in education; the continental universities had a hundred years' head start (Leff 1968). Similarly, since Islam came to India from Arabia and Persia, the madrasa system was already entrenched there before the first madrasas were established on Indian soil.

2. The reason for selecting Oxford over Cambridge, despite both having similar monastic roots, is that Oxford is the older of the two and has been argued to represent the "most complete expression of collegial tradition" (Tapper and Palfreyman 2000).

3. The former in its purest form has been referred to as the "constitutional design" approach, while the latter as "the theory of spontaneous order" or the "self-organization of society" (Bowles 2004).

4. Within NIE, there are two dominant positions on efficiency of institutions. As opposed to Oliver Williamson's (1975, 1985) position, which argues that institutions arise because they provide most efficient outcomes, North (1990) recognizes that institutions do not necessarily lead to socially

change, actors are attributed little control over the direction of aggregate outcomes. Institutions in this approach are viewed to be analogous to languages: evolution of social rules, like the acquisition of an accent, is argued to be the product of countless interactions, the aggregate consequences of which are often unintended (Bowles 2004). The two approaches are not entirely exclusionary: the strategic approach recognizes the potential role of evolutionary forces in shaping institutional change, while the evolutionary approach does not entirely discount the role of deliberative action on the part of individual actors; they differ mainly in terms of the relative emphasis they place on these alternative explanatory forces. Other factors shaping the direction of institutional change include the initial resource endowments of the dominant players trying to influence the direction of change, and the interaction between the formal and informal institutions.

Taking cues from this literature, this chapter examines whether the divergent paths followed by Oxford and the madrasas of South Asia during the twentieth century are best explained through differences in the academic excellence of the ʻulama in South Asian madrasas and the Oxford dons, the varying initial resource endowments of the two organizations, chance events, incentives endogenous to the institution, or external environment, that is incentives exogenous to the institution. Prior to undertaking such an analysis, it is important to establish that the two are indeed comparable.

## Oxford and the South Asian Madrasas: An Apt Comparison?

In the existing scholarship on madrasas within Islamic studies, strong parallels have been drawn between them and the Western colleges and universities and such parallels have been equally fervently contended.[5] The cause of contention is not so much the curriculum or the teaching methods adopted in the two systems but their organizational structure. Madrasa education across the Muslim world remained informally organized around a teacher until the nineteenth century. Conversely, Western colleges and universities moved toward the formation of a formal legal entity as early as the thirteenth century (Hackett 1984). A comparison between the University of Oxford and the madrasas in South Asia reveals no

optimal outcomes. Institutional change is the result of negotiations and competition within actors and organizations with varying interests, and the organizations that have higher bargaining power influence the institution in the direction that best preserves their interests.

5. See Makdisi (1981) for an analysis of commonalities between madrasas and Western colleges; for the critique of this position see Chamberlain (1994).

exceptions: the former acquired the status of a corporate entity as early as the thirteenth century, while the latter made no move in that direction until the late nineteenth century. This section argues why, despite the difference in the level of formality, a comparison between the two can be meaningful in understanding the causes and processes of institutional change.

It took just over a century for the numerous independent schools operating in Oxford to give way to the rise of the University of Oxford as a formal corporation: the presence of the first master to have taught in Oxford is recorded in 1095 and the first Chancellor, Geoffrey de Lucy, whose presence indicates the University's formal recognition as a corporation, was holding office by 1216 (Southern 1984). The Crown made the earliest of its grants of privileges to the University in the person of the Chancellor on 12 January 1231, demonstrating recognition of its corporate status. The medieval corporations were established to secure the groups' professional interests and the objectives of the Oxford masters were the same. These masters, who had so far run independent schools, wanted to defend their collective interests through the corporation; they were now free to elect their own head and other officers, own property, use a common seal, and develop a constitution. Many of the rules that present-day Oxford students obey were enshrined in the University's constitution during this early period: it was made obligatory for every student to matriculate under a regent master, the curriculum became firmer, clear term times were established, and a system was developed for conducting examinations and awarding degrees (Hackett 1984). By 1295, the masters had also started to assert greater autonomy vis-à-vis the Bishop of Lincoln, who initially had the final say in the appointment of the Chancellor;[6] by the end of the thirteenth century the University of Oxford was a fully recognized corporation.

As Oxford was moving toward this centralized system of governance,[7] madrasas were emerging across the sub-continent in response to two developments: conversions to Islam through the preaching of the Sufis who had started migrating to India as early as the eighth century, and the establishment of Muslim rule

6. Compared to Paris, Oxford had an advantage. Paris, due to being at the forefront of international speculative and theological thought within Christianity in the thirteenth and fourteenth centuries, had great difficulty in seeking autonomy from the religious authority, while Oxford being less noticeable for the Church gave the masters a much greater scope to develop an independent institution (Leff 1968: 8). This independence from the Church authority was further extended through the strategic behavior of its masters and due to the constant support it received from King Henry III (Southern 1984).

7. Despite its move toward centralization, until 1500s the University's development was largely ad hoc and unplanned. The colleges evolved gradually; Merton, the first major college, was established in 1264 (Cobban 1988).

in India starting from the twelfth century.[8] Prominent madrasas were already in place by the early thirteen century: the Mu'izzi Madrasa in Delhi established in 1211 is an example of an influential madrasa of the time. Unlike the Oxford colleges, these innumerable madrasas dotting the Indian landscape were not under any central control, nor did any of them seek legal status of a corporation. Further, not even the most prominent madrasas from the early period survived in their individual capacity till the twentieth century. What makes this system broadly comparable to that of Oxford, however, is the continuation of scholarship across madrasas over time: Islamic scholarship produced in the prominent madrasas of each period was systematically transmitted to the next generation through very deep but informal bonds of a teacher-student relationship.[9]

All madrasas covered certain core texts but the teaching was highly personalized and revolved around the teacher (Nizami 1983). There was no attendance register, no degree awarding system, and no fixed curriculum. The respect accorded to an 'alim (Islamic scholar) was based not on a degree certificate or on the name of the madrasa in which he studied but on the recognition of being the student of a well-known 'alim. Students flocked around eminent scholars known for their expertise in teaching certain subjects or core books. On completion of these books, students were issued a certificate (*Ijaza*) stating the subject studied and the name of the teacher who had taught them. Most students considered it their moral obligation to follow the path of their teachers and advance their teachings:[10] scholarship produced within influential madrasas of the time was thus successfully transmitted to the next generation, even when the madrasa itself faced decline.[11] This informality remained the hallmark of the madrasa education system in South Asia until the rise in 1866 of Dar-ul-Uloom Deoband,

8. Initial conversions to Islam in India were mainly through the Sufis who impressed the public as much by their way of life as by their teachings. Starting from the thirteenth century they began organizing themselves into Sufi orders. Some Sufis and scholars from other regions also came as refugees; for example, scholars were displaced to India at the time of Genghis Khan (thirteenth century) and Taimur (fourteenth century). The first Muslim invasion of India took place in the eleventh century but the Muslim empire was established only in the twelfth century. The successive Muslim empires—Delhi sultanate 1173–1351; Regional Muslim powers 1398–1451; Lodhis 1451–1526; the Mughal empire 1526–1707; political fragmentation 1707–1779; and, from 1800–1857 the growth of British influence—laid heavy emphasis on the establishment of mosques and madrasas (Ali 1963).

9. The bigger madrasas generally had a large number of smaller madrasas under their direct influence in the neighboring *qasbats* (small Muslim townships) and towns, which extended their influence beyond the big cities (Nizami 1983).

10. Shaikh Nizamuddin Auliya, the famous thirteenth-century Sufi and scholar, even quoted a hadith, which was not found in standard collections on the authority of his teacher, thereby revealing his trust in the knowledge of his teacher (Nizami 1983).

11. Madrasas could decline within one or two generations or even after nurturing religious scholarship for centuries either due to loss of caliber of 'ulama with successive generations or because of the changing fortunes of the Muslim rulers who patronized them.

which was to become the most influential madrasa during the twentieth century.[12] Unlike its predecessors, Dar-ul-Uloom Deoband had a set curriculum, formal classes, a set examination system, and a formal degree-awarding system. The teaching at Dar-ul-Uloom drew heavily on scholarship developed within the two most prominent madrasas of South Asia from the seventeenth to nineteenth centuries: Farangi Mahall and Madrasa-i-Rahimyya. Thus, though Oxford evolved into a centralized formal legal identity five centuries prior to any similar shift being made among madrasas in South Asia, once the links among major madrasas across different times are taken into account, the different level of formality of the two systems becomes less of a concern in understanding the role the two played in shaping the public interpretation of the religious traditions they taught.

The arguments about their different formal structures also become less relevant for a comparative analysis presented here when it is recognized that, despite the move toward acquiring a formal legal identity, Oxford retained many of the informal characteristics of the madrasa in its everyday routine. The internal organization of the colleges was quite nonbureaucratic where tasks were allocated, according to the skills and aptitudes of the masters rather than to the positions they held (Tapper and Salter 1992). Further, the tutorial system in the Oxford colleges—the weekly face-to-face meetings between the tutor and undergraduate student—which was the centerpiece of its pedagogy, shared the same emphasis on teacher-student interaction present within the madrasa system. The number of students was also not dramatically different: the total number of students in Oxford at any one point during the thirteenth century is estimated to have been between two and three hundred. Most important, the provision of boarding facilities for students through halls and colleges in Oxford was a practice again in common with the madrasa system.

Both Oxford and the madrasas thrived on the study of theology, though both covered other important subjects. Oxford had retained autonomy from the Church, but it exercised great influence over Christian discourse and the shaping of state policy on religious matters. As opposed to the emphasis on medicine and law in the early Italian universities, at Oxford the focus was on the Doctrina Sacra (School of Divinity) (Sager 2005). Between the thirteenth and sixteenth centuries theology was the largest single faculty at Oxford accounting for 2,104 scholars out of a total of 4,614 pursuing degrees in the higher faculties (Cobban 1988).

12. In Pakistan, out of total of 16,000 registered madrasas, 9,500 belong to Deobandi school of thought; in Bangladesh all Qaumi (unreformed) madrasas, estimated to be around 9,000 are Deobandi; the same is the case for India, which hosts the parent Deoband madrasa. Since 11 September 2001, Deobandi madrasas have attained international notoriety for promoting orthodox Islam as key Taliban leaders were trained in Deobandi madrasas in Pakistan.

Similarly, in all but two of the ten colleges founded between the late thirteenth and sixteenth centuries, theology was the dominant subject. The religious orientation of the University is also clear from the fact that, at the time of registration, every student was required to swear on the Thirty-Nine Articles of 1571 to affirm his Anglican beliefs, a practice that continued until 1854 (Cobban 1988). Despite growing secular influences and the rising number of students in other fields, especially law, even in the seventeenth century Oxford remained primarily a clerical seminary where the majority of dons were in holy orders and a high ratio of the junior members planned to join the Ministry of the Church of England. This trend did not reverse until the twentieth century.

This specialization in theology made Oxford an influential player in shaping debates within Church and State: out of the nine Bishops of Lincoln who occupied the seat from 1209 to 1362, at least six had previously been masters in Oxford, and in the fourteenth century at least six Archbishops of Canterbury came from Merton College (Sager 2005). Because the Crown also appointed its chancellors and ministers from the higher ranks of the clergy, the Oxford influence spread further. After the Reformation, when Mary came to the throne and wanted the country to return to Catholicism, Oxford's theologians again played an important role. In 1555, two major figures of the Reformation, Bishops Hugh Latimer and Nicholas Ridley, were sent for trial in the Oxford School of Divinity, resulting in these heretics being burnt at the stake opposite Balliol College (Sager 2005). Six months later the Archbishop of Canterbury, Thomas Cranmer, was also sent to the stake in Oxford. The French Revolution similarly led to the formation of an alliance among the University, Church, and Crown: Oxford was anxious to check the spread of Catholicism; the University still was a bastion of the Church of England (Green 1974). In addition, to this formal association with Church and State, Oxford masters also influenced religious discourse through their teachings, public lectures, and written dialogue on contentious theological debates with Church officials.

Likewise, the madrasas were primarily a place of religious learning. In the absence of a formal religious authority in Islam to parallel the church, the 'ulama trained within these madrasas were central players in interpreting religious texts. They transmitted Islamic knowledge "that made men Muslim and their communities Islamic" (Robinson 2000: 178). At the individual level they defined what it was to be a good Muslim; at the official level they supported the Muslim rulers in establishing a system of judiciary and administration based on Islamic principles. The 'ulama thus staffed the various levels of the judiciary, oversaw the charitable establishment of the empire, acted as prayer leaders at town mosques, and became most influential among the courtiers (Metcalf 1982). In addition, they educated the entire nobility. Much of this authority extended beyond the period of Muslim rule; even during the colonial period, the 'ulama exercised what Metcalf (1982) calls the "concentric circles of influence," whereby their authority trickled through multiple levels including links with students and disciples, occasional solicitation of judicial decisions, public attendance at their sermons, writing and publication of religious literature, and public preaching and debate. The 'ulama thereby have been as critical players in the interpretation of Islam in South Asia as the Oxford-trained clergy has been in the case of Christianity in England.

There are thus solid grounds to argue that despite the differences in organizational forms, Oxford and the prominent madrasas of South Asia shared enough commonalities in their core objectives and outcomes to be used as broadly comparative cases to refine our understanding of processes of change in religious institutions. The purpose of the above analysis is thus not to establish that the two traditions were exactly the same, but to help us better understand the causes of the dramatic shifts in the madrasa system in South Asia by bringing in a counterfactual scenario. At the time of the British takeover of India, the parallels between the bigger madrasas of South Asia and Oxbridge were often captured in the observations of British officers as well as those of Indian scholars:

> They learn through the medium of Arabic and Persian languages, what young men in our colleges learn through those of Greek and Latin—that is grammar, rhetoric and logic. After his seven years of study, the young Mohammadan binds his turban upon a head almost as well filled with the things which appertain to these branches of knowledge as the young man raw from Oxford—he will talk as fluently about Socrates and Aristotle, and [13]Hippocrates and Galen and Avicenna—and what is more to his advantage in India, the languages in which he has learnt what he knows are those which he most requires through life.[14]

After a visit to Farangi Mahall in 1896, Maulana Shibli Nomani, a leading Muslim scholar, declared with a touch of hyperbole: "this is the very Cambridge of our India" (Robinson 2001b).

If at the turn of the nineteenth century the two systems could invoke such comparisons, the real puzzle rests in untangling the causes of their present-day differences where one is recognized as a premier secular academic institution in the West advising state, commerce, and industry, and the other is a stronghold of

---

13. Observations of a British colonial officer noted in Nizami (1983).

14. The demand was confined not just to the urban centers, like Delhi and Lucknow, which occupied a position of intellectual and educational prominence, but also came from the *qasbats,* which were scattered all over the countryside.

orthodoxy with its curriculum purged of modern subjects. To trace the answer to this question it is best to start from the very beginning.

## Starting at the Very Beginning: The Initial Conditions

If the madrasa system evolved gradually, the fact is that the University of Oxford was also not created; it also evolved gradually. The initial demand and supply conditions that led to the rise of Oxford and the prominent madrasas in South Asia bear striking similarities. The catalyst for the demand for higher religious learning was the changing socioeconomic and political conditions in the two societies during the twelfth century. As these societies evolved, higher religious learning became important in the quest for individual piety, as well as for the running of the state apparatus and the formal economy. In England, the public expressed an increased demand for a literate clergy to sing mass, lead the congregation, and to conduct the business of the Church (Southern 1984). Kings, bishops, and monasteries had the provision to recruit an increased number of men, trained at an advanced level of theology, to conduct official affairs. An increasingly elaborate organization of economic activity also called for literate and numerate men (Southern 1984). Similar forces were at work in India. The Sufis' endeavors to spread Islam across South Asia had unbridled a demand for higher Islamic education within the newly organized Muslim community. The establishment of Islamic rule in India starting in the twelfth century had led to the reorganization of judicial and revenue administration, requiring employees trained in the Persian language and in Islamic law[15] (Nizami 1983). The thriving trade, both domestic and regional, required more qualified men to cope with the growing complexities of the market.

This demand triggered a dramatic expansion of parish churches and schools[16] in England and of the madrasas in India; in both categories, most were restricted to the basic level of education. In England, the opportunities were mainly for elementary education in Latin and in the arts of singing and chanting; in India

15. All types of schools in England, as elsewhere in Northern Europe, were closely linked to churches and were under the jurisdiction of local ecclesiastical authorities, which held monopoly over education.

16. The University of Oxford was not the only place of learning to emerge in England during this time. Northampton was among its potential rivals. Similarly, the chain of madrasas selected for this analysis does not represent all madrasas of that time. The focus here is on Oxford and on the three leading madrasas of South Asia, which became the most dominant players in the field to influence the interpretations of Christianity and Islam in their respective contexts over centuries.

many of the initial madrasas were geared toward the imparting of basic Quranic and Islamic education. Neither could produce highly trained scholars of Islam or Christian theology and jurisprudence, who would be capable of meeting the demands of the state, or satisfying individuals seeking higher spiritual learning. An abundance of such schools and madrasas was, however, a prerequisite for producing religious entrepreneurs who led to the rise of the University of Oxford[17] and to the leading madrasas of South Asia. In England, the growth in such schools produced an increasing number of ambitious students who traveled abroad to Paris, Bologna, Liege, and elsewhere in pursuit of higher learning—no English student seeking higher education between 1066 and 1190 stayed in England if he could opt to go abroad, and all school masters in England during this period were trained in foreign schools (Southern 1984). In India, the mushrooming of Sufi hospices across the countryside created a large pool of students out of which the intellectually curious and the worldly ambitious moved to abodes of popular Sufis and scholars in bigger cities.

The first known Oxford school master, Theobald of Etampes, who taught from about 1095 to 1125, was trained in France, the place for higher learning at that time; he was a man with intellectual ambitions who carried on controversies not only with local ecclesiastical magnates like the Abbot of Abingdon and the Bishop of Lincoln but also with the famous logician Roscelin (Southern 1984). He is known to have had a school of fifty to sixty students. The next recorded master, Robert Pullen, was also trained in theology in France. By 1133, Oxford had become a place where an ambitious master might hope to find students in the highest branches of learning and theology. There was a vacuum for the next fifty years until the arrival of Alexander Neckham in 1190. Again, trained in Paris, Neckham was to introduce a type of theology for which Oxford was to become famous (Southern 1984). The caliber of these initial masters at Oxford was critical to attracting students and better teachers to the town. Between 1190 and 1209 at least seventy masters resided in Oxford (Southern 1984).

The story of prominent madrasas is no different: the intellectual caliber of the ʿulama and their formal training in Islamic texts were central to the rise of influential madrasas. From very early on, the scholars and Sufis who attracted

17. One important difference in the charitable giving coming to Oxford and the madrasas was in administrative structure; the former established charitable trusts and the latter waqfs (Islamic endowments). In a charitable trust the institution is governed according to the letter of the trust instrument. In this the trustees cannot perpetuate themselves, being replaced as they come to the age of retirement, or otherwise ending their trusteeship. Conversely, the Islamic notion of waqf provides the founder with complete control. The lack of change arguably stunts growth and development. This, some have argued, has led to the culture of family-based influence in madrasas, and a more broad-based trusteeship among western collegiate universities (Makdisi 1981).

students in throngs were those known for exceptional religious knowledge. The 'ulama of Farangi Mahall inherited a long lineage of prominent scholars before the madrasa became a prominent player within the religious hierarchy. Mullah Hafiz, one of the earlier scholars from the family was acknowledged as a distinguished scholar by the Mughal emperor Akbar as early as 1559; however, the real fame for the madrasa came a few generations later under Mullah Nizam Uddin, who compiled the Dars-i-Nizami—a formal madrasa curriculum that spread across the South Asian madrasas during the eighteenth century—and was a scholar respected for his innate talent. The same was the case for the Madrasa-i-Rahimyya, established by Shah Abdur Rahim (died 1718); the madrasa acquired real fame under his son Shah Wali Ullah again an exceptionally gifted scholar who had received training in the study of Hadith (Prophet's sayings) in Hijaz (Saudi Arabia). The Deobandi 'ulama similarly had established credentials prior to opening the madrasa; they took their lineage from Shah Wali Ullah (Robinson 2000).

There are signs that the geostrategic importance of a location also played some role in the expansion of Oxford and the elite madrasas. Unlike continental universities, Oxford was not based in a central city nor was it a seat of the bishopric; however, the town had its importance. In 1135, the civil wars of King Stephen's reign made Oxford the center of communications in the midlands and one of the main crossings of the Thames; toward the end of Henry II's reign the rapid growth of ecclesiastical courts in Oxford made it an important center for hearing ecclesiastical disputes (Lawrence 1984). The latter development had direct dividends for the university as senior lawyers who came to Oxford for court cases also taught for an additional income. By 1190, the presence of such lawyers had begun to draw students of Canon and Roman law to Oxford. Strategic location also contributed to the expansion of the big madrasas. Most prominent madrasas emerged in Delhi, the capital of most Muslim regimes in India, and the center of education and learning. Shah Abdul Aziz, a leading scholar, said about Delhi: "It has so many madrasas that if any visitor roams about the city he will find books everywhere" (Nizami 1983: 16). Other prominent madrasas, including Farangi Mahall at Lucknow and Dar-ul-Uloom Deoband, emerged in the Indian state of Uttar Pradesh, which was the heartland of the Muslim elite.

That chance events, at societal as well as at an individual level, cannot be entirely ignored in creating new opportunities or ruling out preferred options in the creation of new players, is also visible in the expansion of Oxford and the madrasa system. In England, the tension between the kings of France and England played an important role in making some English scholars remain in their country: Alexander Neckham, one of the prominent masters at Oxford, remained in Oxford not by preference but because the war between the two kingdoms made travel to France impossible. In case of Farangi Mahall, the 1692 murder of the great-great-grandson of a distinguished scholar Mullah Hafiz brought a major shift in the family fortunes: Emperor Awrangzeb compensated Hafiz's sons by assigning them a European merchant's house (Robinson 2001b). Though the family had long been involved in religious education in the small town of Sihali, it was only after the shift to Farangi Mahall in Lucknow, the capital of Awadh, in 1695 that the family established a major teaching center that attracted scholars not only from all parts of India but also from places as far away as Arabia, Central Asia, and China (Robinson 2001b).

Finally, another critical factor shaping the rise of elite organizations was their ability to mobilize financial resources. Oxford and the prominent madrasas were successful in attracting state patronage as well as individual donations, while avoiding core dependence on the state. Although most endowments to colleges came from kings or bishops, this was in an individual capacity, and the same applied to the madrasas. The motives of the givers in the two contexts were ironically also shared; both sought salvation in the next world. It is because of this that, despite being secular colleges, most Oxford colleges had a higher proportion of theology students as their founders often had outlined a religious role in the guidelines of the endowment. As Cobban (1988: 113) notes: "Generally speaking, whether kings, queens, high ranking ecclesiastics or statesmen, or wealthy members of lay aristocracy, they regarded the establishment of a college as a charitable and pious venture which would enshrine their memory and which would result in a foundation in which masses would be said for their souls and for those of their relatives."

Similarly, the emphasis on charity in Islam made affluent Muslims support madrasas as a means of securing their hereafter.[18] Under the Mughal Empire, such support became formalized under the system of *Madad-i-Mash* (revenue-free land) where land was regularly donated for charitable purposes; madrasas were one of the prominent beneficiaries of this policy (Nizami 1983). The Muslim rulers also supported madrasas through establishing grants for the salaries of teachers and scholarships for residential students. In addition, wealthy Muslims (*Ashraf*) supported madrasas in their individual capacity (Nizami 1983). Such donations were particularly feasible for the nobility in both contexts, as Oxford and the bigger madrasas produced educated clerics and lawyers to serve the state. Both attracted funds from a fusion of spiritual motivation with educational purpose.

18. By 1840, over 1,750,000 acres of land given as revenue-free grants to Muslim 'ulama and the elite had been withdrawn by the British state. It is said of Hafiz Rahmat Khan that he had in his time (mid-eighteenth century) patronized five thousand 'ulama, but by the early nineteenth century his descendants were themselves in need of daily bread (Nizami 1983).

The comparison thus reveals striking similarities in the factors shaping the rise of Oxford and the leading madrasas of South Asia. In doing so the comparison also illuminates the processes of an elite formation. It shows that chance events, geostrategic importance of the location, and financial viability are important contributors in the rise of elite organizations. However, the decisive factors shaping elite organizations over time are competence and strategic behavior of the maximizing actors—in this case, the masters of Oxford and the ‘ulama of prominent madrasas—who combined their academic talent with strategic behavior across the centuries to turn changing events into opportunities. The question arises: If it is neither the skill of the players nor their differing initial resource endowments that explain the divergent paths followed by Oxford and the madrasas in South Asia, then what is it that does? Does the answer rest in the nature of the institution itself, in other words in the core principles of Christianity and Islam?

## Incentives Endogenous to the Institution

The argument that the different positioning of Oxford and the leading madrasas in South Asia during the twentieth century is attributable to the basic principles of Islam and Christianity whereby the former restricted free thought and the latter encouraged intellectual inquiry also does not hold. This is reflected among other things in the balance of the curriculum taught at Oxford and in the leading madrasas. Both systems placed emphasis on the teaching of theology but, in addition, covered all the critical subjects of the time; in particular they shared a similar emphasis on use of logic. At Oxford, theology enjoyed the supreme position within all taught subjects, followed by law and then the arts (Cobban 1988). Since the twelfth century both viewed logic or dialectic as critical for understanding other subjects, including theology, law, medicine, natural sciences, and grammar. From the very beginning the curriculum in the madrasas in India had two categories of subject: rational subjects (*maqulat*) and transmitted subjects (*manqulat;* reliant exclusively on the religious texts). The former included subjects based on reason including *mantaq* (logic), *hikmat* (philosophy), *tibb* (medicine), *riyazi* (mathematics), and *hai'at* (astronomy); the latter focused on religious texts like *tafsir* (exegesis), *hadith* (tradition), and *fiqh* (jurisprudence). The actual balance of rationalist and transmitted subjects taught varied among madrasas, but from early on all madrasas covered both: for instance, many madrasas established by Feroz Shah Tughluq (1351–1388) during the fourteenth century included medicine, metaphysics, natural sciences, and mathematics in their curriculum (Nizami 1983).

Oxford and the leading madrasas also had similar conceptions of knowledge. At Oxford, the search for truth was equated with comprehending the core texts through commenting and discussing a prescribed body of writings. The supreme authority was the Bible, in the light of which all other texts had to be judged. Teaching was organized through three forms of lecture: Ordinary (designed to cover core texts); Extraordinary (delivered by masters on books that were not part of the formal course); and Cursory (required lower level of expertise, consisting of a straightforward reading, paraphrase and summary of text, with little commentary) (Cobban 1988). Similarly, central to Islamic learning was the Quran and a series of commentaries, most of which had been written by the end of the eighth century of the Islamic era (Robinson 2000). Scholars relied on a series of commentaries, super-commentaries, and notes to understand these texts. Teaching within madrasas, however, relied on one-to-one meetings instead of lectures. Both emphasized vocation rather than on research; both were expected to make a concrete contribution to society by training clergy, lawyers, and other professionals (Cobban 1988; Nizami 1983).

The sixteenth and seventeenth centuries again marked similar trends within the two systems as both opened up to the study of new subjects. Oxford opened up to humanistic subjects during this period, allowing for the study of classical literature and languages, which had until then been ignored as "a memorial to a dead culture, an indulgence out of tune with the sharper educational objectives of the age" (Cobban 1988: 13). A major achievement of the period was the evolution of high standards in the teaching of Latin grammar so as to facilitate higher Latin humanist scholarship. Conversely, the scholarship within the madrasas of South Asia made a major shift toward rationalist subjects within this period. The trigger for this shift was Fadl Allah Shirazi, an Iranian scholar who arrived at the Mughal emperor Akbar's court in 1583, and became acclaimed for his excellence in rational sciences, such as philosophy, astronomy, geometry, astrology, geomancy, and arithmetic (Robinson 2000). He was equally learned in Arabic, hadith, interpretation of the Quran, and rhetoric. Shirazi encouraged the widespread study of the rational subjects within South Asian madrasas culminating in the rise of Dars-i-Nizami. This period drew the sons of the elite to Oxford and the leading madrasas, as the two had gradually acquired the status of grooming the elite in the two societies (Cobban 1988; Nizami 1983).

It is toward the end of the seventeenth century that the first major divergence in the two systems becomes visible, though in a reverse direction to the one witnessed today: the seventeenth and eighteenth centuries were periods of steady decline for Oxford, and of superior rationalist scholarship within the leading madrasas. Many accounts note the plummeting of education standards in Oxford, making some critics argue that Oxford colleges were no more homes of learning than were the neighboring alehouses, and that secure in the enjoyment of fixed stipends Oxford dons had no stimulus to lecture (Cobban 1988: 87).

The student number in Oxford steadily declined from 500 or more in the 1630s to 300 in 1700 and to 182 by 1750 (Green 1974); even more revealing was the dramatic decline in the admission of the children of the nobility and gentry. For the leading South Asian madrasas, this was a period of constant expansion and innovation within rationalist scholarship. The scholars at Farangi Mahall, which became a major intellectual center of rationalist inquiry, engaged with European sciences: one translated Newton's *Principia* into Persian. A senior scholar of Farangi Mahall, Mullah Nizam Uddin (d. 1748), consolidated the Dars-i-Nizami during this period, providing instruction in grammar, rhetoric, philosophy, logic, scholasticism, tafsir, fiqh, hadith, and mathematics. The teaching method also recorded a shift toward argumentation and discussion to encourage the use of reasoning, and it discouraged concentration on textual matters. This period also witnessed expansion within the study of traditional subjects under another prominent scholar, Shah Wali Ullah (d 1762) at Madrasa-i-Rahimyya. As opposed to the emphasis on philosophy within Dars-i-Nizami, Shah Wali Ullah's teachings focused on the Quran and hadith. This curriculum better suited the students especially those interested purely in religious subjects; it did not completely ignore logic and philosophy while emphasizing the importance of going back to the "literal word" (Robinson 2000). (Different emphases on rationalist and traditional sciences in the two madrasas is presented in table 2.1.) Thus, during the period when Oxford suffered a decline in educational standards, leading

**TABLE 2.1** Curriculum in Indian madrasas in the Eighteenth Century

| | MADRASA-I-RAHIMIYYA | DARS-I-NIZAMI |
|---|---|---|
| SUBJECTS | NO. OF BOOKS | NO. OF BOOKS |
| Exegesis (tafsir) | 2 | 2 |
| Hadith (traditions of the Prophet) | 3 | 1 |
| Philosophy (falsafa) | 1 | 3 |
| Logic (mantiq) | 2 | 11 |
| Scholasticism (kalam) | 3 | 3 |
| Rhetoric (balaghat) | 2 | 2 |
| Etymology and Syntax | 2 | 12 |
| Medicine (tibb) | 1 | |
| Astronomy and mathematics (ha'at aur hisab) | Few small brochures | 5 |
| Jurisprudence (fiqh) | 2 | 2 |
| Principles of jurisprudence (usul-l-fiqh) | 2 | 3 |
| Mysticism | 5 | |

*Source:* Nizami (1983).

South Asian madrasas boasted of vibrant intellectual debate and excellence in rationalist subjects.

What then explains the entirely divergent paths followed by Oxford and the madrasas of South Asia during the twentieth century when Oxford became the leader in scientific inquiry and progress, and the active reasoning and debate within the leading madrasas gave way to orthodoxy and emphasis on literal interpretation of the divine text?

## Incentives Exogenous to the Institution

Comparison between Oxford and the leading madrasas of South Asia illustrates that the direction of religious change is shaped not so much by the ideological conviction of the religious leaders but by their maximizing behavior in response to changing incentives. Both excelled in rationalist inquiry during periods of political stability and resorted to orthodoxy and stagnation during periods of political instability. Oxford engaged in intellectual debate and opened up to humanistic scholarship during the fourteenth and fifteenth centuries when it was comfortably placed vis-à-vis the monarchy; it stagnated during the eighteenth and nineteenth centuries, when weakened by the Reformation it became ultra-royalist and orthodox; and it had a revival in the twentieth century when, severed of the links with the monarchy it had to ensure its survival through responding to demands of the Parliament (Green 1974). Developments of the leading madrasas of South Asia record similar trends: rationalist subjects expanded within the madrasas in the period of political stability of Muslim empires reaching a peak in the Mughal period; they gave way to transmitted subjects during the nineteenth and twentieth century with the decline of the Mughal Empire and Muslim political power. The phenomenon is not just specific to Oxford and to the leading madrasas of South Asia but is also visible in the case of the Ottoman and Safavid empires: the rationalist sciences tended to flourish when Muslims were confidently in power; the transmitted sciences flourished when Muslims felt that Muslim state power was threatened or destroyed as the upholder of Islamic society (Robinson 1997).

Twentieth-century Oxford awoke from the slumber caused by the insecurities it had faced during the Reformation, when monarchical rule was superseded by the Parliament (Green 1974). The latter, cognizant of the stagnation within the University, forced it to reform. Two royal commissions, one in 1854 and the other in 1871, brought dramatic changes within the University. One of the most important shifts made during this period was that Oxford fellowship was no longer a prize but required the holder to engage in advanced study and research; prior to this, only 22 out of 542 fellowships at Oxford were fully open to competition

(Green 1974). Many other reforms ensued including an increased emphasis on natural sciences in the curricula, long resisted by Oxford dons. The replacement of royal patronage with formal dependence on the Treasury, the demands from industry and technology, two World Wars, societal changes opening up space for women—the first society for the Higher Education of Women in Oxford was formed on 22 June 1878 and, in October of the following year, two residential halls, Lady Margaret Hall and Somerville were opened—created incentives for Oxford dons to adapt to the contemporary society (Green 1974). Oxford masters thus recognized that if they were to survive in the changing context, they had to respond to what Tapper and Palfreyman (2000) call the "3Ms": marketization (the push to tailor scientific inquiry to the demands of industry), managerialism (the managerial and accountability pressures from the state due to formal financial dependence on the Treasury), and massification (the increasing number of students and inclusion of female students).

The move by the ʻulama during this period from emphasis on rationalist inquiry to textual interpretation was similarly triggered by the changing political conditions. With ascendancy of the East India Company, the Mughal Empire gradually gave way to the establishment of the formal British Empire, dramatically altering political and economic context in which the madrasas had to operate. Not only did the official sources of support dry up and Muslim elite was marginalized,[19] more important madrasa education became irrelevant for securing positions within the formal economy (Metcalf 1982; Nizami 1983; Robinson 2000). The colonial administration not only retrieved much of the land given as revenue-free grants to madrasas, it introduced a Western system of education that made the madrasa education, formally a prerequisite for gaining elite positions, entirely irrelevant. The Shariʻa law was superseded by Anglo-Muhammadan law and the Unani Tibb (Greek medicine) taught in madrasas was displaced by biomedicine (Robinson 2007b). The abolition of Persian in 1837 as the language of administration removed any remaining worldly significance of madrasa education that had an excessive bias toward Persian and Arabic learning. The direct consequence of these shifts was that, in order to retain its status, the Muslim elite had to withdraw from the madrasas to attend Western educational institutions.

It is in this context that the decline of rationalist subjects within the madrasas and the renewed emphasis on the study of the texts, as witnessed within Deoband, has to be understood. The decline of Muslim political power initially spurred the

19. The separation of Islam from the working of the state under colonial rule led to fragmentation within Islamic thought. The three dominant schools of thought within Sunni tradition in present-day South Asia—Deobandi, Barelvi, and Ahl-i-Hadith—emerged in this period. In the sphere of madrasa education, the Deoband tradition became most influential.

'ulama into action to fill the vacuum; 'ulama from leading madrasas like Farangi Mahall tried to respond by writing new textbooks, but all eventually crumbled under the pressures of weakening financial support base (Robinson 2000). Thus, Deoband, a madrasa that later grew into a movement creating sister madrasas across South Asia, came into existence. Deoband followed British bureaucratic style of education and developed a set curriculum, separate classes for students of different levels, an academic calendar, annual examinations, and networks of affiliated madrasas; however, it replaced the emphasis on rationalist subjects in vogue among the 'ulama with an emphasis on hadith and the Quran (Metcalf 1982; Robinson 2000). To some extent the 'ulama of Deoband being from the lineage of Shah Wali Ullah of Madrasa Rahimyya, which historically placed greater emphasis on study of the transmitted subjects, were following an ideological position. A closer examination of their choices reveals that this shift was the most strategic choice to ensure survival under the changed circumstances.

For the 'ulama, any strategy aimed at competing with Western educational institutions was likely to be both financially and practically unviable: the introduction of new subjects, especially the English language, required heavy investment in the learning of new subjects with no guaranteed pay off; Western schools established by missionaries were bound to always have a head start. In such a context the optimal strategy for the madrasas was precisely that executed by the 'ulama of Deoband: consolidate and expand what they knew best and for which they were still in demand in the society, that is the teaching of Islamic texts. Their decision to disengage with the state and focus on individual piety also made strategic sense in a context where it was clear that the Muslims were in no position to regain the political power they had lost to the British. The decision of Deobandi 'ulama to consolidate their attention on study of transmitted subjects, therefore reflects an optimal response given that, under the changed incentives in the new climate, 'ulama had to incur much higher costs in pursuing rationalist subjects than they did during the Mughal period, without surety of any reward. Such a strategy worked particularly well for 'ulama of Deoband who anyway drew inspiration from Waliullahi reforming tradition, with its emphasis on transmitted subjects.

Once focused on the transmitted subjects due to the changed political context, the Deobandi 'ulama drew more on the Quran and old commentaries, given the importance attached to the former as the ultimate guide to Muslims. Seeking answers to the reasons for the decline of the Muslim political power and society, the Deobandi 'ulama thus sought guidance in the original texts. This emphasis on the original texts was noted by a senior Deobandi scholar in Karachi as late as 1970, "We do not want modernism (tajaddud) but rather to go further back (tagadum [in search of authenticity])" (Zaman 1999: 318). The reversion to the Quran in a time of crisis in intellectual scholarship reflects that specific characteristics of an institution—in this case the emphasis placed on the Quran in Islam as the ultimate word of God—also do play some role in setting the direction of change. That incentives within an institution, and not just the external context, matter in setting the direction of change was also visible among other actions of the ʿulama and Oxford dons, many of whom made material sacrifices to defend their ideological positions: Oxford dons were burned at the stake for supporting the Reformation and many ʿulama risked their lives by participating in the 1857 mutiny against the British; others, like Muhammad Ishaq (1778–1846), grandson of Shah Wali Ullah and his spiritual successor, migrated to Mecca to live under an Islamic state (Robinson 2000).

These cases however were the exceptions. In general dons were politically compliant: the majority wished to keep their fellowships to enjoy the fruits of patronage, and they had no wish to taste the dubious charms of either exile or martyrdom; most adapted to changes brought by the Reformation despite their ideological resistance (Green 1974). The ʿulama were similarly willing to operate within the parameters set by the Muslim rulers and benefit from positions in state bureaucracy (Robinson 2000). Some did seek these positions as a means to promote their interpretation of the religious beliefs within the ruling elite, but most were driven by the desire for material prosperity (Metcalf 1982). This survival strategy was followed not only under Muslim rulers but also under the British Empire; some ʿulama took on government positions and issued many fatwas (religious rulings) to oppose anti-government fatwas while others, including the Deobandi ʿulama, chose to stay quiet rather than be confrontational (Robinson 2000). Thus, the moves toward rationalist inquiry within the corridors of Oxford and that toward orthodoxy within the madrasas of South Asia during the twentieth century, were direct consequences of the political context in which the ʿulama and Oxford dons found themselves. Further, the maximizing behavior of the ʿulama and Oxford dons to best secure their material interests as well as religious beliefs was central to setting the direction of religious change.

## Conclusions

The analysis of divergent paths followed by Oxford and the madrasas of South Asia during the twentieth century supports the underlying position within an institutional perspective—whether within the NIE framework or the broader field of political economy—that an institution alone does not determine the choice set for the organization and actors within it; rather what makes a stable choice set is the total package of formal and informal constraints (Bates 1990; North 1990; Ostrom 2005). The incentives initiating institutional change are not just endogenous to an institution; equally important are the incentives exogenous to the institution. The current-day problems of madrasas cannot be attributed to Islamic precepts as they were themselves contingent on the interpretations given to them by the ʿulama, who were interpreting the text to best preserve their personal interests as well as those of their faith in the context of changing political conditions.

The comparison between Oxford and the leading madrasas of South Asia demonstrates that the ascendancy of reason in the former and that of orthodoxy in the latter during the twentieth century cannot be attributed to different emphasis on use of reason in the two religions; nor can the difference be attributed to different origins or objectives of Oxford and the leading madrasas. Their differing positions in the twentieth century was a product of the different incentives induced by the political environment in which Oxford dons and the ʿulama within the madrasas had to operate. Oxford dons being part of an industrial society were increasingly drawn upon to provide solutions to today's needs, while the ʿulama were completely marginalized from the modern economy and society under the new education and economic policies of the colonial rulers. The two thus had to develop different survival strategies. This argument supports strategic theories of institutional change, which argue that the kind of knowledge, skills, and learning acquired by members of an organization will reveal the payoffs and the incentives imbedded in the institutional constraints (North 1990). It is thus differing context, and not different recourse to reason, that explains the divergent choices pursued by the ʿulama and Oxford dons.

Evolutionary forces, including sudden disruptions and chance events, do instigate the process of change; however, whether the change is discontinuous, radical, or incremental, it is the maximizing behavior of the dominant players at those points in time that determines the direction of change. The madrasas were marginalized due to sudden disruption caused by colonial rule, yet it was the strategic behavior of the Deobandi ʿulama that ensured that this change gave way to a more individual centric and puritanical form of Islam. The importance of players' strategic behavior in understanding institutional change also becomes evident in the process of elite formation. The Oxford dons and the ʿulama of elite madrasas had what North (1990) defines as tacit knowledge, which requires possession of special skills in a subject, as opposed to communicable knowledge, which anyone can pick up through conversation. Chance events, location, and financial viability all contributed to the rise of Oxford and the leading madrasas as elite players, but central to this process was the specialized knowledge that Oxford dons and the ʿulama of the leading madrasas possessed of the rules of the game.

The chapter thus shows that religious beliefs are not fixed; rather they adapt to and change with changing context. This shows the limitations of purely structuralist accounts of religious behavior. At the same time, the analysis also records that religious beliefs can make some endure great material sacrifices, thereby ruling out very narrow conception of utility. Why religious beliefs can induce materially sacrificial behavior is a critical question, which is addressed in detail in part three of this book. The more immediate question of interest, however, is why after the demise of colonial rule the South Asian ‘ulama did not revert to the rationalist scholarship practiced under Mughal rule. It is to the subject of institutional stickiness that we turn in chapter three.

3

# EXPLAINING THE STICKINESS

## State-Madrasa Engagement in South Asia

> **Institutions are the engine of history because... they constitute much of the structure that influences behavior, including behavior leading to new institutions. Their independent impact and their interrelations with social and cultural factors imply that we cannot study them as reflecting only environmental factors or the interests of various agents.**
>
> —Avner Greif, *Institutions and the Path to the Modern Economy* (2006: 379)

> **There is an alternative method which treats the decisions and criteria dictated by the economic system as more important than those made by the individuals in it. By backing away from the trees—the optimization calculus by individual units—we can better discern the forest of impersonal market forces. This approach directs attention to the interrelationships of the environment and the prevailing types of economic behavior which appear through a process of economic natural selection. Yet it does not imply that individual foresight and action do not affect the nature of the existing state of affairs.**
>
> —Armen A. Alchian, *Uncertainty, Evolution and Economic Theory* (1950: 213)

On 14 August 1947, the British left India, drawing over two and a half centuries of colonial rule to a close. Their exit, however, did not remove their imprints on the local system of governance (Barlas 1995; Cohn 1996). They left entrenched a post-colonial civilian and military elite, which having been trained at Oxbridge and Sandhurst, had not only mastered the vocabulary to negotiate with the British within the English constitutional framework[1] but had also picked up Western cultural sensibilities including a secular worldview. For Jawaharlal Nehru, the first prime minister of India, religion was one of the causes of India's economic backwardness (Gellner 1982); Mohammad Ali Jinnah, the leader of the nascent Islamic

1. For an account of the role played by Western educational institutions established by the British in the rise of a new Indian elite and associational culture that culminated in Indian nationalist resistance see Seal (1968). This experience in India arguably made the British reluctant to invest in establishing Western education institutions in later colonies, such as, northern Nigeria (Tibenderana 1983).

Republic of Pakistan led a secular lifestyle (Wolpert 1989). Later in 1971, when East Pakistan broke away to become a separate state of Bangladesh, a leader with a socialist outlook, Sheikh Mujibur Rehman, was to be at the helm (Ali 1973; Wright 1987). The exclusion of madrasas from formal economy and society, a process that started under British rule, continued in the independence period: the secular elite across the three countries attempted to reform the religious elite to make it reinterpret orthodox religious beliefs in line with the demands of modernity.[2] Yet, to date, across the three countries, the traditional ʻulama exercise control over the interpretation of Islamic texts.

Why inefficient institutional paths persist has long intrigued economic historians. The maximizing assumption inherent in the standard economic theory suggests that, since rational individuals make choices keeping in view their total choice set, and the long-term implications of those choices, actors will invest in choices that record a shift to a higher equilibrium provided the actors are aware of the possibilities, i.e. there will be no remedial errors (Liebowitz and Margolis 1995). Why then inferior paths persist remains a subject of serious scholarly debate. The most plausible explanation for the persistence of inefficient institutions within institutional economics has come to rest in the idea of path dependence:[3] "what happened at an earlier point in time will affect the possible outcomes of a sequence of events occurring at a later point in time" (Sewell 1996: 262–63). Put simply, path dependence implies that past choices have consequences for future choices. There is little difference of opinion on this (Liebowitz and Margolis 1995); however, what remains contested is the cause of path dependence.

One group of scholars attributes path dependence to historical factors, where "lock-in by historical events" leads individuals to opt for sub-optimal choices even when they are aware of more efficient alternatives (Arthur 1989; Libecap 1989; Pierson 2000). Studies supporting this framework identify that in shaping individual choices, specific patterns of timing and sequence matters and that large consequences may result from relatively small or contingent events, and most important that a particular course of action once introduced may be virtually impossible to reverse. Such a view identifies the limits to individual pursuit of most efficient equilibrium. The opposing view, grounded within the neoclassical assumptions, maintains that if one of the two options is superior in the long run but not in the short run, then market arrangements will generally assure

2. Since September 11, these programs have gained support of international development agencies, including United States Agency for International Development (USAID) and UK Department for International Development (DFID), as part of their counter-militancy programs (Bano 2007a, 2007b).

3. For the widespread application of the concept to study political processes overtime see Pierson (2000).

the adoption of the superior path.[4] Remedial path dependence, in view of these scholars, is a rarity and the explanation for path dependence rests not so much in the historically determined factors but lack of sufficient incentives for the actors to make the due investment to lead to the superior path within the given endowment or technological constraints (Liebowitz and Margolis 1995). Here the optimal path is eventually chosen as under these assumptions technology responds to scarcities, techniques respond to price, and so on.

This chapter explores the explanatory power of these competing positions on path dependence to illuminate the factors that shaped the 'ulama's resistance to state madrasa reform programs in Pakistan, India (Uttar Pradesh and West Bengal) and Bangladesh.[5] Such an analysis helps assess whether the incentives in the given environment made resistance to the adoption of a revisionist interpretation of Islam an optimal strategy for the religious elite, that is, whether resistance was a result of conscious choice. Or does it represent the human tendency to unquestioningly adhere to certain historically shaped and culturally transmitted ideas and beliefs?[6]

## Madrasa Reforms: Three Countries, One Story

Inspired by the economic progress of colonial rulers, the leaders of the newly independent South Asian states sought rapid economic prosperity and industrial

4. Liebowitz and Margolis (1995) differentiate among three types of path dependence where the first degree path dependence (initial conditions put an individual on a specific path that cannot be left without cost but that path happens to be optimal) and the second degree path dependence (where inferior path is chosen due to lack of information) do not imply that the outcome has to be inferior. Third degree path dependence—there exists or existed some feasible arrangement for recognizing and achieving a preferred outcome, but that outcome is not obtained—is the only form of path dependence that conflicts with the neoclassical position and is, in the view of the authors, very rare in practice.

5. The analysis draws on fieldwork conducted in Bangladesh (districts of Dhaka and Chittagong, the former provides a good sample of 'Aliya (reformed) madrasas, the latter of Qaumi (unreformed) madrasas; India (states of Uttar Pradesh and West Bengal because of the presence of leading orthodox madrasas in the former and a well-developed state madrasa board running reformed madrasas in the latter); and Pakistan. Interviews were conducted with the leading 'ulama for and against these reform programs. Other respondents included government officials responsible for conception, design, and implementation of the madrasa reform program, public intellectuals, journalists, and academics. During visits to both reformed and unreformed madrasas, group discussions were conducted with students and parents.

6. This analysis of interaction between formal and informal institutions has particular resonance for students and planners within the field of international development, who in an attempt to improve the quality of life in developing countries, often are required to design policy interventions to reform apparently inefficient informal institutions, such as female genital mutilation and honor killings.

growth (Kochhar 1999; Rao 2008), and any platform averse to modern scientific inquiry was considered suspect (Sinha 1991). In both India and Pakistan, the political elite soon initiated debates to demark the appropriate role of religious establishments (Engineer 1998). Cognizant of the political repercussions of a policy seen to target a specific religious community, the political elite in the multi-religious India[7] preferred to set broader parameters for the working of minority educational institutions within the national constitution instead of setting out to reform a particular minority institution. These constitutional provisions were followed in 1978 with the establishment of the Minorities Education Commission to regulate issues related to minorities, including streamlining of any state funds channeled to minority religious institutions (Nair 2009). The discussions around a reform program explicitly geared toward madrasas officiated at the national level in the early 1980s though some Indian states, especially those with a high Muslim population, had a much older and more complex history of engagement with madrasas.[8]

The political elite within Pakistan and Bangladesh, where both countries had an overwhelmingly Muslim population, were less vulnerable to the pressure of being accused of malicious intent and thereby were at greater liberty to critique the educational standards within madrasas and pursue the reform agenda. A reflection of the state's disregard for madrasa education in Pakistan, from the very outset rests in the state's decision to classify the madrasa graduates as illiterates, thereby excluding them from the electoral register in the country's first election (Bano 2007a). Formal government deliberations on madrasa reform started as early as 1962 with the establishment of the first formal state committee to review the madrasa curriculum.[9] In the case of Bangladesh, within eight years of the inception of the country, the Bangladesh Madrasa Education Board was securely in place (Bano 2008a).

Over the decades, the rhetoric of madrasa reform across the three countries has been couched within concerns for economic security of the madrasa graduates. Government documents justified the reforms based on concern about economic insecurity faced by the madrasa graduates due to an exclusive focus on religious subjects in the madrasa curriculum, rendering these graduates incapable of securing employment within the modern economy (Malik 1997). The real impetus for these reforms, however, rested in the desire to curtail the power exercised

---

7. Muslims constitute 12 percent of total population of India.

8. States running Government Madrasa Boards include West Bengal, Uttar Pradesh, Madhya Pradesh, Bihar, Rajasthan, and Assam (Nair 2009).

9. In 1962 the governor of West Pakistan established the Committee for Recommending Improved Syllabus for the various Dar-ul-Ulooms and Arabic madrasas (Malik 1997).

by the ʻulama over believers by virtue of interpreting religious texts[10] (Hefner and Zaman 2007; Robinson 2000, 2007b). The ʻulama across Muslim societies have historically enjoyed the power to influence individual and collective choices of the believers; for the ʻulama, as Robinson (2000, 2007a) notes have traditionally defined what it is to be a good Muslim. In terms of institutional literature, the ʻulama are the elite players who enjoy maximum bargaining power to shape the rules of the game of Islam. Changing public conception of the dominant Islamic precepts either requires winning over some ʻulama to promote revisionist interpretations of Islamic texts or cultivating an entirely new religious elite, groomed to reinterpret the text to match the demands of modernity.[11] Investment in madrasa reforms was thus a strategic intervention on the part of the state designed to create players who could reinterpret the very rules of the religion.

Although deliberations on reforms initiated early across the three countries, the state's ability to roll out a reform program and the degree of acceptability of these reforms within madrasas has varied enormously. Ironically, Pakistan—where political leadership was most vocal in its critique of madrasa education—was the last state to roll out a reform program. The national government had trialed a madrasa reform program under the auspices of the Ministry of Education in the early 1980s, but a formal program was launched only in 2002 with a provision of US$225 million aid package made by the United States under the banner of the war on terror (Bano 2007a). It is also in Pakistan that reforms have met the severest resistance from the religious elite. The program has failed to record noticeable success: by 2007, only 250 out of the 16,000 registered madrasas in Pakistan had accepted the state reform program (Bano 2007b) and the program was closed in 2009.

The Indian government, despite the misgivings at intervening in a minority educational institution, launched a madrasa modernization program in 1993–94 with the inception of the Area Intensive Madrasa Modernization Program. The state of West Bengal had a madrasa board—West Bengal Board for Madrasa Education—in place as early as 1927 to manage state-supported madrasas (Nair 2009). The Modernization program, despite being pronounced suspect by many prominent Indian Muslims,[12] has had a relatively higher level of acceptance within madrasas than in Pakistan. While the leading madrasas—for instance,

10. Such attempts to curtail the power of religious elite have not been specific to South Asian states; for review of similar tensions in other Muslim majority countries see Hefner and Zaman (2007).

11. The former approach is illustrated in the reform of Al-Azhar in Egypt where the state gradually implemented rules to check its independence and the latter in the Turkish experience where Kamal Ataturk closed down all the madrasas replacing them with state regulated Islamic schools (Agai 2007).

12. Such concerns, voiced frequently by prominent Muslim personalities, such as Syed Shahbudin (2001), were shared by the president of Jamaat-i-ʻUlama Hindi, the leading Muslim political party in India: "The state does not support our efforts to establish secular educational schools for Muslim

Dar-ul-Uloom Deoband and Nadwa-tul-'Ulama in Uttar Pradesh—stay distant from the modernization program, the government-run madrasa board in West Bengal has been able to create a system of reformed madrasas which, in terms of the number of the affiliate madrasas, rivals the orthodox (Karzai) madrasas: by 2007, 500 madrasas were reported to be registered with the government madrasas board and 550 with Rabata-e-Madaris (the board of Karzai madrasa).[13]

Compared to the experience in India and Pakistan, the Bangladesh madrasa reform program records yet another variation—the last country to emerge on the map of South Asia was ironically the first one to roll out a national-level madrasa development program. By 1978, the Bangladesh Madrasa Education Board was in place and process of enrolling the madrasas interested in joining the reform program started the following year. Interestingly, Bangladesh is also the country where the reforms have had highest acceptability within madrasas: over the past three decades, 'Aliya madrasas (reformed madrasas) have recorded a steady growth so that today there are 9,000 'Aliya (reformed) madrasas against 10,000 Qaumi (traditional) ones.[14] 'Aliya madrasas, which operate under the Ministry of Education, represent over 30 percent of the total secondary-school enrolment in Bangladesh (Bano 2008a).

The greater analytical challenge is not to understand the differing ability of the states to roll out the reform program and their differing levels of acceptance among the 'ulama, but to explain why the ultimate outcome of these efforts has been the same: the political elite has failed to disinvest the orthodox 'ulama of the authority to interpret Islamic texts. In Bangladesh, Dar-ul-Uloom Moinul Islam Hathazari, Al-Jamia Al-Islamia Pattia, the oldest Qaumi madrasas in Chittagong (viewed to be the heartland of orthodox Islam in Bangladesh), and their likes, and not 'Aliya madrasas, remain the citadels of Islamic education. In Pakistan the oldest and most prestigious of traditional madrasas, the likes of Banuri Town and Jamia Dar-ul-Uloom Karachi in the metropolitan city of Karachi, enjoy this status. The reality in India is no different; the ultimate arbiters of valid interpretation of Islamic texts are the 'ulama of the leading madrasas, including Dar-ul-Uloom Deoband and Nadwa-tul-'Ulama and their likes in the other sects. Enough students of the reformed madrasas in Bangladesh and the Indian state of West Bengal have graduated who, arguably, could have displaced the orthodox religious 'ulama but as yet have no voice in shaping Islamic discourse of the time; the positions within mosques and madrasas are securely in the hands of

---

communities, so when the state repeatedly reiterates a commitment to supporting madrasa education it makes Muslims uncomfortable (interview with Mahmood Madni, Delhi, March 2007).

13. Rabata-e-Madaris, West Bengal.

14. Bangladesh Madrasa Education Board.

students of Qaumi and Karzai madrasas. This means that, even where reforms have been seriously implemented and have been accepted by a significant number of madrasa leaders, the new players have failed to change the rules of the game: the voices interpreting Islamic texts that are capable of winning a public following are overwhelmingly conservative. To understand whether the explanation for this resistance rests in the weakness of the material incentives introduced by the state or the strength of ideological commitment of the religious elite, it is best to start by exploring the reasons for the different pace with which the reform programs were rolled out in the three countries, as this has a bearing on the nature of the incentives introduced in the three states.

## Push to Reform

Studies within economics and psychology indicate that commitment to ideals or altruistic behavior can waiver the higher the cost of such adherence (Frey 1994)—a fact noted within institutional economics as one of the explanations for institutional change (North 1990) and also recorded in the changing behavior of the 'ulama in response to changing political contexts (see chapter 2). The explanation for the differing levels of commitment of the leaders in the South Asian states to impose the madrasa reform agenda rests precisely in this. Across the three countries, the reforms were primarily initiated due to the ideological conviction of the ruling elite to disinvest the society of the orthodox religious worldview: Nehru was a secularist and proponent of restricting religion to the private sphere (Edwardes 1971); in Pakistan, apart from the General Zia-ul-Haq era, the state has been in the hands of leaders of a secular bent (Haqqani 2005);[15] and in Bangladesh, the founding father, Mujibur Rehman, was an ardent socialist and his successors—despite using Islam for political ends—were of a liberal outlook (Evans 1988). The varying level of commitment to initiate such reforms across the three countries is thus not reflective of the differing levels of ideological conviction of the elite to the idea of reform; the difference reflects the varied costs the political elite in the three countries incurred to pursue their ideological commitment. Across the three countries, the 'ulama exercise some degree of influence in determining outcomes at the ballot box (Haqqani 2005; Hassan 1987; Misra 2003; Shaheed 2009)[16] and this has had a direct bearing on the

15. General Zia-ul-Haq, who initiated an Islamization drive to gain popular support for this eight-year military rule, was the only exception.

16. Across the three countries, the 'ulama influence electoral outcomes through formation of Islamic political parties and through influencing the voting behavior of their followers (Haqqani 2005; Yadav 1999).

political elites' willingness to push the madrasa reforms. Madrasa reforms have been pushed mostly in the context where the secular elite did not have to sacrifice their political interests in pursuing these reforms.

Pakistan's political history is marked with repeated military coups: out of sixty years of existence, forty have been under military governments. Devoid of constitutional legitimacy, the successive military rulers have repeatedly cultivated coalitions with influential political groups—in particular the feudal and religious elite—to establish some form of parliamentary democracy to legitimize their government (James and Lyon 1993; Talbot 2000; Waseem 1994). Creation of a country in the name of Islam bears evidence of the rallying power of Islam within the Pakistani public where, devoid of political legitimacy, military leaders have attempted to gain public legitimacy through associating with religious ideology—in the process, making Islamic political parties powerful players within the political arena (Haqqani 2005; Misra 2003; Shafqat 2002). The oil boom in the Gulf states, which ensured the flow of petrodollars to Pakistan due to its Islamic identity created additional incentives for the secular elite to cultivate close ties with the religious elite. In such a context, the desire to protect their political interests outweighed the secular elite's ideological commitment to reformist ideas; they did not seriously pursue the madrasa reform program despite expressing verbal support for it.[17] The reform program was rolled out post–September 11, when the then-president General Pervez Musharraf's decision to join the U.S.-led war on terror made it awkward for him to delay the imposition of these reforms.

In India, the political elite faced a dual challenge in implementing the reforms: not only were the strategic interests of the secular elite better protected by maintaining cordial relations with the Muslim religious elite (Yadav 1999),[18] whose support could be critical in the case of closely contested elections, over-interventionist policies also exposed the political elite to the risk of being tainted as an anti-minority. The minority status of the Muslims made a madrasa reform program suspect in the eyes of many of them, with the result that the Indian states that have pushed the reform program have employed the language of strengthening the Muslim educational institutions rather than that of reform (Nair 2009). In India, as in Pakistan, the political elite were not in a position to

17. In Pakistan, the political significance of the religious elite is visible in numerous measures put in place by various governments to appease them. As early as 1962, General Ayub Khan set up an Islamic Advisory Council, apparently to initiate reinterpretation of Islamic texts according to "modernist" parameters, but its main purpose was to absorb political dissent by giving senior 'ulama a stake in the system (Haqqani 2005).

18. In India, 12 percent of Muslim voters, especially in the states with high Muslim concentration, are important players in determining the electoral outcome (Yadav 1999).

push the madrasa reform agenda because the political costs of pushing the secular agenda were quite high.

The primary explanation for the quick rolling out of the reform program in Bangladesh is that the ideological interests of the secular elite in Bangladesh matched those of dominant players within the religious elite making the reform program a win-win strategy (Bano 2008a). In Bangladesh, the political elite were less reliant on the use of Islamic discourse to legitimize their rule for four reasons. First, in the friction between the elite of East and West Pakistan, the West Pakistani elite had justified their actions in the name of Islam and referred to Bengali liberation fighters as *kafirs* (infidels). Second, Islamic countries had resisted the Bangladesh liberation movement. Third, Islamic political parties had become controversial in Bangladesh when they supported West Pakistani leadership in its attempt to crush the war of liberation. This association of traditional Islamic forces with the anti-liberation struggle opened up a space for a modernist interpretation of Islam (Ganguly 2006; Huque and Akhter 1987) within an otherwise ardently Muslim population.[19]

In this context, the shift of power from Mujibur Rehman, the socialist leader, to General Zia ur Rahman (1977–1981) and later General Hussain Muhammad Ershad (1982–1990), with both the military leaders drawing on Islamic discourse to gain some legitimacy for their rule, enabled the government to present the madrasa reform program as a sign of genuine commitment to advancing modern scholarship within Islam. In 1988, General Ershad declared Islam the state religion of Bangladesh, changed the weekly holiday from Sunday to Friday, and, removed the ban on Islamic political parties. It was in this context, where Islam was highly valued within the society but there was also acceptance of revisionist interpretations of Islam, that the military regime best maximized its political interest by making a serious investment in rise of the reformed madrasas. The ordinance for establishment of Bangladesh Madrasa Education Board was passed in 1978. Within traditional madrasas the continued emphasis on imparting education in Urdu, the language of the Indian Muslims, which had become irrelevant in Bangladesh where Bengali had become the state language, further increased the appeal of the state-initiated reform package, which provided education in Bengali. The other factor galvanizing support for these reforms was their approval by Jamaat-i-Islami, the largest Islamic political party in South Asia, at present an influential player in Bangladeshi politics.

During the course of my fieldwork, many 'ulama and employees of the governmental madrasa board noted links between Jamaat-i-Islami and 'Aliya

19. For an account of high observance of Islam in Bangladeshi society see Huque and Akhter (1987).

madrasas. In the words of an employee of the board, "It is an ideological support. 'Aliya madrasa teachers are of the Jamaat-i-Islami mind-set." The Jamaat's support for 'Aliya madrasas was also clear from an interview with a senior official of the party, "Qaumi madrasa education does not represent the true spirit of Islam. The student coming out of a madrasa is a misfit in the society and incapable of competing with others. The person who comes out of a madrasa should be able to go to Oxford. Islam does not forbid you from learning English, mathematics, and other subjects. Islam is a modern religion."

The last factor shaping higher acceptance for the reform program within Bangladesh and the West Bengal state of India is the old history of 'Aliya madrasas in this region: the first 'Aliya Madrasa, initially known as the Calcutta Madrasa, was established by Governor-General Warren Hastings in October 1780; he also bore its expenses before the government of Bengal formally took over the program in April 1782.

The three-country analysis supports the theoretical position that the higher the price of ideological commitment, the lower is its prevalence: despite being equally committed to the idea of secularization, the political elite in the three countries pushed the madrasa reform agenda at a pace that minimized the political cost incurred in pursuing that commitment. This means that institutional equilibrium persists, where given the bargaining strength of the players and the set of contractual bargains that make up the total exchange, none of the players find it advantageous to devote resources to restructuring the agreements. This has been the case in India, and especially in Pakistan, where given the strong presence of the 'ulama in the public sphere the political elites' interests are best secured by retaining the support of the religious elite. Although Muslim minority context in India posed additional challenges to the government-led reform program at the federal level, the federal government as well as governments in selected states were nonetheless able to advance the reform program much more effectively than in Pakistan. The respective governments in Pakistan despite being in a strong position to lead the reforms due to Muslim majority context did not push the reforms in order to protect their political interests. Thus, the differing ability of the governments across the three countries to lead the reform program was shaped not so much by Muslim majority or minority context but by how well the political interests of the respective governments were served by the reform agenda.

I now turn to the other important question as to why the religious elite resisted the reform program despite financial incentives from the state. Was the resistance purely ideological, thereby showing that a religious actor is more committed to ideas (thus demonstrating that path dependence is shaped by historical forces) than a secular actor, or were the financial incentives introduced by the state too weak (i.e., path dependence is a result of strategic calculations)? Prior to undertaking such an analysis, it is important to first rule out that the explanation for this difference rests in the content of the reforms across the three countries.

## Why Resist? The Madrasas' Response

The proposition that the difference in the level of acceptance of the reform programs across the three countries rests in the content of the curriculum reforms introduced by the state is easy to rule out as the reform program has had a similar objective in all three countries: namely, to introduce modern subjects—English, mathematics, social studies, and general science—into the madrasa curriculum so that the students "integrate into the mainstream economy and society."[20] In Pakistan, the first phase of the program, initiated in 1983, focused on primary classes and, during the second phase, the focus shifted to secondary education. The experience has been similar in India and Bangladesh. The different level of acceptance of the reform program is thus not explainable by the differing ideological content of the reformed curriculum. What then explains the difference?

Analysis of the reform programs across the three countries reveals the importance of strategic behavior where actors respond to financial incentives; the stronger financial incentives offered by the Bangladeshi state did have a role to play in making a greater number of Bangladeshi 'ulama accept the reforms as compared to the experience of the other two countries. It is in Bangladesh that the state provides most concrete financial incentives to the madrasas: the state bears the cost of the salaries of all the teachers appointed in the madrasas and, occasionally, it also provides the funds for the school infrastructure. The financial incentives that the state provides in the case of Pakistan and India were very limited. In Pakistan, the reform program provided for the training of 28,000 madrasa teachers of only secular subjects and textbooks, stationary, computers, and furniture for the madrasas. The national level madrasa modernization program in India similarly offers weak financial incentives: the scheme includes 100 percent support for two qualified teachers with a salary of Indian Rs 3,000 per month (US$54), and a one-time lump sum grant of Rs 7,000 (US$127) for science and math teaching kits, but it does not provide for the salaries of religious teachers. Given that in a madrasa most teachers are hired to teach religious subjects, by making no provision for salaries of religious subject teachers, the reform programs in the two countries leave the main financial burden intact

20. For details of the reforms, the incentives offered, and the subjects introduced at each degree level see Bano (2007b, 2008a) and Nair (2009).

on the madrasa administration. The head of the madrasas and the teachers of religious subjects therefore have weak incentives to accept the reform program. The current incentives in fact have the potential to create a managerial dilemma for the heads of the madrasas, where teachers of secular subjects drawing state salaries can earn a higher income than Islamic studies teachers, whose salaries are contingent on fluctuating donations.

This varying commitment of the state is also reflected in the investment each state has made to ensure smooth administration of the reform program. In Bangladesh, the formal Madrasa Education Board operated under the auspices of the Ministry of Education as early as 1979. In Pakistan, the program falls under a project director within the Ministry of Education and the program has been beset with numerous problems including the release of approved funds and an insufficient number of staff. In India, the modernization program is under the supervision of the Ministry of Minority Affairs rather than an independent board. In West Bengal, however, where the state madrasa support program has expanded the most, the state has a separate madrasa board just as in the case of Bangladesh.

Neither in Pakistan nor in India have the incentives or the administrative structures to pursue these reforms been clearly worked out and the result is a weak acceptance of these programs within the religious community. In India, female teachers were appointed to madrasas in remote places which, apart from making these jobs physically taxing for these teachers, consumed a major share of their meager remuneration (Indian Rs 1,000 [US$18]). In addition, many teachers did not know Urdu, making communication with the largely Urdu-speaking madrasa students difficult (Nair 2009). In a context where Bangladeshi madrasas were also financially more insecure,[21] the combination of strong financial incentives and a weak financial resource base, coupled with the political support of Jamaat-i-Islami made the shift toward reform a more efficient strategy for many madrasas.

The strength of these financial incentives, though it partly explains the greater acceptance of reforms within Bangladesh, does not help answer the perseverance of orthodox Islam across the three countries. Rather the continuation of the orthodox madrasa tradition in Bangladesh, despite the strong financial incentives offered by the state illustrates that the pursuit of religious ideals also has

21. During the fieldwork the obvious differences between the buildings of the leading orthodox madrasas in Chittagong as compared to those in Pakistan reflected the former's weaker financial resource base; another sign of the relative strength of Pakistani madrasas rests is the traditional flow of a noticeable number of students from Bangladeshi madrasas to bigger madrasas of Karachi while a movement in the reverse direction is rare. Further, out of the three countries as yet only in Pakistan have the madrasas succeeded in getting their master's degree recognized by the state.

some inherent rewards. That the 'ulama were ideologically opposed to reform across the three countries is clear; the 'ulama and the state officials clashed on the very conception of what knowledge is (Zaman 1999). For senior 'ulama, knowledge demands the pursuit of truth for its own sake with little consideration of employment matters. The walls of many madrasas visited during the fieldwork were engraved with quotations emphasizing the pursuit of Islamic scholarship in the search for knowledge, and not as a means of employment. Interviews with leading 'ulama across the three countries reveal the concern that the state-initiated reform programs were aimed at secularization and commercialization of madrasa education rather than at improvement of the madrasas' ability to train more learned 'ulama. The 'ulama also repeatedly expressed the practical limitations of the proposed reform programs, where inclusion of secular subjects in the curriculum beyond matriculation level was argued to lead to madrasa graduates excelling in neither religious nor secular education. In the view of Maulana Jalandari (2006), secretary of Wafaq-ul-Madaris Al-Arabia:

> Today is the time of takhassus [specialization]. Every teaching institution selects the curriculum according to its objectives. No one questions why a doctor graduating from King Edwards Medical College is also not an 'alim, the same should hold for the madrasas. Specialization in religious subjects demands devoted scholarship that cannot sustain inclusion of secular subjects at the higher levels without seriously compromising the quality of religious education taught within the madrasas.

Interestingly, the resistance to the state-initiated reform programs within senior 'ulama rests additionally on the recognition of the strong pull of material incentives. During the interviews, the 'ulama repeatedly recorded concerns that acceptance of state funds could in the long term lead to compromises on core religious principles, even if in the initial phase the reforms were within acceptable limits. There was a recognition that, once the head of a madrasa becomes used to a regular income from the state, the seduction of that regular income can lead to compromise on religious beliefs; therefore, it is thought best not to get used to such comfort. To justify their resistance, senior Pakistani 'ulama quote examples of the relative secularization of madrasas over time in states where 'ulama have accepted state money (Zaman 1999).

The analysis so far supports the emphasis on the power of material incentives within economic theory and much of public policy, where despite the inclusion of other motives such as altruism in the utility model (Becker 1993), the policy recommendations remain highly skewed in favor of financial incentives (Bowles 2004). However, once we take into account the fact that even in Bangladesh, the prominent madrasas, which were financially more secure, have resisted the reforms the analysis starts to expose the limitations of those conceptions of human nature and policy predictions that fail to take into account nonfinancial incentives. It is madrasas with a weak financial base across the three countries that have been more inclined to accept reforms. It is impossible to explain the adherence to orthodox religious beliefs among the 'ulama in the bigger madrasas of Chittagong and their refusal to accept the financial incentives provided by the state without accounting for the appeal of Islamic beliefs for them and their followers.

Whether this adherence to orthodox Islamic interpretations was entirely the result of 'ulama's own ideological commitment or public expectations also had a role to play is debatable. Islamic scholarship provides detailed guidelines to shape most aspects of individual and collective conduct. Although Islamic teachings were orally preserved from earlier period, the active use of print by the 'ulama in South Asia starting in the late nineteenth century led to an extensive body of written scholarship across the different schools of thought especially in Urdu language (Robinson 2000). Just as North (1990) argues that the inability to achieve compromise solutions may reflect not only a lack of mediating institutions but also limited degrees of freedom of the entrepreneurs to bargain and still maintain the loyalty of their constituent groups, this tradition of textual scholarship in Islam gives the followers an independent means of acquiring Islamic knowledge thereby reducing, though by no means removing, the dependence on the 'ulama to act as the ultimate arbiters of Islamic rules. In such a context, the religious elite have to demonstrate a good knowledge of the text and argue for change by using the Quranic verses if they are to convince the followers. This textual tradition does not make the belief unchanging; it just requires more learned leadership to convincingly defend the reinterpretation of the text. Thus, the more formalized the institution, that is the more formally recorded and written its rules of the game, the less free is the elite to bargain on core institutional rules without fear of losing its power over the followers.

The financial security ensured by the popular following has enabled the 'ulama in South Asia to organize madrasas under wafaqs (collective platforms) to safeguard their interests, including effectively resisting state pressure to reform the madrasas. Wafaq ul Madaris Al Arabia, Bangladesh, currently has 9,000 registered madrasas; Rabata-ul-Madaris Al-Islamia, the last wafaq to be established in Pakistan, has over 1,000 registered madrasas, while Wafaq ul Madaris Al Arabia has 10,000; and in West Bengal, Rabata-e-Madaris has around 550 Kharzi madrasas. These collective platforms have further strengthened the bargaining capacity of the religious elite vis-à-vis the state. It is the office bearers of these wafaqs that have regularly negotiated with the Pakistani state since it launched an initiative to register all madrasas after 2001, just as it is through the platform of

Wafaq ul Madaris al-Arabia Bangladesh that the 'ulama of Qaumi madrasas are negotiating with the Bangladeshi government to recognize their degrees (Bano 2007b and 2008a).

The 'ulama's ability to resist state pressures to reform indicates that informal institutions often have followers within the formal institutions, making the religious elite more confident as is seen in the cases of Pakistan and Bangladesh. One of the reasons for the reform program to record slow progress in Pakistan is that many ministry officers responsible for implementing the reform program, due to being practicing Muslims, respect the senior 'ulama and are themselves not convinced of its objectives.[22] Due to their knowledge and practice, the 'ulama have been able to build up a mass following not only within the community but also from among the government officials in the Muslim-majority countries of Pakistan and Bangladesh.[23] Thus, the ideological appeal of Islamic texts for some, a strong tradition of written rules in the given informal institution, namely Islam, and presence of a large number of followers are factors that have played an important role in ensuring the institutional stability of orthodox Islam in South Asia. The question remains, however, concerning the madrasas that did accept the reforms: Why, after three decades of state support for producing graduates taught under the reformed curriculum in Bangladesh and four decades of such an exercise in the case of West Bengal in India, has the state not been able to displace the power of the orthodox elite? Why have the new religious actors failed to redefine the rules of the game?

## Why Reformed Madrasas Failed to Displace Orthodox Elite

The field visits to both reformed and orthodox madrasas reveal that the explanation for the inability of the graduates of the reformed madrasas in Bangladesh and West Bengal to displace the hold of the Orthodox 'ulama, rests in the state's inability to understand the significance religion has for the public, making it misdirect its efforts toward secularizing the madrasas rather than improving the quality

22. In India, bureaucrats interviewed (who happened to belong to Hindu faith) were also lukewarm about the program but for different reasons; they were of the view that the state is unnecessarily supporting Muslim institutions, when the secular educational institutions were themselves in need of support.

23. During the fieldwork in Pakistan, many 'ulama quoted examples where government officials allowed them to carry on with their activities (such as expansion of mosque beyond the officially allocated land) or allowed them special concessions because they found it a convenient way to contribute to an Islamic cause.

of religious learning within them. Instead of aiming at producing more learned scholars of Islam within these madrasas, the state has tried to reduce the role of religion itself. The result is that the graduates of the reformed madrasas are not equipped to address the religious needs of the society, leaving it to the traditional madrasas to continue to meet that need.[24] In Bangladesh the control of Qaumi madrasas over the religious establishment is clear: the leadership of Wafaq-ul-Madaris Arabia, which represents the religious establishment in Bangladesh, comes from Qaumi madrasas. Even in the international and regional Islamic networks, it is the representatives of Qaumi madrasas that are taken seriously; 'Aliya madrasas have not displaced their authority and respect within the public.

During my fieldwork, the differences between the philosophy and practice of reformed and traditional madrasas were striking. Traditional madrasas aimed at grooming the religious leadership, but reformed madrasas were concerned with preparing their students to compete for positions in regular economy. The heads and teachers of the reformed madrasas took pride in highlighting the reduced religious content within the curriculum, and interviews with parents and students within 'Aliya madrasas revealed a preference for employment positions within the regular economy. These children were not aspiring to secure religious positions, they wanted to compete with children from regular schools; in the absence of reformed madrasas, these children would have been in secular schools rather than in Qaumi madrasas. Interviews with parents, especially in West Bengal, highlighted that those opting for state madrasas found them a better option over secular schools, where their children would have been otherwise admitted, because these madrasas provided some religious training along with secular subjects in an otherwise secular society. These were not the children who would have ever opted for regular madrasas. Also, like their counterparts in Bangladesh, the teachers and principals of reformed madrasas in West Bengal proudly noted the relative secularization of the reformed madrasa, making frequent references to the fact that in some 'Aliya madrasas as many as 40 percent of the students and teachers are non-Muslim.

In Bangladesh, 'Aliya madrasa students are encouraged to join secular professions and compete with children in regular schools. The whole philosophy of

24. Nelson (2006: 720) notes similar reasons for the failure of the state madrasa reform program in Pakistan, which is supported by international development agencies: "Unfortunately, the dominant thrust of current efforts seeks to *avoid* Islam more than seeking to constructively *engage* it." Demonstrating the high demand for Islamic education within Pakistani public, he argues that the reformers have only two choices: "On the one hand, they can simply announce that the notion of 'demand' does not include 'demands in favor of religion' as it relates to international assistance.... On the other hand, however, they could attempt to ... work *within* the language of Islam—not apart from it or against it." He concludes that the latter will be a more effective strategy.

'Aliya madrasas is that religious studies should not mean religious employment and that children from madrasas should be able to enter into regular economy. The number of 'Aliya madrasa students goes down dramatically at master's degree level, when the emphasis shifts mainly to religious studies.[25] There is no evidence to suggest that 'Aliya madrasa students enter the traditional religious hierarchy in Bangladesh and exercise control over mosques spread across the country. Both 'Aliya and Qaumi madrasas belong to the Deobandi school of thought and follow the same religious textbooks, but differ in terms of the time spent on the study of religious and secular subjects. According to the present syllabus of the 'Aliya madrasa at the Dakhil level (grades 9 and 10), out of the total exam marks 500 are for religious studies and 500 for general education; at the Fazil level (bachelor's degree), 600 marks are allotted to religious studies and 200 for Bengali and English and the remaining 300 for one subject chosen from economics, political science, Islamic history, philosophy, English, sociology or social welfare; and, at the Kamil level (master's degree), out of the total of 1,000 allotted marks 800 are for religious related subjects and 200 for Islamic history.

Not only do 'Aliya madrasas teach more secular than religious subjects, the content of religious texts that are taught is not covered as comprehensively as in Qaumi madrasas. Parents as well as the 'ulama noted that 'Aliya madrasas taught only parts of the religious text, enough to make the children pass the exams, a normal practice in South Asian schools,[26] while in Qaumi madrasas the entire text is studied. The comprehensive coverage of the religious texts within Qaumi madrasas is made possible due to the residential facilities where the students' study hours stretch from sunrise until after dinner with prayer and recreational breaks; in 'Aliya madrasas the students have a regular school day from 9 am until 2pm.

The consequence is that Qaumi madrasa students, being more specialized in religious education than those of 'Aliya madrasas, are in higher demand in the community when it comes to filling a position at a neighborhood mosque or madrasa; in North's (1990) vocabulary it is they who acquire tactic knowledge in Islamic Studies. In the words of the son of Sheikh ul Hadith, a prominent 'alim and political figure in Bangladesh, "the real purpose of the madrasa is to impart the teachings of the Quran and Hadith and not to primarily be worried about the degree. If a child wants the degree to secure a job he will go to 'Aliya madrasa,

---

25. Data made available by the Bangladesh Madrasa Education Board show that only a small fraction of 'Aliya madrasas impart education up to the master's level: Ibtidaiya (6,713), Dakhil (9,169), 'Alim (2,629), Fazil (1,216), Kamil (189).

26. Across the three countries, the state schooling system suffers from problems of access and quality (UNESCO 2008).

if he wants only Islam he will come to Qaumi madrasa. In our country, one did not become a good 'alim in 'Aliya madrasa nor did one become a good master's graduate, one became a hybrid." Precisely the same views were expressed by the 'ulama about reformed madrasas in West Bengal.

Here it is also important to understand the role the 'ulama have to play for the believers. For the believers, the 'ulama not only lead the Friday prayers, they are also the authority to clarify Islamic principles and give guidance on issues dealing with modern life, which are not explicitly addressed in the Quran and Sunna (practice of the Prophet Mohammad). These *fatwas* have to be provided in the light of religious texts. For a believer, an 'alim who is known for his religious specialization is more important than the one who is seen to have followed a divided curriculum. During the interviews, the officials of the state madrasa board in Bangladesh, as well as parents of the students attending 'Aliya madrasas, acknowledged that the students in Qaumi madrasas are better trained in religious texts. As noted by a junior officer at the Bangladesh Madrasa Board, "When it comes to religious matters even I will seek guidance from an 'alim who is more specialized in Islamic texts."

'Aliya and Qaumi madrasas also differ markedly in their relationship with the community. Traditionally, the head and teachers of a madrasa not only teach the regular students, they also provide Quranic recitation classes in the evening for the neighborhood children. The madrasa imam also leads the Friday prayer at the mosque. This association is not necessarily present in the case of 'Aliya madrasas, as most of them do not belong to a mosque nor do they provide afternoon Quran classes to community students. This difference is critical in determining the relationship between the two types of madrasas with the community. This means that the mosque network remains under the control of the traditional 'ulama, and when there is an opening at a mosque, Qaumi madrasa students attached to that mosque have the strongest chance of securing that position. 'Aliya madrasa students fail to develop any relations with the community which, as is shown in chapter 4, has direct bearing on giving an 'alim the liberty to reinterpret Islamic principles.

The relationship of 'Aliya madrasas graduates with the community is also affected by their mannerisms and behavior as students of 'Aliya madrasas are argued to follow more secular norms. Interviews show that these cultural and attitudinal changes of 'Aliya madrasa students also play an important role in reducing public trust in the competence of the graduates of 'Aliya madrasas (for more on this, see chapter 4). In Bangladesh, apart from the three state managed 'Aliya madrasas, the rest are co-educational, a practice that does not enjoy much respect among the staunch believers—given the emphasis on purdah and gender segregation within traditional Islamic texts. According to the ‘ulama of Qaumi madrasas, the very attitudes of the students within ‘Aliya madrasas have changed, the latter have become just like schools. Student dress, their mannerisms, and their way of speech do no differ from the school children. The point to note, however, is that though ‘Aliya madrasa students seem to have become relatively secular in the eyes of the Qaumi madrasa leadership they have not become entirely free of religion either. Comparing the attitudes of ‘Aliya madrasa students with those of students from secular madrasas, Asadullah and Chaudhary (2006) argue that ‘Aliya madrasa graduates have conservative views compared with the children of secular schools; they are less favorable to ideas of higher education for girls and working mothers, have a preference for large families, and seek an Islamic democratic political system. Thus, they are different in their professional orientations from Qaumi madrasa students but in terms of their mind-set, they follow many of the orthodox Islamic principles as in case of the Qaumi madrasas thereby showing a dual failure of the reform program.

The reformed madrasas have therefore failed to display orthodox ‘ulama because they are not equipped to meet the demands of the community. Traditional Islamic interpretations still serve a purpose for people in the given context, supporting North's (1990) claim that many informal constraints have great survival tenacity because they still resolve basic exchange problems among the participants, be they social, political, or economic. The bargaining power of the graduates of ‘Aliya madrasas vis-à-vis the public is thus very weak when compared to that of the graduates of Qaumi madrasas, who offer specialized knowledge of Islamic Studies. The shift to a new equilibrium could be galvanized either by making a huge financial investment in reforms and engaging the ‘ulama in designing the reforms, or by having the reformed madrasa graduates demonstrate such sophisticated understanding of traditional Islamic texts that they win the believers' confidence.

## Why Madrasas Failed to Reform

Thus far I have tried to provide an explanation for the persistence of orthodox religious views despite the financial incentives introduced by the state. This should, however, not be interpreted to mean that the senior ‘ulama see no need for improvement in the existing system of madrasa education. During the interviews with senior ‘ulama across the three countries, in line with some existing studies (Sikand 2002), I found them critical of the state of madrasa education and cognizant of the need for improvement. During the interviews, though most senior ‘ulama started the conversation by defending the education provided within the madrasas,[27] most justified their position in context of the limited resources with which they operate. I found many 'ulama were aware of the fact that the general public has a poor impression of madrasa education and the madrasas no longer produce scholars of great repute; others also recognized that the children at the madrasas at times feel to be inferior to students in secular schools. These 'ulama recognize the need for improvement in the madrasas education system but for them the optimal reform is not to make a child learn less of a religious content and more of secular subjects but one where a student becomes well-versed in a greater range of Islamic texts and develops a better command of the Arabic language. Although the emphasis of the state-led reform is on secularization of the madrasas, I found that the 'ulama's vision of reform revolves around producing learned Islamic scholars, who specialize in Islamic studies and are well-versed in a much broader array of religious texts. Why these voices of reform among ranks of senior 'ulama have not led to actual changes within the madrasa curriculum is best explained by Arthur (1989): (1) large set-up costs, which give the advantage of falling unit costs as output increases; (2) learning effects, which improve products or lower their costs as their prevalence increases; (3) coordination effects, which confer advantages to cooperation with other economic agents taking similar action; (4) adaptive expectations, where increased prevalence on the market enhances beliefs of future prevalence.

To broaden the religious horizons of the graduates within the madrasas implies providing them with the means to understand a variety of authors exposing them to various interpretations of the religious texts. It is much less costly to continue to teach the traditional curriculum of Dars-i-Nizami than to start teaching texts by al-Ghazali (d. 505/1111) and other such Islamic philosophers who provide a more philosophical than literal interpretation of Islamic texts. Ensuring such a shift requires large-scale initial investment, in the absence of which there can only be continued investment in the teaching of traditional texts. Further, there are coordination effects as, given that all five schools of thought running madrasas in Pakistan teach jurisprudence, for any one school of thought to take a plunge in a different direction would involve high costs. The adaptive expectations also play a role in the continued investment in the study of Islamic fiqh (jurisprudence), as given the high demand among the public for the fatwa services provided by the 'ulama, their expectation is that the public will continue to demand a more traditional interpretation of Islamic texts, which does not take a radical departure from existing practices.

---

27. One senior representative of the Deobandi wafaq countered state critique of the madrasas by noting, "Today we are giving to the entire world, very good 'ulama while our students from secular schools have to go and study in foreign universities" (Jalandari 2006).

The reluctance of the ‘ulama to shift to a new equilibrium of learning, despite acknowledging the need for it, illustrates that path dependence is not just a product of chance events but of a process of conscious calculation or the optimal choice under the circumstances of the time. Prolonged investment in certain equilibrium, as seen in the case of Dars-i-Nizami during two centuries of colonial rule, created a lock-in that has prevailed beyond colonial time. The Deoband tradition opted for an inwardly puritanical Islam due to the displacement of Islam from being the state religion to becoming completely irrelevant to politics and economics under the colonial government. In doing so, it recorded a major shift from the rationalist scholarship, which had dominated Islamic scholarship on the subcontinent under the Mughal rule. Over time, path dependence has developed, and reverting back to the study of rationalist subjects has become a very high investment strategy. Drawing on the historical analysis developed in the previous chapter, the only way that the ‘ulama will be motivated to make the investment to move toward a new equilibrium will either be the birth of such a remarkable reformist theologian as Shirazi in the Mughal period, or such a dramatic shift in the external context as was seen with the advent of colonial rule, that the very survival of the madrasas requires making that shift.

There are signs that the hostility in the external context due to the policies of the war on terror is providing such a changed context: exposed to serious criticism by the state and international forces, ‘ulama in the Pakistani madrasas, as noted during the fieldwork, have started taking some measures to initiate an internally led reform process by placing greater emphasis on teaching English language and exposing the children to computers and information technology so that their graduates can better defend their viewpoint vis-à-vis the secular elite. Thus historically determined factors have played a role in creating institutional inertia within the ‘ulama but the opportunity for breaking out of this inertia seems to be in the making due to the dramatic changes in the external context by a chance event, namely September 11. The direction of change will, however, be determined by the competence and strategic calculations of the ‘ulama leading the religious hierarchy at the time.

## Conclusions

The causes of institutional stickiness as evident in persistence of orthodox Islamic teaching in South Asian madrasas in the post-independence period support theories of path dependence, which note the role of historical factors but place greater emphasis on the strategic behavior of the institutional elite. Ideological conviction in orthodox Islamic beliefs and a genuine difference between the secular elite and the 'ulama regarding what is real "knowledge" did play a role in making 'ulama resist the state-led reform, even in contexts where there were strong financial incentives. Similarly, the historical endowment of the 'ulama, which as noted by Arthur (1989, 1990) led to large investment costs, learning effects, coordination effects, and adaptive expectations, did play a role in creating institutional inertia. However, the fact that these 'ulama took these factors into consideration (some consciously and other sub-consciously) in refraining from initiating internal reform is reflective of the importance of strategic calculations rather than chance events in creating institutional change and inertia. By noting that elite madrasas in Pakistan have started an internal process of reform in response to the hostility meted out to them since September 11, the research shows that institutional lock-in to an inefficient equilibrium is not irreversible (Liebowitz and Margolis 1995): the 'ulama within elite madrasas are adjusting to these changes just as their forefathers did when suddenly displaced from position of power under colonial rule, and in this process there will be changes to the very rules of the game, namely interpretation of Islamic texts. Thus, Liebowitz and Margolis (1995:223) are correct in emphasizing that "the endowment of one generation is the bequest of another, and there is value in learning what actions previous generations took that increased or decreased their wealth." The only issue is that in focusing on the actors it is important not to completely neglect the impact of the initial endowments and uncontrollable macro events—a neglect that Liebowitz and Margolis (1995) demonstrate, given their emphasis on neoclassical assumptions.

That it is not just the strategic behavior of the institutional elite but also that of followers that is critical in determining institutional inertia and change is also borne out by the fact that the institutional elite is not necessarily free of checks in setting the direction of change. The 'ulama's adherence to orthodox beliefs partly represented their own ideological conviction but it also reflected their recognition of the expectations of followers (especially the bigger patrons), thereby supporting two of North's (1990) propositions: one, the inability to achieve compromise solutions may reflect not only a lack of mediating institutions but also limited degree of freedom of the entrepreneurs to bargain and still maintain the loyalty of their constituent groups; two, the institution still serves a purpose for people. What my analysis has shown is that informal institutions, which have written rules, restrict the elite's freedom to dramatically change the rules of the game as followers (especially big patrons) have access to written works interpreting those rules. Even though many Muslims in South Asia might not be able to read or write due to high illiteracy rates, the large patrons usually come from affluent families, are literate, and have access to prior learning. However, this is not to argue that beliefs engrained in written texts are unchanging; rather the point is to highlight that in such a context the institutional leadership needs to be able to argue from within the text to justify new interpretations.

Islam has an advanced tradition of written scholarship; the complex set of commentaries by a number of reputed scholars available to followers reduces their reliance on one 'alim as an ultimate arbiter of Islamic rules (Cornell 2007; Donnan 2002; Esposito 1999; Gordon 2002). Informal institutions, which have written codes of behavior, are therefore more likely to resist dramatic shifts to new equilibrium especially when they serve a clear purpose as seen in the case of state failure in the three countries to produce credible centers of theology. The state reform programs have ended up secularizing the madrasas whose graduates seek to enter the formal economy instead of producing more enlightened scholars of Islam capable of convincing the broader public with their knowledge; the result is that the 'ulama trained in orthodox madrasas continue to serve a purpose in the followers' lives. Thus not just the behavior of the elite but also that of the followers shows reflective rather than habitual behavior.

In addition, the interaction between the secular and religious elite over the madrasa reform program across the three countries supports existing research that argues for recognizing the importance of power asymmetries in setting the direction of institutional change (Ensminger 1992). As North (1990) notes at times path dependence results because given the bargaining strength of the players and the set of contractual bargains that make up the total exchange, none of the players find it advantageous to devote resources into restructuring the agreements. Despite ideological commitment to the ideas of madrasa reform, the secular political elite in India, Pakistan, and Bangladesh consciously chose not to push these reforms, because their political interests were best served within the prevailing structures of interaction between the political and religious elite. How elite interests are affected by the proposed institutional changes play a critical role in determining whether or not a shift to higher societal equilibrium would occur. Power asymmetries thus do impede shift to socially optimal equilibrium.

The study of interaction between the secular and religious elite also highlights that informal and formal institutions employ different mechanisms to gain public legitimacy. Formal institutions rely on formal authority, whereas informal institutions rely in most cases on voluntary compliance—with the result that the elite in the formal institutions are in a position to enforce rules and regulations through formal apparatus, while the elite in the informal institutions have to win compliance not just through demonstrating their efficiency but also by establishing model behavior. It is due to the latter that adoption of secular norms within graduates of reformed madrasas reduces their ability to mobilize public following. My research suggests that broadly, the strength of a formal institution rests in three main characteristics: political legitimacy (the more representative the formal institutions, the less they have to rely on informal institutions to gain public legitimacy); bureaucratic efficiency; and, the ability to provide financial incentives. Conversely, the strength of the informal institution depends on the practical relevance of the institution in followers' daily life, financial independence of the elite, and the ideological appeal of the ideas that the institution presents.

These findings have important policy implications. In South Asia, the states have tried to change the rules of the game of orthodox Islam by creating new players in the field, while a more effective strategy requires developing the incentives that make it worthwhile for the elite among the old players to adjust the rules of the game. It would be more efficient to engage with those ʻulama who themselves voice the need for change, and support an endogenous reform process rather than imposing an agenda from outside. The failure of the state to reform orthodox Islam is evidence not of the rigidity of the ʻulama but the failure of the South Asian states to provide the ʻulama with appropriate incentives to invest in diversification of religious learning. Given the importance of the elite in initiating institutional change and setting the direction of this change as well as in creating institutional inertia, chapter 4 develops an understanding of the working of the religious elite and the organization of the religious hierarchy in Pakistan.

4

# ORGANIZATION OF RELIGIOUS HIERARCHY

## Competition or Cooperation?

> **Thus, the central theme that runs through my remarks is that complexity frequently takes the form of hierarchy, and that hierarchic systems have some common properties that are independent of their specific content. Hierarchy, I shall argue, is one of the central structural schemes that the architect of complexity uses.**
>
> —Herbert A. Simon, *The Architecture of Complexity* (1962: 468)

> **Markets and Hierarchies are presented in some courses as fundamentally different "pure types" of organizations. Not only are these types of institutional arrangements perceived to be different but each is assumed to require its own explanatory theory... Thus, the time is ripe for an effort that attempts to draw on the foundations of many disciplines... to attempt to answer the core question... What are the underlying component parts that can be used to build useful theories of human behavior in the diverse range of situations in which humans interact?**
>
> —Elinor Ostrom, *Doing Institutional Analysis* (2005: 820–21)

Pakistan is a land of diversity—in income, geography, ethnicity, and languages[1]—and its madrasas are no exception. In a small village situated in the scenic hills of Murree with 3,000 inhabitants, a one-room hut serves as a madrasa, in which the imam of the local mosque gives Quranic lessons to 50 children. This is the only madrasa in the entire village. In the sprawling city of Karachi with its 13 million residents there are 2,500 registered madrasas; the largest among these, which provide education up to the doctoral level, have as many as 4,000 students who gravitate toward these madrasas from across the country. The unregistered madrasas in Karachi are countless: on every major street corner there is a mosque with an adjacent room for the teaching of basic Quranic education. Both the one-room hut and the sprawling buildings in Karachi are referred to

1. For a good review of the political economy of Pakistan see Noman (1990) and Zaidi (1999).

as madrasas. However, I could simply walk into the former, but I had to make repeated requests and use my connections within the wafaq to be granted access to the latter. Are the two the same? And, how do they relate to each other, if at all? In this chapter I present the complexity of the madrasa network in Pakistan to identify the basis of religious hierarchy.

Neoclassical economic theory begins with the market where free agents bargain and trade in a manner that maximizes their utility under the given price constraints; a horizontal structure unaffected by any power relations where individuals engage in exchange until they achieve the optimal outcome. The rise of the firm, an institutional arrangement where individual agents voluntarily coordinate their activities under a hierarchical structure of production, has thus been an analytical puzzle, which has led to the rise of the dynamic field of organizational economics. The primary explanation for rise of this voluntary hierarchical structure has come to rest in the idea of transaction costs, that is the cost of negotiating and enforcing contracts (Coase 1937). Although generating a complex set of literature such as represented by Alchian and Demsetz's (1972) work on role of team production externalities, and Williamson's (1975) work on informational asymmetry in giving rise to these transaction costs, the main focus within this literature has been on noting the importance of setting the right financial incentives that make the supervisors and subordinates coordinate their activities to meet the firm's objective (Miller 1992).

Anthropologists, sociologists, and political scientists, however, highlight the importance of moral authority and cooperation within the working of noneconomic hierarchies. Ensminger (1992), an economic anthropologist who despite working within the NIE framework argues that how exactly competition works and what it rewards depends on the structure of the specific institution so that nonmarket hierarchies are not necessarily a product of competitive behavior. Pierson (2000) draws a similar distinction between outcomes in the economic and political spheres, arguing that the central features of political systems are compulsory rather than voluntary where exercise of authority—generally combined with a complex array of complementary institutions designed to circumscribe and legitimize that authority—rather than financial incentives form the basis of political authority. In this approach the explanation of the rise of hierarchy rests in moral or legislative authority rather than efficiency.

The existing studies on madrasas in Pakistan though rarely framed in an explicit theoretical framework share the assumptions of an authority obeying rather than efficiency-based conceptions of the madrasa hierarchy. The 'ulama in the madrasas are viewed to exploit their moral authority to convince students of the benefits of enrolling in jihad for promises of rewards in the other world; these studies assume rather than systematically study the working of authority within the madrasa hierarchy. Whether religious authority is free from all competitive pressures whereby the elite command unquestioning obedience among the followers is an important issue to settle empirically if the claims regarding movement of madrasa students to jihad are to be properly analyzed. An empirically grounded analysis of working of noneconomic hierarchies focusing on the actions of individual actors involved in the hierarchy also has the potential to address Ostrom's (2005) concern about the need to develop a consistent theory of human behavior that can explain the existence of markets as well as hierarchies.

One attempt at such a bridging exercise rests in the work of Gary Miller (1992) who drawing on theories of leadership from other social sciences records that even economic hierarchies are not simply based on financial incentives; rather firms where managers can use noneconomic incentives to inspire cooperation enjoy a competitive advantage over those that do not. In this chapter I undertake a similar analysis but in a reverse context: applying the analytical tools of NIE to a noneconomic hierarchy, namely that of religion, I explore whether the competitive forces are less important in the working of the religious hierarchy or is the latter just as much a product of competition as the market; is behavior dominated by different consideration in the religious sphere as opposed to the market?

There are 16,000 registered madrasas in Pakistan, that is madrasas that have registered themselves with the five central wafaqs (collective platforms). These wafaqs are semi-autonomous bodies run by the ʻulama and are recognized by the government. The unregistered madrasas, normally one-room schools attached to mosques referred to as *maktabs,* exist in much greater number. The existing literature on madrasas, however, rarely demonstrates cognizance of these variations or an understanding of rules determining the interactions within the complex network of the madrasa system; at best, brief footnotes are introduced to qualify claims about links between militancy and madrasas (ICG 2002; Stern 2000). Despite featuring prominently in the global counterterrorism discourse and the war on terror, whereby madrasas have been the target of drone attacks (such as in Bajour) besides being subjected to curriculum reforms, very basic but important empirical questions about madrasas in Pakistan—their number, geographical spread, rules of engagement within the madrasa system—remain unaddressed. How actors within the madrasa network differentiate among madrasas and the ranking criteria remain unexplored. Analyzing the data on the number of madrasas available within the five wafaqs, this chapter addresses inter-wafaq and within-wafaq differences among madrasas and explains the factors shaping the rise of the elite madrasas and the retention of this status over generations. In addition, by looking at the motives and decision-making processes of the ʻulama to join the wafaq, the chapter develops an understanding of the basis of religious hierarchy.

## Hierarchy as a Response to Complexity: The Madrasa Landscape

Herbert Simon (1962) in his groundbreaking work on hierarchy identified the existence of an informal hierarchy within complex systems as a natural response to complexity. Drawing a distinction between a formal and an informal hierarchy, he argued that all complex systems end up having a hierarchy where the sub-systems do not have formal reporting requirements but are interdependent: "If we make a chart of social interactions, of who talks to whom, the clusters of dense interaction in the chart will identify a rather well-defined hierarchic structure" (Simon 1962: 469). Contrary to the exiting studies of madrasas in Pakistan, which fail to develop an analytically meaningful classification, the analysis developed here validates Simon's position that actors within a complex network have internal mechanisms to differentiate and coordinate among themselves—even when to actors outside the system those signs are unintelligible. The mere scale of madrasas in Pakistan indicates the existence of some internal coordinating mechanisms.

The registered madrasas in Pakistan have 1.5 million students.[2] Situated within the total school-going population, this figure at first loses its significance as the share of madrasa students within the total population of school-age children has been argued to be between 1 percent[3] (Andrabi et al. 2005) and 2.6 percent (Cockcroft 2009). Such claims, however, need a cautions engagement, given the methodological limitation[4] of the studies on which they draw. Further, when the afternoon Quranic education classes held at the madrasas for the neighborhood children are taken into account, along with the system of home schooling whereby most middle- and upper-income families engage a madrasa 'alim or a student to teach Quran to their children, the sphere of influence of the teachings imparted within madrasas becomes quite extensive (Nelson 2006). It is also worth remembering that in terms of absolute number, 1.5 million is by no means a small number.[5]

There are two criteria to conceptually organize the 16,000 registered Pakistani madrasas: one is based on the school of thought, the other on the differing scale of madrasas within the same school of thought; in other words, it is important to understand inter-wafaq as well as within-wafaq differences. The decline of

2. The Pakistani government provides data for 2003/4. Because the government figures also draw on the data maintained by the five wafaqs, where possible the book draws on the data directly acquired from these wafaqs during 2007–8 because it is more recent.

3. The comparative figure for India is 4 percent of school-age Muslim children (Sachar 2006).

4. Most estimates draw on publicly available data sources, such as population census, instead of using instruments especially designed to ask questions about madrasa enrollment.

5. For instance, the entire school-age population in Sweden (including children in pre-school and secondary schools) is less than 1.7 million (UNICEF 2008).

Mughal Empire and gradual withdrawal of state support for Islam saw fragmentation within nineteenth and twentieth century Islamic thought: the prominent schools of Islamic thought in South Asia including Deoband, Barelvis, and Ahl-i-Hadith emerged in this period (Metcalf 1982). In the 1940s, Jamaat-i-Islami emerged, which represents a sociopolitical organization rather than a distinct school of Islamic thought.[6] However, by virtue of establishing a large number of madrasas of its own, it has successfully negotiated the status of a wafaq. These five schools of thought to date dominate the madrasa network in Pakistan. The largest number of madrasas are registered with the Deoband school of thought (9,500), followed by Barelvis (4,500), Jamaat-i-Islami (1,000), Ahl-i-Hadith (500), and Shia (500).

The interesting dimension about the strength of madrasas within each school of thought is that the spread does not correlate to the popular adherence of that belief within the public. A large number of Pakistanis, especially in the most populated province of Punjab, is estimated as following Barelvi practices, which place heavy emphasis on visiting shrines and revering the Sufi saints, yet it is the puritanical Deobandi sect, which denounces such practices, which has the largest number of madrasas in Pakistan. A satisfactory explanation for this puzzle requires an in-depth historical analysis, though interviews with leading 'ulama provide useful indicators: one, Deobandi madrasas have been more successful in producing a larger number of prominent personalities among 'ulama in Pakistan than the other sects; two, this outcome could be the result of the process of self-selection. Because madrasas in South Asia revolve around 'ulama rather than Sufis (though there are close connections between the two), it is more likely that the families who opt for madrasa education are predisposed toward the puritanical Islamic school of thought, thus creating a higher demand for Deobandi madrasas.

During my fieldwork I found that those schools of thought that have the largest number of madrasas also tend to have madrasas with a larger number of students. The biggest Deobandi madrasas—Banuri Town, Jamia Karachi, Korongi Town—have up to 4,000 students each. Conversely, the leading Shia madrasa, Jamia al-Muntazir in Lahore has only 350. The difference results from the differing approaches to learning within these madrasas: Shia madrasas, unlike the Sunni madrasas, place little emphasis on the memorization of Quran (the process of hifz) with the result that—unlike the madrasas from the other schools of thought—they mainly admit students seeking training in theology. A Shia theologian can become a mujtahid (a person qualified to form an opinion in Islamic law) without having to memorize the Quran; in fact, I found the Shia

6. Jamaat-i-Islami claims to work across the sectarian divides, and its membership is open to all Muslims—its theological positions however are closest to that of the Deoband school of thought.

ʿulama critical of the emphasis placed on hifz in the Sunni wafaqs. In the words of Maulana Mohammad Ishaq, a Shia scholar in Islamabad:

> The Shia madrasas in the cities mostly admit children after they have completed matriculation. We do not take small children because hifz is not part of our syllabus. We do not believe that memorization of the Quran has an important role in the training of an Islamic scholar, we focus on developing a deeper understanding of the Quran and Islamic texts. This is the reason that even in our biggest madrasas there are only 200–300 children. A small madrasa, on the other hand, can have only 25–30 students. In rural areas there might be some madrasas that take very small children.

A Sunni scholar, however, would seriously compromise his authority if he were not a hafiz (a person who memorizes the Quran). It is the process of hifz that attracts a large number of students to Sunni madrasas (for details see chapter 5) and, when Shia scholarship does not place much emphasis on this, the number of potential students is understandably fewer than that in madrasas of the other schools of thought.

Another noticeable variation I found was the geographical spread of the madrasas across these five schools of thought. Apart from the Deobandi madrasas, which in line with their high number record a presence across the country, I found that the madrasas from other schools of thought have specific geographical pockets as their stronghold. Deobandi madrasas are spread across the provinces, with the most prestigious madrasas concentrated in Karachi; Barelvi madrasas, which are the second largest in number among the five schools of thought, are also spread across most parts of the country though they record the strongest presence in Punjab followed by Khyber Pakhtunkhwa and Sindh and comprise a very small number in Balochistan (see table 4.1).

**TABLE 4.1** Distribution of madrasas across the provinces[1]

| | DEOBANDI | AHL-I-HADITH | JAMAAT-I-ISLAMI | BARELVI | AHL-I-SHIA |
|---|---|---|---|---|---|
| Punjab | 3,218 | 302 | 150 | 3,579 | 210 |
| Sindh | 1,746 | 45 | 155 | 302 | 81 |
| Balochistan | 663 | 5 | 30 | 137 | 14 |
| Khyber Pakhtunkhwa | 1,815 | 22 | 245 | 391 | 13 |
| Islamabad | 107 | 2 | 14 | 70 | 7 |

*Source:* Data gathered from the five wafaqs (2008).

[1] The data on Federally Administered Tribal Areas (FATA) and Azad Kashmir is not included. By 2011, the total number of madrasas registered with the government had increased to 19,366. The recent registration data, however, does not provide breakdown by sect.

I found that the role of prominent personalities played a critical role in determining the popularity of a specific school of thought in a given geographical area. Either learned ʻulama or leading political or social figures in the locality play an important role in ensuring the spread of that particular school of thought in a given locality or region. During the interviews, for instance, the spread of the Shia sect in Parachinar, a city in the tribal belt bordering Afghanistan, was attributed to a prominent Shia theologian who heralded from an affluent background and also became a leading Shia politician. He is viewed as having played a central role in the spread of the Shia school of thought in this area, which is otherwise surrounded on all sides by Sunni Islam, in particular the Deoband sect. According to the head of a prominent Shia madrasa in Peshawar, "In Khyber Pakhtunkhwa, Arif Hussain Al Hussaini has played a very important role in the spread of Jafaria school of thought. Not only was he a highly respected scholar, he was also a very dynamic leader of the Shia community. He also became the leader of Teehrik-i-Jafaria Pakistan [political party] and played a central role in preserving Shia school of thought in Parachinar. His assassination was a huge loss for the Shia community in the area." Senior ʻulama from the Ahl-i-Hadith school of thought explained the stronghold of Ahl-i-Hadith in Kasur, a small city in central Punjab, in similar terms: "The local population accepted the Ahl-i-Hadith school of thought under the influence of a financially affluent notable who over time became a strong follower." Similarly, ʻulama repeatedly explained to me that the concentration of elite Deobandi madrasas in Karachi was the result of settlement of senior ʻulama from the Deoband school of thought in Karachi on their migration from India, thus making this metropolitan city a central player in Deobandi scholarship (Usmani 2004).

The presence of prominent ʻulama and political figures appears to be a critical contributor to the spread of a particular school of thought in an area, though my interviews with the ʻulama also highlighted the importance of historical and cultural trends: the natural affinity between the initial resource endowments of the local community and the religious ideology of a specific school of thought appeared to be the most plausible explanations for the overwhelming influence of the Deoband school of thought in Khyber Pakhtunkhwa and Balochistan, the two provinces in Pakistan that host the traditional Pathan and Balochi tribes. This relation has an old foundation, wherein many Afghani students traveled to India to enroll at Deoband during the colonial period (Metcalf 1982). An important explanation for the dominance of the Deobandi madrasas in the two provinces seems to rest in the close affinity between Deoband's puritanical interpretations, which place emphasis on a direct link with God and equate saint worship to *shirk* (associating partners with God), and the tribal culture with its emphasis on honor and equality. It therefore appears that the closeness of an idea to the historical traits and cultural attributes of a population, that is the proximity of the rules of the new institutions to the existing ones, seems to facilitate its widespread acceptance.

Where I found the five wafaqs record fewer differences than expected is in their curricula. All five schools of thought teach the Dars-i-Nizami, using different selection of textbooks. In addition, they differ in terms of the exposure the 'ulama from these wafaqs have to higher theological training in reputed centers of learning in the Muslim world. The Shia tradition makes it mandatory for all madrasa students to undertake the last two years of education in Qom (Iran) or Najaf (Iraq). Among Sunni madrasas some students do pursue higher education in universities in the Arab states, but such access is limited and contingent on the individual efforts of the students. Despite the formation of Ittihad-i-Tanzeemat Madaris-i-Deenia, a collective platform formed by leaders of the five wafaqs in 2003, the five schools are natural competitors in the hands of astute 'ulama where the real competition is to outshine each other in the pursuit of religious scholarship and win over converts from the other schools of thought. Central to such an exercise is *radd,* a process of argumentation based on logic and reasoning to counter the other party's theological position on an issue of Islamic jurisprudence. Ideally kept within the confines of scholarly refutation, such argumentation can at times degenerate into acrimonious debate where the scholars from one group label the other heretic.[7] During the interviews, I could often sense friction among the leaders of the different schools of thought despite them showing solidarity on the collective platform. The leaders of the Shia wafaq, in particular, often recorded concerns about being labeled heretic by the Sunni 'ulama; they also at times expressed concerns about the standards of education in the other wafaqs. Maulana Mohsin, a senior Shia scholar, was very blunt in his critique of Sunni 'ulama: "In some schools of thought even a maulvi (prayer leader) with very basic education can give fatwas. Our mufti is not sitting in every gali [road] and kucha [corner]. Our mufti is Mujtahid-i-Azam, who is selected very carefully." However, the 'ulama were able to put aside their differences when it came to cooperating on the platform of Ittihad-i-Tanzeemat Madaris-i-Deenia to confront the Musharraf government.

I also identified differences within the madrasas of the same school of thought. The internal organization of madrasas belonging to any wafaq represents a pyramid

---

7. A senior member from the Shia wafaq especially brought to attention a government report, which based on curriculum review of the five wafaqs, noted the biases against Shias in the Deobandi text, but failed to initiate any corrective measures from the government side. These ideological differences can at times lead to violence between Shia and Sunni groups—though in Pakistan such violence often has been politically engineered (Jaffrelot 2002).

**TABLE 4.2** Hierarchy of madrasas

| LEVEL OF MADRASA | DEGREES |
|---|---|
| Elite madrasas | Most reputed madrasas at 'Alimiya level, often include option for PhD level research (Takhassus) |
| Level 4: 'Alimiya | Master's degree |
| Level 3: 'Aliya | BA |
| Level 2: Khasa | Senior Secondary |
| Level 1: Ibtida'iya | Hifz and basic Islamic education |

*Source:* Based on the fieldwork (2006–2008).

structure, where the number of madrasas steadily tapers off as one moves up the pyramid. The madrasa system is no different from the secular schooling system in having distinct levels of education with a clearly specified curriculum: Ibtida'iya (primary), Khasa (senior secondary), 'Aliya (bachelor's degree), and 'Alimiya (master's degree). In addition, the elite madrasas, which represent the very tip of the pyramid, and offer takhassus (specialization; PhD level research), are estimated to be no more than 150 in number[8] (see table 4.2).

In Punjab, for instance, there are 1,680 registered Deobandi madrasas at the primary level, while there are only 681 madrasas at the matriculation level and 558 offering master's degree.[9] Similarly, a census of educational institutions conducted by the Ministry of Education estimated 21,552 madrasa students at the master's degree level as opposed to 74,782 students at the primary level[10] (Ministry of Education 2006). Given that most primary level madrasas are least likely to register while the bigger madrasas do, this suggests that when taking the total pool of madrasas in Pakistan (i.e., taking into account registered as well as unregistered madrasas) this difference will be even more significant. The largest number of madrasas (60%), thus, operates at Ibtida'iya level and in rural areas their ratio is even higher. That the elite madrasas are few and those offering takhassus facility are even fewer was noted by the head of an 'Alimiya madrasa in Rawalpindi, which despite belonging to the ranks of elite madrasas had only recently started to offer this facility: "For takhassus, you need reputed teachers and it is not easy to find teachers of that caliber. We finally started to offer this facility because otherwise our students had to go all the way to Karachi. Initially,

8. The wafaq data do not differentiate madrasas that teach takhassus from madrasas imparting education up until 'Alimiya level; this estimate is based on the 'ulama's own assessment.

9. Wafaq-ul-Madaris Al-Arabia (2006).

10. The census did not cover all the registered madrasas, thus these figures should not be interpreted to represent the total madrasa enrollment in registered madrasas at these levels.

takhassus facilities were available only in the bigger madrasas in Karachi and even today only a few madrasas in other cities are in a position to offer this facility."

Not only does the organizational structure of the madrasas parallel the secular schooling system, I also found that the spread of the madrasas across rural and urban areas follows the same pattern: elite madrasas like prominent universities tend to cluster in big cities. Sixty-eight percent of the Pakistani population lives in rural areas, but a madrasa offering education in Islamic theology is mainly an urban phenomenon. The directories of the madrasas available within the five wafaqs showed that while looking at madrasa population in rural area, 75 percent of the total operate at Ibtida'iya level. According to a senior Barelvi scholar, the reason for such distribution is obvious:

> You do not find universities within villages—it is the same for madrasas. The community in the rural areas is less affluent, therefore it cannot afford to make significant financial donations for the working of madrasas; the physical infrastructure is underdeveloped so students from urban areas do not have the incentive to migrate to rural areas though the reverse is routine; and, for similar reasons good teachers are more inclined to gravitate toward urban rather than rural areas.

In the directories of the four wafaqs,[11] over 80 percent of the 'Aliya level madrasas were located in the cities.

Karachi, the largest city and Pakistan's financial capital, is home not only to the largest number of madrasas across the five sects but also to some of the most prestigious madrasas within each sect. After Karachi, the next highest concentration of madrasas is in the federal and provincial capitals with Lahore—the second largest city and provincial capital of the most populated province of Punjab—securing lead position (see table 4.1). In addition, southern Punjab and rural Khyber Pakhtunkhwa represent other areas with a high concentration of madrasas. The high demand for religious education in these regions is often attributed to poverty and the presence of the strong feudal elite, which has restricted access to and provision of regular schooling in the area. A valid explanation but it alone is inadequate to explain the heavy concentration of madrasas in these regions when the performance of the other two provinces, namely rural Sindh and Balochistan, on economic indicators is not very different (World Bank 2002). The alternative explanation, provided to me by many 'ulama, rests in the historical specificities of these regions. Southern Punjab has been home to and the burial place of many early Sufi saints who spread Islam in South Asia,

11. The Wafaq-ul-Madaris Al-Arabia (Deoband wafaq) provided only the total figures rather than giving access to a directory listing all madrasas.

and Khyber Pakhtunkhwa is the resting place of Shuhdah-i-Balakot, a group of Islamic scholars known in the popular folklore for fighting to protect Islam in the region. During the interviews with senior ʻulama, the presence of the graves of Shuhdah-i-Balakot was repeatedly recorded as an important explanatory factor for the "love of Islam" and for Islamic learning in that region. Economics as well as historical factors thus seem to have played a role in determining the demand for madrasas in these two geographical settings.

I found that the madrasa network has a clear educational hierarchy, and records important inter-wafaq and within-wafaq differences in the organization of madrasas. These findings are arguably commonsensical, but recording these facts attains academic significance when the existing literature fails to register any cognizance of these variations. I now turn to the organizing principles of the madrasa hierarchy in Pakistan.

## Rise of Elite Madrasas and Retention of Elite Status

My survey of 110 madrasas (see Appendix A for samples selection)[12] across the eight districts with highest madrasa concentration upholds the argument established through the historical analysis in the preceding chapters: I found the tacit knowledge of the ʻalim is central to the rise of elite madrasas. Even quick reviews of the evolution of these madrasas, which from their very beginning acquired elite status or which gradually grew to have one, show them to have been established either by prominent scholars or by potentially aspiring graduates who established their credentials as each madrasa evolved.

In conversations with the ʻulama as well as the followers I discovered that they use numerous criteria to judge the competence of an ʻalim, namely, the power of logical reasoning, writing ability, command of historical texts and references, the volume and quality of the publications, oratory skills that are tested at the Friday *khutbas* (sermons), and the quality of the *qira'at* (vocalization of Quranic text). Qira'at skills have more emotive value for the believer and are important criteria in the selection of imams and prayer leaders. To reach the rank of elite ʻulama, however, one has to demonstrate a sound knowledge of Islamic texts, which determines the course of rightful actions for the believer. In the words of an ʻalim leading a small Barelvi madrasa, "Some of my most ardent followers are those who are very inspired by my Qira'at. They tell me that they come to pray

12. See Appendix for a review of sample selection and other methodological details.

in my mosque because they love my Qira'at. They say my Qira'at brings tears to their eyes." The 'ulama of the elite madrasas were also often appreciated in the interviews for their Qira'at skills but in their case this attribute was mentioned as an additional feature; the main emphasis was instead placed on their knowledge of the complex Islamic texts.

Madrasas run by 'ulama with a combination of these capabilities expand dramatically, drawing a large patronage base. On how donors judge the credentials of the 'ulama for various roles, see chapter 7. Here it is sufficient to note that the expansion of a madrasa is contingent not just on the theological knowledge, Qira'at, or oratory skills of the 'alim but also on his ability to mobilize a large number of patrons. I found ample evidence to show that the rise of elite madrasas, such as the prominent Deoband madrasas in Karachi, is a result of the mixing of caliber with capital. A large number of senior 'ulama from Deoband in India, many of whom were noticeable figures within the religious circles, on migrating to Pakistan did indeed settle in Karachi but the rapid expansion of their madrasas was ensured due to the financial support made available by the traders and businessmen in this port city, which is the center of commercial activity in Pakistan. An Islamabad based Deobandi 'alim commented on the rise of elite madrasas in Karachi, "The elite madrasas are not financially dependent on anyone. Over time they have been supported by patrons, who have also helped the leaders of these madrasas establish independent income generating activities. Remember, it is in the tradition of the Prophet to engage in trade and commerce. The 'ulama of elite madrasas make their living often from independent businesses. In establishing these businesses they have been supported by affluent patrons." 'Ulama interviewed across the eight districts, repeatedly identified the importance of the alliance between prominent 'ulama and the patrons from rich business families, as being critical to the rise, consolidation, and survival of the elite madrasas in Karachi. The big madrasas of Karachi are thus a product of not just the theological excellence of the respected 'ulama but also of their strategic maneuvering to attract a large pool of stable donors.

The survey results illustrate that, once a successful alliance has been negotiated between 'ulama and patrons, the rise of elite madrasas is guaranteed. As expected within secular educational institutions, the survey of 110 madrasas shows that the higher the madrasa is placed on the pyramid the higher the qualifications of its teachers; a larger percentage of them have received education abroad, and a higher number of them are involved in research and publications.

The heads of the five wafaqs had received education in foreign lands, and profiles of the 'ulama heading the elite madrasas included within the survey reveal that 80 percent had studied in the original Deoband madrasa or other parent schools and around 30 percent had gained education in universities in the Gulf and the Middle East as compared to none in the smaller madrasas. The data show that, out of the three tiers of madrasas surveyed, it was also the ʿulama from elite madrasas who were invited to give advice on national level government committees, including the zakat (Islamic alms) committees, which are responsible for the disbursement of annual zakat funds collected by the government, the Ruhat-i-Halal Committee (committee for the sighting of the moon for Islamic festivals), and other consultative committees. The committee formed by the government to negotiate with the ʿulama of the Red Mosque when it was under siege also drew on ʿulama from these elite madrasas.

In comparison, the head of the medium madrasas (Levels 2 and 3) also had teachers with master's degrees; however, they differed in terms of the volume of literature produced. The reason that the qualifications of the ʿulama between these two levels of madrasas do not record significant differences is that the madrasas evolve gradually from junior to higher levels of Islamic education; therefore an ʿalim leading a medium-scale madrasa often demonstrates the same qualifications as those of senior madrasas because he would be aspiring to make his madrasa evolve to the highest level. None of the heads of these madrasas were appointed to advisory positions vis-à-vis the government; if they were this was mostly at the local government level, for instance, the district level zakat committee. The leaders of madrasas represented in the bottom tier (Level 1), which focused primarily on the process of hifz, were normally (70%) trained only as hafiz. The survey results thus demonstrate that it is the more qualified ʿulama who demonstrate their expertise through sermons as well as through publications that come to lead the religious hierarchy; the elite madrasas acquire this status due to the academic excellence of the leading ʿulama in interpreting religious texts.

The survey results showed similar distribution of teachers across the madrasa hierarchy, so that the bigger madrasas register a higher number of teachers who are also more qualified (table 4.3). Twenty percent of the teachers in the elite madrasas had gained a master's degree or a PhD in a secular university, and had pursued higher training overseas. Twenty-five percent of the teachers from these madrasas had contributed to some Islamic magazine or brochure as compared to none in the Ibtida'iya or Khasa madrasas, though only a few had produced research publications. The smaller madrasas, not surprisingly, drew on a much smaller number of teachers; 80 percent of the Ibtida'iya madrasas were one or two teacher initiative having between ten to fifty students as opposed to presence of over 1000 students on average in the bigger madrasas. For example, Jamia Hafsa, a leading madrasa for females established in late 1980s, had 175 teachers and 50 assistant teachers where the teachers were recruited based on their qualifications and experience.

**TABLE 4.3** Comparative data on teachers

| TEACHERS' PROFILES | ELITE (%) | 'ALIMIYA AND 'ALIYA (%) | KHASA (%) | IBTIDA'IYA (%) |
|---|---|---|---|---|
| Teachers from rural areas | 60 | 60 | 75 | 75 |
| Teachers from urban areas | 40 | 40 | 25 | 25 |
| Teachers who studied overseas | 20 | 7 | 0 | 0 |
| Teachers who produced publications | 25 | 15 | 3 | 1 |

*Source:* Based on the fieldwork (2006–2008).

In discussions with the 'ulama and the students I found that the high demand for elite madrasas, which was visible in the case of the madrasas in Karachi, results in attracting students from across the country. Discussions with wafaq officials revealed clear within-province and cross-provinces migratory flows among the madrasa students. Conversely, the province of Khyber Pakhtunkhwa draws very few students from other provinces except in the cases of exceptionally renowned madrasas like Dar-ul-Uloom Haqqania in Akora Khattak. Similarly, during visits to Balochistan, another small province, I found that it attracts an insignificant number of students from other provinces, while students from both these provinces record a high presence in elite madrasas in Sindh and Punjab (see maps 4.1 and 4.2). At the same time, the provincial and federal capitals were the main base for attracting students from other parts of that province. This result is not surprising given that these cities have a higher concentration of reputed madrasas. This means that the bigger madrasas can afford to set more rigorous entry requirements. As noted in an essay on the admission process in the *Wafaq-ul-Madaris Weekly:*

> Every year there are new admissions whereby special focus is on madrasas in the following cities: Peshawar, Akora Khattak, Lahore, Faisalabad, Multan, Rawalpindi, Islamabad, and Karachi. In big madrasas, the admission process is more competitive and lasts longer. At the first stage there is a written test, then there is a test in *tajweed* [pronunciation of Quran] and qira'at [vocalization of Quran], after which the student's competence is further tested through careful assessment of his character certificate and transcripts of degrees from the previous madrasas. After that the student has to appear for a *takreeri* [debating] competition on at least two important books.

The difficulty of securing admission in an elite madrasa was repeatedly noted by the parents. One mother, whom I met at an elite female madrasa in Peshawar while waiting for the principal, said: "I am quite keen to have my daughter admitted to this madrasa. But it is not easy to secure admission here. I was told that people enter the name of the child a year before the child is to be admitted. I therefore stay in touch with the principal of this madrasa to ensure that my daughter will be admitted next year." The story for the smaller madrasas was very different. I found that as opposed to the luxury of picking the best students, the very small madrasas at times admit any child or actively mobilize students for enrollment, because it is the student presence that enables a madrasa to attract donations. The head of a small madrasa in Multan, southern Punjab, had for instance brought many children from his home village in Khyber Pakhtunkhwa to join the madrasa as the presence of the students provided him with the pretext to seek donations.

The elite madrasas thus attract academically the brightest and financially the most affluent classes. Forty percent of the students enrolled in the Hifz program in elite madrasas surveyed came from upper middle income or elite families. I found that the elite madrasas initiate a self-reinforcing mechanism where, by virtue of attracting the best students from the available pool, they end up growing the cream of the next generation of scholars and forming financially and intellectually affluent alumni that further strengthens these madrasas.

These madrasas thus have the highest bargaining power vis-à-vis the state, students, teachers, and donors. The government wants them on state committees to gain legitimacy; the donors prefer to make donations to these madrasas because they have more confidence in entrusting the ʿulama of these madrasas with their money, the brightest students want to enroll there, aspiring to be taught by the leading ʿulama in the field; and the best teachers end up gravitating toward these madrasas. In the words of an ʿalim from the Ahl-i-Hadith school of thought, "When a madrasa acquires a good reputation, it attracts everyone—students, teachers, and donors. Those who are the brightest want to be based at a place where others are of the same caliber. The reputed madrasas therefore attract the best teachers and students." In addition, the elite madrasas also have more influential networks because the more prestigious a madrasa the more renowned the mosque attached to it, and the greater the number of influential donors who utilize the services of that mosque. The donors of big madrasas are also well-connected socially and politically thus they are able to facilitate the working of madrasas in numerous ways.[13]

13. These connections are very useful in winning concessions from the state, as well as restricting undue state intervention, in a context where corruption within the state bureaucracy requires recourse to bribes to gain required permissions. During the fieldwork, the heads of most small madrasas recorded having confronted numerous problems when attempting to get a registration certificate from the government; none of the ʿulama leading the bigger madrasas faced any such problem.

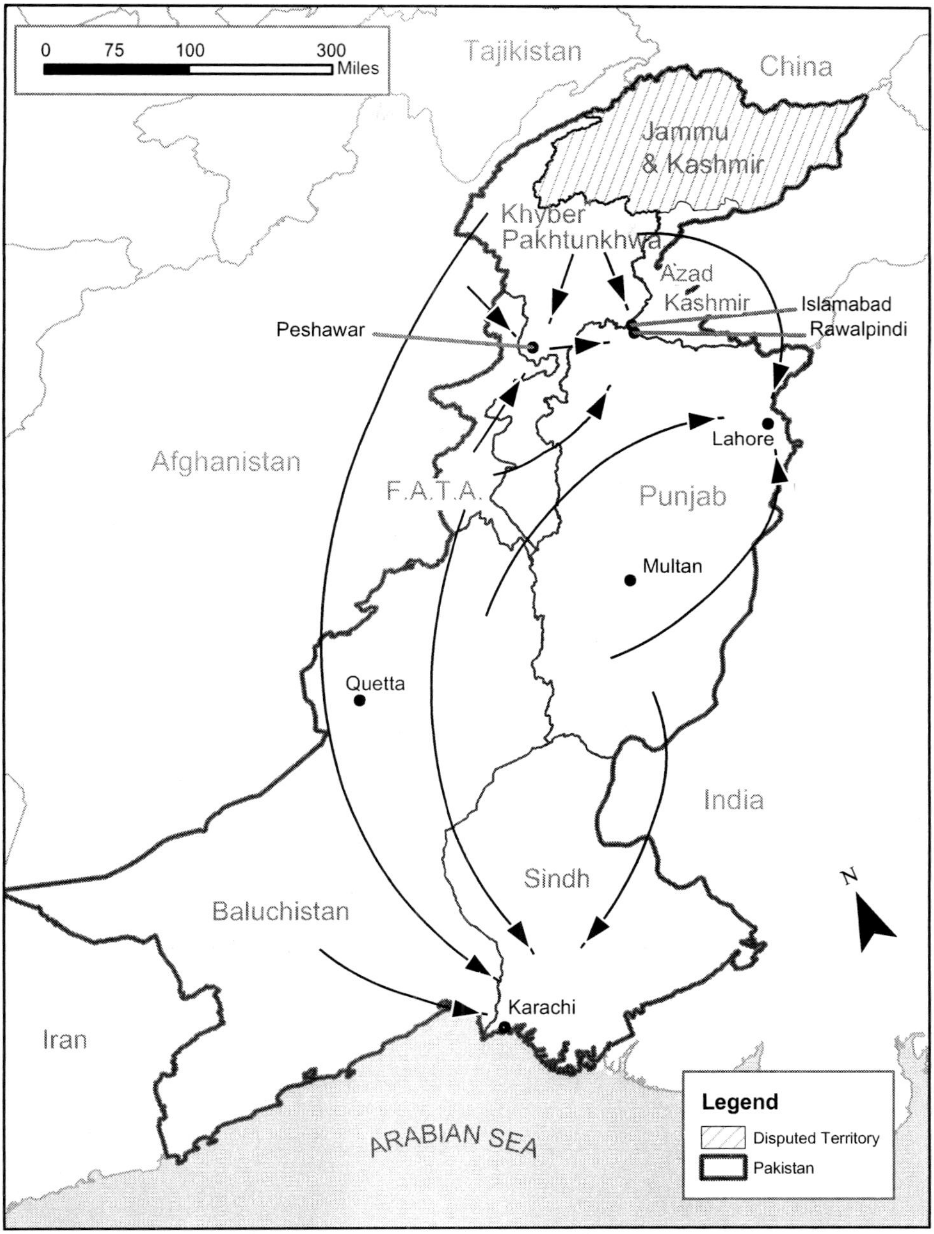


**MAP 4.1** Inter-provincial migratory flows among madrasa students since 1947
*Note:* FATA stands for the Federally Administered Tribal Areas. Until 2010 Khyber Pakhtunkhwa was known as the North-West Frontier Province.

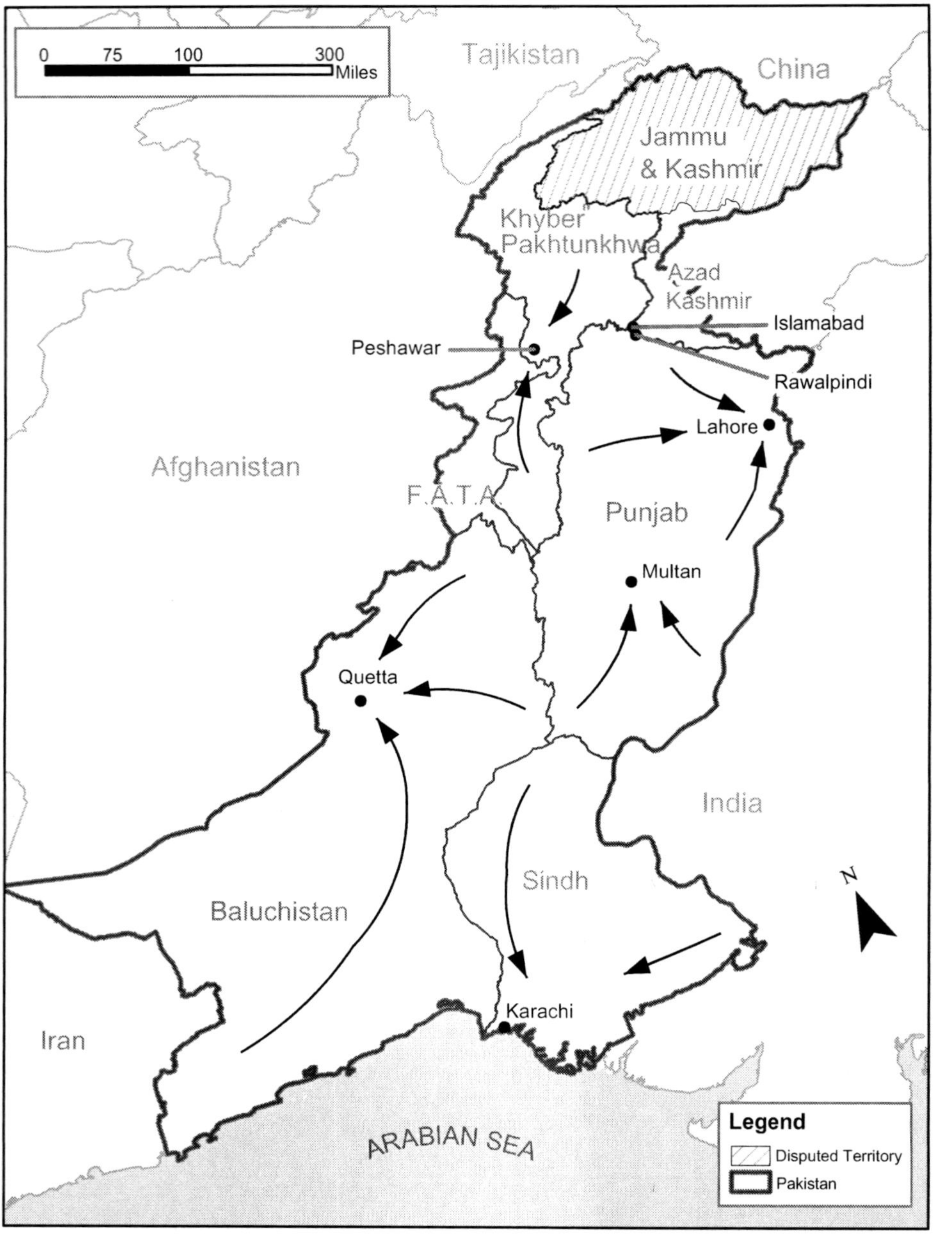


**MAP 4.2** Within-province migratory flows among madrasa students since 1947
*Note:* FATA stands for the Federally Administered Tribal Areas. Until 2010 Khyber Pakhtunkhwa was known as the North-West Frontier Province.

The elite madrasas, as the survey reveals, also have the most comfortable physical infrastructure, with more spacious classrooms, better boarding conditions, and libraries with impressive collections of Islamic texts. During the field visits it was impossible not to note the sprawling buildings of the elite madrasas, often specifically designed for teaching purposes. Most buildings were set amid spacious lawns, had well-aired and sunlit classrooms; though due to the high student numbers even the bigger madrasas convert classrooms into bedrooms at night. The leading madrasas in all five wafaqs were based in very spacious and often very aesthetically appealing buildings. The Dar-ul-Uloom Karachi, one of the most prominent Deobandi madrasa in Karachi, has a sprawling campus as does Jamia Ashrafi, the most prestigious Deobandi madrasa in Lahore. Jamia al-Muntazir, the madrasa hosting the Ahl-i-Shia wafaq is based in Model Town, a posh locality in Lahore, and has a well-planned architecture; Jamia al-Kousar, a newly built madrasa-cum-university in Islamabad belonging to the Shia school of thought has an extremely elegant architecture with Persian style motives adoring the exterior of the building. Jamia Naeemia, the madrasa hosting the Barelvi wafaq, similarly has a spacious and aesthetically appealing campus, and so do many other Barelvi madrasas such as Jamia Rizwia Al-Noor in Multan. The Jamaat-i-Islami wafaq is based in Mansura, where the Jamaat maintains a large independent complex. Jamia Al-Salafia in Faisalabad, which hosts the Ahl-i-Hadith wafaq, similarly has a sprawling campus. One of the differences often noted with pride by the ‘ulama of the larger madrasas was the presence of a well-resourced library, a facility which was limited in the cases of the medium-scale madrasas, and completely absent in the small madrasas. Dar-ul-Uloom Haqqania in Akora Khattak had over 4,000 volumes of books, many of which were expensive texts produced across the Muslim countries.

The infrastructural standards expected from a good madrasa, as described by the head of a prominent Barelvi madrasa, are quite high:

> The classrooms should be spacious and there should be a good system of lighting within them. The library should be so designed that the students can sit there to undertake their research and writing. The library should have many books in which the madrasa specializes as well as general knowledge books. The teachers’ place of residence should be within the madrasa because if the teachers come from afar they will find it difficult to concentrate. There should be a playground and place for extracurricular activities. For example, in our madrasa we have a place for extracurricular activities but it is not enough for playing cricket, a popular sport among students. There should also be a shop for the students to have easy access to essential items. Ideally, the madrasa should be located at some distance from populated areas.

The differences among the madrasas across the three tiers thus puts into question the validity of the claims that noneconomic hierarchies—cultural, religious, or political—are shaped by authoritarian rather than by competitive forces. The basis of religious hierarchy is academic excellence of the ʻulama in the religious texts. I, however, found one difference between the working of religious and economic hierarchy, which rests in the expectations that followers have from the religious leaders. Historical texts as well as interviews conducted during the course of this fieldwork highlight an emphasis on the personal behavior of the ʻulama, where important criteria establishing their stature was their personal piety and abstinences from excessive pursuit of material and bodily comforts. The obituaries of prominent ʻulama are littered with evidence of their personal virtues and self-sacrificing behavior. A collection of obituaries of prominent Pakistani ʻulama, by a reputed Islamic scholar Maulana Taqi Usmani, provides ample evidence:

> A good writer who translated *Bheeshti Zaewar* [a popular Islamic text] in Bangla, Maulana Sham-ul-Haq Faridpuri of East Pakistan who was a graduate of Deoband and Saharanpur, was not only a good-hearted and well-wishing individual, but saying the truth and courage were his special characteristics. He was on good terms with the rulers but when it came to issues of religion he was very firm in stating his positions.... He lived in a small room in the corner of the mosque, with just a small wood bench, serving as his bed, and next to it was a floor mat, on which he used to sit. And, when I visited him the last time,... he was eating some lentils and light gravy with simple bread. That was all. (2004: 11–13)

The emphasis on personal piety and a strong sense of responsibility is also illustrated in the obituary of Maulana Zafar Ahmad Usmani, a student of Deoband:

> He wrote prominent books in Tafseer, Hadith, and Fiqh. In addition, he had written many books on different religious issues in Urdu as well as Arabic. Works that cannot be produced by groups of scholars at big academies were produced by him single-handedly. His political and social contributions were numerous. He was an active member of the movement for the establishment of Pakistan and his commitment to prayer was exemplary. Even at the age of eighty-five when he was very frail he said all five prayers in the mosque with the congregation and led the *Zuhur* [mid-day] and ʻ*Asar* [afternoon] prayers. Until the very end he gave *dars* [lessons] in *Saheeh Bukhari* [a prominent Islamic text]. He was very punctual in responding to any letters until the very end. (Usmani 2004: 16–21)

The most comprehensive account of the high expectations from a leading ʿalim is, however, available in the obituary of Maulana Syed Mohammad Yusaf Banuri, the founder of the famous Banuri Town[14]madrasa in Karachi:

> He was a treasure of knowledge in every field of Islamic learning. His power of memory, his breadth of knowledge, his taste for book reading, his Arabic writing and spoken skills, his sense of humor, his knowledge of the modern demands, despite solid conviction in Deobandi principles, his ability to engage with others, his devotion to religion, his clean and simple living, his style of hospitality, and his vibrant gatherings, out of this what can we forget. He did not just gain knowledge to acquire the degrees, he made it his discipline to serve his teachers and gain from their companionship. The biggest demonstration of his knowledge was his *Saahra of Jamia Tirmazi Maruf-ul-Sanan*, which is spread over 3,000 pages and has been published in six volumes. His Arabic writings are in particular fluent, simple, and gentle. He was part of the independence movement. It was because of him and Shafi Usmani that Karachi became the center of theological debate.... He was also generally very knowledgeable. He was very affectionate toward the young,... he took my brother to Chittagong when due to limit of space within the train compartment only one person could sleep properly, he asked my brother to take the spot. When my brother refused preferring the Maulana to take some rest, the Maulana forced him to lie down and gently kept a hand on his legs so that he could not get up. (Usmani 2004: 85–110)

This emphasis on intellectual excellence as well as on the strength of the moral character of the leading ʿulama shows that the criteria shaping the basis of religious hierarchy go beyond competition. The moral behavior of the executive of a commercial firm is unlikely to dramatically affect a consumer's decision to purchase a product of that organization,[15] but if the imam of a madrasa manifests a lack of moral integrity he will inevitably sacrifice some of his authority within the religious hierarchy even if he is an expert on the text. The more stringent the checks on the working of the religious elite, the more these senior ʿulama are

14. Arguably one of the most revered madrasas within the Deobandi ʿulama in Pakistan, but in the Western discourse primarily known for alleged links of one of its graduates to the murder of the U.S. reporter Daniel Pearl.

15. The increasing emphasis placed on corporate social responsibility in recent years does indicate that even consumers within the market can allow moral and ethical considerations to impact economic decisions; however, research also suggests that these considerations become secondary the higher the price to be paid for seeking a more ethical alternative (Bowles 2004).

able to galvanize a level of respect among the broader community, which is difficult to win within the economic market. It is important to understand the cause of this difference in the working of economic and religious hierarchies in order to explain the behavior of a religious actor, a subject addressed in detail in chapter 7. The immediate concern is to see if the elite status once acquired can be sustained unchecked. An exploration of some prominent cases where the leadership of a leading madrasa was handed over from father to son suggests that the answer to that is negative.

Elite madrasas are established by prominent ʿulama; however, they consolidate over a period of a few generations. Often the leadership of these madrasas passes from father to son. My attempts to trace the performance of some of the prominent madrasas in Pakistan over a period of a few decades indicated that once a madrasa establishes a name for religious learning, the reputation persists beyond the lifetime of the ʿalim who established it. Still, the future of a madrasa remains heavily contingent on the competence of the inheritor who on failing to sustain public expectations, can risk losing the elite status. This highlights the fact that the reputation of madrasas is constantly in flux; if the son fails to show the intellectual excellence of the father or his integrity of character, the word gets around. During my fieldwork, imams of medium and small madrasas often commented on the leaders of the elite madrasas and those who had best carried forward their father's scholarship. It appeared that the longer an elite madrasa has been managed by a competent ʿalim, the fewer the chances that it will face a sudden decline in the hands of an incompetent inheritor—mainly because of the fact that the longer the duration of competent leadership, the higher are the chances of the system having been institutionalized primarily through a self-reinforcing mechanism marking the working of elite madrasas. As noted by Dr. Sikander, head of Banuri Town madrasa, Karachi, "The reason these madaris [in Karachi] are big is due to caliber, the *ikhlas* [purity] and personality of the people who set them up. They had knowledge and they taught with a real jazba [devotion]. The people they gathered around them for teaching were also *mukhlis* [sincere] and competent. They had both *ʿilm* [knowledge] and *ʿamal* [action]. Thus, during their lifetime they gathered a core pool of scholars and supporters around them who sustained the reputation of the madrasa overtime."

For example, during my fieldwork, I found a senior representative of the Deobandi wafaq, who was the son of a prominent Deobandi scholar and had inherited the leadership of the madrasa established by his father, was exposed to heavy criticism because of his apparent closeness to the state agencies. This leads to an argument that the ʿalim's decision to abide by Islamic rules is not necessarily voluntary, but rather is at times a result of conscious calculation. As long as they are reliant on donations, which was the case for the ʿulama who established an elite madrasa, religious leaders are more likely to live by the people's expectations as compared to conditions of relative affluence inherited by the sons of the elite ʿulama. Interestingly, this transformation in preferences from one generation to the next occurs in an even more pronounced manner within the Sufi tradition in South Asia. Profiles of the prominent Sufis record their simple lifestyles and renunciation of ostentatious living; their inheritors, instead, used this religious clout over the followers to support British colonial government in regulating the peasantry in return for generous land grants (Sherani 1991).

## Hierarchy by Choice: The Rise of Wafaqs

Unlike Catholicism, Islam does not provide for a religious hierarchy. Each individual is required to form a direct link with God with no provision for mediators.[16] In practice, however, there is a clear role for ʿulama in conducting Islamic rituals and leading prayers within Muslim societies. Although madrasas are independent entities, except for some established by religious political parties, most voluntarily join the collective platform of wafaq, which presents a hierarchical structure enabling some madrasas to exercise greater control in setting the rules of the game within the religious hierarchy. There are five government-recognized madrasa boards in Pakistan. These boards, which represent the four dominant schools of Islamic thought that developed in South Asia during the nineteenth and twentieth centuries (except Jamaat-i-Islami that came into being in the 1940s as a social and political movement instead of a distinct school of Islamic thought), were established between the 1950s and the 1980s. Wafaq-ul-Madaris Al-Salafia (Ahl-i-Hadith) was established in 1955, Wafaq-ul-Madaris Al-Arabia (Deobandi) in 1959, Wafaq-ul-Madaris Al-Shia(Shia) in 1959, Tanzeem-ul-Madaris Ahl-i-Sunna-wal-Jamaat (Barelvi) in 1960, and Rabata-ul-Madaris Al-Islamia in 1983.

These wafaqs are hierarchical structures where a madrasa's influence over the decisions within the wafaq is determined in proportion to its placement within the three-tiered hierarchical structure of the wafaq. As stated by a senior ʿalim from the Ahl-i-Hadith school of thought, "The authority for each level is determined according to the responsibility shouldered by members at that level. The eligibility to be elected to the higher levels of the wafaq is in turn shaped by

16. Quran specifies, "In God's eyes, the most honoured of you are the ones most mindful of Him" (Surah 49:13). All quotes from the Quran are taken from M. A. S. Abdel Haleem's translation (Oxford: Oxford University Press, 2010).

a madrasa's ability to represent the collective interests." At the top, the Majlis-i-Amalah (Council of Executives), which represents the office bearers of the wafaqs, is the most influential but also the most exclusive body comprising representatives from the elite madrasas. The second tier, called Majlis-i-Shura (Consultative Council), includes all madrasas that impart education up to the master's degree level, and the office bearers appointed to this council come from within its ranks. The third tier, Majlis-i-Umumi (General Body), is most comprehensive in terms of representation where all madrasas affiliated with the wafaq enroll one representative; this council has the least authority.

Wafaq membership is voluntary, which raises the question as to why this voluntary religious hierarchy emerged and still persists. In other words, why do madrasas at the bottom of the hierarchy willingly adopt a subordinate role? The answer rests in the very calculated cost-benefit analysis of participation in the wafaq by the madrasas across the three tiers. The most important role of a wafaq is to conduct examinations of madrasa students affiliated to the board and to issue degree certificates, but it also undertakes many other functions. It sets the curriculum to be taught in the madrasas belonging to that school of thought. More important, the wafaq is the main body to negotiate demands of the madrasas vis-à-vis the state—the wafaq, in other words, becomes the representative for that school of thought. In the words of the head of a small madrasa in Rawalpindi: "The benefit of joining the wafaq is that the bigger madrasas can take our message to the powerful people. They take our demands and problems to the government."

The wafaq also plays an important networking role within the madrasas, facilitating information sharing through monthly newsletters and other social gatherings. For example, a sample issue of the *Wafaq-ul-Madaris Al-Arabia Tarjaman* (2006), a monthly publication of the Deobandi wafaq, published examination results, disseminated information about examination entry requirements, included a tour report of the president of the wafaq in Iceland where he not only visited Islamic and religious centers but also reviewed the conditions of ordinary Muslims, carried essays on theological issues, such as *Rozay-ke-Haqeeqat* (the reality of fasting), as well as on current political concerns, for instance a review of the Women's Protection Bill and state-led military operation that killed Akbar Bughti (a senior political figure in the Balochistan province), and contained a separate section for book reviews. As argued by Irfan-ul-Haq, one of the senior leaders of Dar-ul-Uloom Haqqania in Akora Khattak, "The purpose of joining the wafaq is that there will be common understanding among all madrasas. The madrasas are now being targeted from all directions so they should stand united. The wafaqs also help maintain educational standards within the madrasas. They hold exams at one time and unlike the state education system where papers are sold out and degrees can be bought, in the wafaqs there is no problem of papers being leaked prior to the exams."

Wafaq membership requires going through an assessment process. The membership application form for the Wafaq-ul-Madaris Al-Salafia, for instance, requires information about the address, registration number, details of the building, land area, number of rooms, land ownership (whether it belongs to an individual or is registered in the name of a society), the number of books in the library, the number of teachers and their educational backgrounds, a copy of the curriculum, and details of the existing system of examinations followed within the madrasa. Although all madrasas can seek wafaq membership in shouldering the duties of running the wafaq, I found the elite madrasas in the top tier bear the most burden; thus the question is raised as to why the bigger madrasas give more time and make higher monetary commitment to the running of this hierarchy. The answer rests in identifying the many tangible benefits attached to occupying the elite position.

First, the elite madrasas get the right to design the curriculum to be followed by madrasas within that school of thought; they thus come to decide and regulate which religious ideas or interpretations are to become dominant within that school of thought. The offices of the wafaqs are often located close to the premises of the elite madrasas, and the office bearers are responsible for producing the wafaq publications, which brings added prominence within the religious hierarchy. In addition, these madrasas get the maximum opportunity to engage with the government on behalf of the madrasas from their sect. They are thus in a position to use the strength of the wafaq to their advantage in negotiations with the government as well as with potential donors, especially the external donors including the Saudis. It is the senior officials of the wafaqs who are invited to join the government zakat committees and the Ruhat-i-Halal Committee, and become part of the official delegations sent to undertake umra or hajj (pilgrimage to Mecca).

If the formation of wafaq enables these bigger madrasas to consolidate their control over the religious establishment and utilize this clout to bargain with both the state and external donors, why do other madrasas—if religious actors are assumed to be forward-looking and utility maximizing—join a system that enables the bigger madrasas to further consolidate their position? Do the leaders of the smaller madrasas join out of deference for the bigger madrasas, out of unquestioning obedience, or is this decision the result of strategic cost-benefit calculations? My discussions with the ʻulama on the history of wafaqs in Pakistan and study of documents from these wafaqs show that the high transaction costs of bargaining with each other and enforcing certain quality standards in the absence of centrally recognized degrees and curriculum, combined with the need to defend their interests against the state, were the central factors leading to their rise.

Pakistan was established as the result of a movement for a separate homeland for Muslims. The political elite, however, inherited a colonial mind-set. Educated in the Western educational institutions that had displaced the madrasas during colonial rule, post-independence leaders of Pakistan had little appreciation for madrasas. The marginalization of madrasas thus continued in the newly independent state of Pakistan, where the political elite often formed committees to give recommendations for the reform of madrasas to make them embrace modernity. This neglect, combined with the emphasis on reform raised apprehensions among the ʿulama who soon realized the need to form a united platform to defend their demands against the state. Just as the onset of colonial rule galvanized the energies of the ʿulama to move toward puritanical interpretations of Islam, the animosity of the formal institution of the state was critical in mobilizing the ʿulama to consolidate their position through the establishment of collective platforms.

Presenting a united front was only one of the objectives. Equally important was the desire to reduce the costs of coordination within the madrasas. Due to the informal nature of madrasa learning, which placed great emphasis on the relationship built with individual teachers, the madrasa system has historically witnessed a high migration of students—students move from one madrasa to another in search of better teachers or to pursue specific subject specializations. During the interviews with students, I repeatedly heard about movements in the past from one madrasa to another or plans for one. When I asked about the reasons for the moves, the explanations given highlighted practical concerns or academic interests. Some had moved because their families had moved to this city, some had moved on their own because they wanted to come to a bigger city and the more ardent students had moved because gradually they learned that a given madrasa offered better expertise in their area of academic interest. One of my respondents, who was seventeen years old explained, "I am from Bahawalpur. There are some very nice madrasas in Bahawalpur and Multan area. However, I moved to Lahore because I had friends who had studied in this madrasa and had told me that it has very good teachers for the study of Hadith. I want to specialize in Hadith. It is also a good experience to be in Lahore, it is a bigger city and there are more opportunities here." The smooth flow of such movements is contingent on mechanisms that facilitate assessment of the prospective students' credentials. As the number of madrasas grew and increased transportation facilities enabled students to travel long distances in search of suitable madrasas, the process of student assessment increasingly became more cumbersome. The old informal networks, which allowed the assessment of a student by a reference to his teacher, were no longer adequate. This constrained possibilities for the prospective students as well as those for madrasa graduates seeking teaching positions.

The establishment of a centralized examination system that could judge madrasa students on a set syllabus and issue standardized degree certificates was thus an efficient mechanism to reduce the information-gathering costs for the transacting parties. The benefits of establishing such a regulatory system were central to winning support of most madrasas for the establishment of a wafaq. The wafaqs networked the madrasas and facilitated information sharing within them. It was these clear benefits of forming a wafaq that convinced the small madrasas to join the network, even when they knew that the wafaq platform would enable bigger madrasas to perpetuate their individual interests. The factor overriding their competitive concern was the realization that they had as much to gain from the wafaq membership as the bigger madrasas. The latter, by virtue of being better financed and networked, were better placed to defend their positions individually; the challenges were toughest for the smaller madrasas. The bigger madrasas were better known so their students faced fewer problems in establishing their credentials when migrating to other madrasas.

Moreover, I found that the bigger madrasas were better known to the government officials, most of whom used the mosques attached to these madrasas to say the Friday prayer. This enabled them to better defend their individual cases vis-à-vis the government. They were more naturally networked within the religious establishment by virtue of hosting leading scholars in the field and producing authoritative literature; the smaller madrasas had no choice but to engage with them to enhance their own learning. The bigger madrasas also compensated by bearing the higher financial burden for running the wafaq: for example, within the Deobandi wafaq, the annual affiliation fee varies from Rs 50 (US$.62) for Ibtida'iya madrasas to Rs 200 (US$2) for Jamias, while the donation fee varies from Rs 200 (US$2.5) for Ibtida'iya madrasas to Rs 1,200 (US$15) for Jamias.

Since their inception, the wafaqs have played a critical role in putting forward views of the madrasas and defending their demands. They have both successfully resisted unfavorable government policies and won major concessions. During the 1980s, under the Zia–ul-Haq regime, which followed an Islamization agenda, the wafaqs successfully lobbied to gain official recognition for the madrasas' degrees—the highest degree of the wafaqs was given equivalence of the master's degree (Malik 1996). Since September 11, due to the external pressure on the government to regulate and reform madrasas, the wafaqs have been playing a central role in negotiating concessions from the government and defending the position of the madrasas. The wafaqs resisted government demand for compulsory registration of all madrasas for three years and eventually when they did agree to cooperate, they did so on their own terms[17] (Bano 2007b). They also played a central role in leading resistance against the government-led madrasa reform program. During these periods, the five wafaqs, which otherwise view each other as rivals, have shown relative solidarity.

It has to be noted that although the benefits of the wafaq do make the smaller madrasas stay within its fold, this does not prevent them from constantly monitoring any gains the bigger madrasas accrue in their position as leader of the wafaqs. As mentioned earlier on in the analysis, during the interviews, many ʻulama of the smaller madrasas expressed concerns about one particular senior official of the Wafaq-ul-Madaris Al-Arabia. Many believed he was too close to the government and was accepting financial contributions from it, though the wafaq had taken a stance not to accept state grants. The doubts about this particular official came to be expressed publicly when the latter was perceived to have supported the state position when called to act as a negotiator between the state and the representatives of the Red Mosque during the final days of the military operation.[18] The doubts were compounded due to his heavy spending on foreign visits, the use of official cars for personal travel, and his acceptance of a paid position on a government board while holding an executive position within the wafaq. The smaller madrasas are thus always suspicious of the intention of the leading ʻulama, and that is why they judge the caliber of the ʻalim not just by his knowledge of the text but also by his personality traits.

The study of inter-wafaq interactions reveals same signs of strategic behavior as seen in the case of intra-wafaq transactions. Since September 11, the five madrasa boards have been strategically collaborating to defend their joint interests. Despite their differences, in the post-September 11 context, the five wafaqs have shown flexibility and cooperation in resisting the growing pressures from the state for accountability and reform through the establishment of Ittihad-i-Tanzeemat Madaris-i-Deenia. The number of madrasas affiliated with each wafaq has determined its position within the organization. The secretary of the Deobandi wafaq, which has the largest number of affiliate madrasas, became the main spokesman of this collective wafaq. This period has seen the wafaqs, which have traditionally blamed one another for promoting hatred against the other, hold regular weekly meetings. There is the realization that despite their differences when it comes to survival, it is better to be strategic and

---

17. The Madrasa Registration Ordinance issued in 2001 was revised twice in 2005 (Bano 2007b) to accommodate the demands of the madrasas.

18. These critiques were vocal enough to find space within the newspaper columns and different Pakistani websites; during August 2007—two months after the military operation against Jamia Hafsa—there were also speculations about a possible break-up of the wafaq (Interface 2007).

work collectively to strengthen their position vis-à-vis the state rather than to stand in isolation but their ideological differences and the competition with the elites of these wafaqs would never allow for their complete merger. During the interviews, the ʿulama from across the five wafaqs, noted the benefits of forming this central platform despite their differences. This platform had enabled them to resist government pressure on a number of issues, most noticeably the government attempts to change the madrasa curriculum. During my follow-up visits in 2009 and 2010, I found that the platform had become even stronger. On asking about the status of this collective platform during my 2010 visit, a senior Barelvi ʿalim explained, "Yes, it is still central to our working, in fact it has become even stronger. All discussions with the government now happen through this platform. It is very important for all five wafaqs to stand together if they are to resist internal and external pressure in the present times." The working of this collective wafaq thus shows that, when their interests are severely threatened, the ʿulama are willing to be strategic and set aside their ideological differences, though by no means to abandon them, to ensure their strategic survival.

## Conclusions

Taking the case of the religious hierarchy as represented through the madrasas, I suggest that explanations that attribute the existence of noneconomic hierarchies to forces other than competition—such as moral authority or charisma—need to be scrutinized more closely. I have argued that the basis of religious hierarchy is competition and that deference or voluntary compliance, which often becomes associated with noneconomic hierarchies, should not be interpreted to mean that individuals show a blind adherence to the moral or political authority; rather the acceptance of the authority rests in the relevant elite establishing its worth through a very competitive process. The institutional elite is thus rarely ever completely free of all checks.

The study of the internal networks and working of madrasas has come to support Herbert Simon's (1962) analysis that every complex system has an informal self-reinforcing hierarchy. The research has shown that this informal hierarchy emerges naturally because any complex system consists of actors with different initial endowments and personal competence, who have different capacity to make use of the opportunities that become available—due to historical patterns or chance events—in the external environment. In addition to noting the existence of the informal hierarchy I have also identified that at times actors consciously choose to enter a formal hierarchical structure such as represented by the wafaqs. Close examination of both this informal and formal hierarchy marking the madrasa network in Pakistan makes me argue that both types of hierarchies are shaped by competitive forces, and actors emerging as the elite are those able to demonstrate a better understanding of religious texts, that is they possess specialized skills and understanding of these texts—what North (1990) identifies as "tactic knowledge"—and also are strategic enough to successfully mobilize the required financial resources. It is this combination of skill and capital that guarantees the rise of the elite madrasas. Overtime, the elite structure does become self-perpetuating where elite madrasas attract better teachers, the most competent and economically the most influential students, and end up having an influential alumni network, which further perpetuates their influence. However, their reputation remains sensitive to the actions of the current leaders. This supports the findings presented in chapter 3 that a choice at any point in time is a product of choices made in the past but in selection of a specific choice at any point in time the role of the caliber and strategic behavior of the actor making that choice is paramount.

Study of the factors shaping rise of the formal hierarchy of the wafaqs, in addition, supports the transaction cost literature—as represented most prominently by Coase (1937), Williamson (1975), and North (1990)—that institutional arrangements arise due to the information and monitoring costs involved in enforcement of any contract: heads of madrasas of all sizes entered the hierarchal structure of the wafaq, despite many having to relinquish authority to a few elite madrasas, because they all gained more through this participation than the cost they incurred in the process. The primary motive leading to the rise of the wafaqs was to reduce the internal costs of transacting as well as the high costs of transacting as individual organizations with the formal institutions of the state. Presence of wafaqs and a centrally administrated examination system helped reduce cost of information gathering and monitoring of the degrees of other madrasas thus facilitating the process of student admissions and teacher recruitment among madrasas. At the same time by investing in the wafaqs, all madrasas were able to negotiate better terms vis-à-vis the state than they could as individual organizations. This supports the position that when actors recognize enough incentives to invest in change, new organizational and institutional arrangements duly emerge—when it became too costly to work individually, the madrasas across the five dominant schools of thought in Pakistan moved to establishment of the wafaqs.

In arguing this, I have also noted that in the study of any informal institution, where the hierarchy is not so visible to outsiders as is the case in formal institutions and where the hierarchy is often shaped by formally defined constitutional rules, it is important to identify the elite and the organizing criteria within the hierarchy—as only knowledge of these criteria can help develop an understanding of the incentives that motivate the actors within the hierarchy.

Finally, in studying the working of the madrasa hierarchy I have demonstrated that though noneconomic hierarchies are driven by the same competitive forces as the economic hierarchy, they do record one major difference: namely, the nature of the religious good is such that once a scholar establishes his credentials he often wins the deference of those below him on the hierarchy, an unlikely trait within the economic market. The religious elite is expected to adhere to high ethical standards of behavior and not just preach religious values. This suggests that, in many ways, acquiring elite status within a religious hierarchy is more challenging than becoming a leader in a commercial organization where elite status is primarily dependent on the delivery of a sophisticated product and is largely insensitive to the behavior of the entrepreneur. However, it appears that the rewards vary in proportion to the investment.

The religious elite is eventually more capable of overcoming competition and converting it into cooperation and deference than a corporate executive can ever hope to achieve vis-à-vis the competing firms. What incentives noneconomic hierarchies offer to their members is an important question, which will be addressed in the next chapter. Here it is important to note that Miller's (1992: 265) work on factors shaping efficiency of the firms shows that noneconomic incentives play an important role here: "organizations whose managers can inspire cooperation and the transcendence of short-term interest among employees enjoy a significant competitive advantages." It is to the study of the role of these noneconomic incentives in shaping individual preferences that we now turn in the second part of this book; before that a quick review of the core argument advanced in the first part would be useful.

In chapters 2 and 3 I had set out to identify the factors leading to institutional change and stability while given the importance placed on religious elite; in this chapter I unpacked the working of religious hierarchy itself. The findings presented in these three chapters support the position that the process of institutional change as well as stability is primarily shaped by incentives made available to the institutional elite by the given socioeconomic and political context. Religious elites experiment with liberal interpretations when they are financially and politically secure; they tend to revert to orthodox interpretations when placed in hostile conditions. In such contexts the margin of error is small; survival is better ensured through consolidation on familiar grounds. The South Asian governments failed to transform the madrasa education system because they have not provided strong incentives to the 'ulama to engage with the rationalist scholarship. The 'ulama in turn failed to initiate internal reforms because their widespread following provides little incentive to invest in pursuing a new form of scholarship. However, as seen in the case of ‘ulama of South Asia confronted by British rule, religious beliefs are adjusted and reinterpreted but they are often not entirely abandoned. In order to understand the working of beliefs, it is therefore as important to understand the determinants of demand and conviction in religious beliefs as it is to recognize that beliefs do change in response to economic and political incentives.

# PART II
# DETERMINANTS OF DEMAND FOR INFORMAL INSTITUTIONS

**For a new behavioral foundation to be a contribution to the social science rather than an invitation to ad hoc explanation, we need more empirical information about preferences and how we come to have them as well as more adequate models of behavior under less restrictive preference assumptions.**

—Samuel Bowles, *Microeconomics: Behavior, Institutions and Evolution* (2004: 98)

**Institutions exist to reduce the uncertainties involved in human interaction. These uncertainties arise as a consequence of both the complexity of the problems to be solved and the problem-solving software . . . possessed by the individual. There is nothing in the above statement that implies that the institutions are efficient.**

—Douglass C. North, *Institutions, Institutional Change, and Economic Performance* (1990: 25)

5

# FORMATION OF A PREFERENCE

## Why Join a Madrasa?

**He was the first one to lead the Taraweeh [special night prayer during Ramadan] at home. When people in the neighborhood heard his voice so many came to pray behind him. Then gradually people also started to come from the neighborhood mosque.**

—Mother of a hafiz

**The fazeelat [blessings] of it as described by the 'ulama is that the children who have done hifz [memorized Quran], there will be crowns on their heads and those of their parents on judgment day. The crowns will sparkle just as in this world the sun comes out and sparkles. People will ask if these people are prophets or saints, and they will be told that it is all the fazeelat of this Quran. Thus, God will give the parents of the hafiz such high fazeelat [blessed status].**

—Father of a hafiz

Manzoor, son of a daily laborer at the brick-manufacturing factory, has been enrolled in a hifz course at a madrasa for the past two years, and so have been Ahmed, son of an industrialist, and Shakeel, son of a junior government clerk. These three respondents in Karachi represent the diverse population I found enrolled in madrasas across the eight districts of Pakistan. All three were involved in the process of hifz but to pursue this education the three had incurred different opportunity costs. If not here, Manzoor would have been engaged in child labor, Ahmed would have been a student in an elite private school preparing for higher education abroad after completing his O' level (high school) exams, and Shakeel would have been a student at a medium, fee-charging private school with aspirations to secure a stable job within the state or private sector. Each of the three also had different recourse to educational facilities: Manzoor was enrolled in a small neighborhood madrasa, Ahmad was in one of the most prestigious madrasas in Karachi led by reputed 'ulama, and Shakeel was enrolled in a medium-size city madrasa. Why did these children from different socioeconomic backgrounds pursue a madrasa education, which apparently offers little monetary compensation, and did the different opportunity costs they incur to pursue this education have any bearing on their choices? Equally important, how was the choice made in favor of a specific madrasa? The first question provides the means to explore the factors shaping the preference for a religious education and the basis of appreciation for nonmonetary preference; the second illuminates the decision-making processes that parents undergo in executing their religious preference. The former is about exploring the rationality of the ends, the latter about the means to attain that end.

One of the most serious critiques of neoclassical conception of a rational actor has revolved around its emphasis on utility maximizing behavior, which at its simplest implies pursuit of happiness (Bentham 1982)—though in practice, more often than not, it is taken to imply maximization of material interests (Bowles 2004). This emphasis on pursuit of self-interest is what gives the theory its predictive power. Critics, however, argue that such an emphasis on utility maximization neglects other motives for action such as altruism (Alkire and Deneulin 2002; Bowles 2004), commitment (Sen 1977), and ideology or pursuit of ideals (Ensgminer 1992; North 1990). The most serious concern has been that policies based primarily on such material conceptions of human well-being could actually crowd out other motives for undertaking the given action (Alkire and Deneulin 2002; Frey 1994; Titmuss 1970). Against such critiques, Becker's (1993) attempt to include nonmaterial motives within the utility calculus was well received within neoclassical economics; it was now possible to explain acts of material sacrifice within the rational framework by adjusting the self-interest assumption so as to record that such individuals have a higher preference for nonmaterial sources of utility. In fact, as Harford (2008) points out, today no economist will argue that rational actors pursue only material goals.

Within NIE, it is now widely recognized that it is not just the price mechanisms but also ideologies and other-regarding preferences that impact individual preferences and that we need to adjust this core assumption of self-interest if causes of institutional change and stability are to be fully understood (Bowles 2004; Greif 2006). As North (1990: 20) argues, "Human behavior appears to be more complex than that embodied in the individual utility function of economists' models. Many cases are ones not simply of wealth-maximizing behavior, but of altruism and of self-imposed constraints, which radically change the outcomes with respect to the choices that people actually make." Similarly, Bowles (2004) emphasizes the role of "other-regarding" preferences in shaping institutions. Further, he argues that not only does neoclassical economics fail to acknowledge "other-regarding" preferences, the assumption of utility remains heavily biased toward material conceptions of well-being rather than truly accommodating other sources of well-being within the utility calculus.

By undertaking a close study of the factors that shape parental and student preference for madrasa education—a choice, which at least for some, comes at the cost of pursuing material ambitions—this chapter identifies the sources of such a preference to see if Becker's (1993) attempt at grouping pursuit of all action as self-interested helps us develop a realistic model of human behavior. The choice to study in a madrasa presents a particularly good reference for undertaking such an analysis because existing studies quickly reduce such a choice to economic deprivation (ICG 2002; Singer 2001; Stern 2000). Based on my fieldwork, I develop an alternative explanation for the demand for religious education.

## Choosing a Madrasa: The Economic Argument

The existing literature explains the parental preference for madrasa education primarily in economic terms, where this preference is viewed to be a result of poverty (ICG 2002; Stern 2000): some studies explain the choice simply as a means to ensure food and shelter for the child, while others relate the preference for a madrasa to the poor quality of education offered within the state schools (World Bank 2002). The minor differences notwithstanding, the underlying message of these reports is the same: material conditions rather than a genuine appreciation of religious rewards are the primary shapers of the demand for religious education. The widespread acceptance of these arguments, which are otherwise based on extraordinarily weak evidence, is partially understandable given the high poverty figures and the poor standards of education in Pakistani state schools.

With a 2.1 percent population growth rate, Pakistan is among the countries with the fastest expanding population, and 33 percent of the country's population of 150 million lives below the poverty line (World Bank 2002, 2007b). Wealth is highly concentrated, with a significant difference between the earnings of the middle and high-income groups, and education system is mired with multiple problems around access as well as quality where education provided within schools and universities bears no link to the employment market (UNESCO 2008; World Bank 2002). The state's inability to meet the society's educational needs has left the field open for the entry of private education providers whereby private schools are estimated to shoulder one-third of the total primary education provision. The low fee charged by some private schools—as little as US$1.5 per child per month—has made some proponents of private schooling present their expansion as a silent revolution in providing access to education among the poor (Andrabi et al 2006). More recent surveys, however, check this optimism by showing that private schools cater to more affluent groups even within the poor (Andrabi et al 2008). Thus, even taking into account the expansion of the private school industry in Pakistan, opportunities for good quality primary and secondary education for the poor and middle-income groups remain inadequate.

The combination of this high level of poverty and the poor state education system has helped popularize the claims that madrasas, which offer free education and full boarding facilities, provide an economically appealing option for the poor.[1] A closer scrutiny of factors shaping parental preference for madrasa education, however, quickly reveals the inadequacies of strictly material explanations. The survey of the socioeconomic profile of students from 110 madrasas shows that rather than it being the absolute poor it is the middle-income groups that record the highest presence within the Pakistani madrasas: 60 percent of madrasa students come from lower middle-income families (Rs 5,000–10,000 [US$63–125] per month), 30 percent from poor families (less than Rs 5,000 [US$63) and 10 percent from upper-middle-income and relatively affluent households (Rs 20,000 [US$250] and above). In interpreting these results, it is important to view the middle-income class as a three-tiered structure (lower, middle, and upper). It is the children from the lower-middle and the middle tiers who record the highest presence within the madrasa system. Only 24 percent of the fathers of the children surveyed were illiterate, while the national illiteracy rate is 50 percent (UNESCO 2008). In addition, only 5 percent of the fathers of the surveyed children were madrasa educated (table 5.1).

I also found that more than 60 percent of madrasa students come from rural areas—a fact that can arguably help reduce the decision to attend the madrasa to economic motives, where madrasas become a conduit for facilitating the process of rural to urban migration. The recognition that admission into a city madrasa means upward mobility for students from the rural areas was captured by one of the ʻulama in the following words, "they learn to dress, talk, and cope with modern life when they move to urban madrasas." In addition, the survey shows a much higher concentration of madrasa students from Khyber Pakhtunkhwa and South Punjab, which are economically backward regions. These facts and observations do not justify reducing motives of the students or their parents to economic considerations as they need to be interpreted in the appropriate context: 68 percent of the Pakistani population resides in rural areas, which means that the higher presence of children from rural areas within madrasas partly reflects the general population ratio. In addition, it is important to recognize that migration from rural to urban areas implies prior resources—namely, information about madrasa hierarchy, social networks in the city that can host both students and parents until admission is secured, as well as financial ability to pay for the cost of transportation. As argued by one respondent in Swabi: "There are a number of things we had to work out in choosing a madrasa for my son. We

1. For review of literature advocating this position see Bano (2007a).

**TABLE 5.1** Student data from elite madrasas

| MADRASA STUDENTS | % |
|---|---|
| Rural/Urban background | |
| Students from rural areas | 60 |
| Students from urban areas | 40 |
| Education level of students at entry | |
| Joined after primary | 22 |
| Joined after middle | 30 |
| Joined after secondary | 40 |
| joined with no prior education | 3 |
| Educational background of fathers of madrasa students | |
| Not having madrasa education | 95 |
| With secondary degree or more | 40 |
| Illiterate | 24 |
| Age of joining madrasa | |
| Between 4 and 9 | 5 |
| Between 10 and 14 | 31 |
| Between 15 and 20 | 50 |
| Between 21 and 25 | 11 |
| Stated motivation for joining | |
| Education for employment | 10 |
| Religious motives | 90 |
| Career aspirations | |
| Teaching in madrasas | 82 |
| Professionals/Army | 10 |
| Tableeg | 5 |

*Source*: Based on the fieldwork (2006–2008).

wanted to send him to a good madrasa, which meant that we were looking for a madrasas in the city because the larger madrasas are there. However, I wanted to be able to ensure I place him in a city where we had relatives because then in case of an emergency someone could reach him. In addition, I wanted the city to be close enough so that he could occasionally visit home. Finally, the decision also depended on which of the bigger madrasas would admit him." The significance of these multiple constraints on moving to reputed madrasas in the cities was repeatedly recorded in the interviews.

The other factor exposing the limitation of a strictly economic explanation for the preference of madrasa education rests in studying the parental decision to send a child to a madrasa along with the choices being made for the child's siblings. The survey showed, in 90 percent of the cases the child surveyed was the only one from his household to be studying within a madrasa while the siblings were either enrolled in regular state or private school or were engaged in economic activity. Other studies have found similar trend (Andrabi et al. 2005). If the preference for madrasa education were a response to deprivation and a route out of poverty, the rational response would be to send all the children to a madrasa. The fact that this is not the case suggests that material incentives alone are not an adequate explanation for preference for madrasa education.

The limits of these causal links between poverty and choice for madrasa education are further exposed when explaining the presence of madrasa students who herald from the economically well-off class. In the survey I found that 10 percent of the student population in madrasas across the eight surveyed districts came from financially very affluent classes, including sons and daughters of big industrialists and landholding families; such students were concentrated in elite madrasas. Close to 40 percent of the students enrolled in the hifz program in the elite madrasas of Karachi belonged to financially affluent families. These respondents commuted instead of availing the free boarding facilities. The fact that 60 percent of madrasa students enrolled in the theology program as teenagers reported having done so out of their own choice rather than that of their parents further shows the limits of the purely economic arguments. Finally, during fieldwork among the poorest families I found that children from certain categories of urban poor can spend a much more comfortable life at home than at a madrasa. Some of the poorest students in the urban areas, whose parents were working as daily laborers or household help, had easier and more appealing options to spend their time at home than to attend a madrasa, most popular of which was to get together with friends from the area and watch movies on the cable channels (a very popular hobby, especially among the lower-income groups). Further, I found that their mothers, who worked as domestic workers, were as reluctant to let them leave the house to board in a madrasa, as would be the mother of a child of an affluent family background. For one mother, "the thought of my son not returning home each night is too emotionally difficult a proposition." When a child from this context opts for the more demanding option to enroll in a hifz program at a madrasa, where he is required to spend most of the day in a classroom reciting the Quran, clearly income poverty alone is not a sufficient explanation for this choice.

Here it is also important to note that the process of hifz is not only demanding, but it comes with a lifelong obligation: to remember the Quran for life. To forget the Quran after having memorized it once is believed to attract serious punishment for the child as well as for the parents. There is immense pressure on the child, parents, and teachers to minimize the chances of the child making a mistake as the Quran is believed to be the untouched word of God, and making a wrong pronunciation, especially when the child does not know the Arabic language, could alter the meaning of the written word.[2] During the interviews, many parents expressed the responsibility they felt to ensure that their children daily recited portions of the Quran, and a significant number would help the child by listening to their recitation while following a copy of the Quran to catch any mistakes. One mother said, "I get up with her every day for the *fajar* [morning] prayer to help her recite a portion of the Quran. She can easily recite the whole *para* [chapter] in half an hour. This requires commitment on my part but I am very particular about it. I want to ensure that she never forgets her responsibility to recite and remember the Quran now that she has been blessed to memorize it." Another respondent from the middle-income background, whose son had completed hifz, but as a teenager had become less committed to participating in religious rituals, was extremely worried about the likelihood of his son forgetting the Quran, "We know that the hafiz has a religious obligation to ensure he remembers the Quran once he has completed hifz. This requires reciting a portion of the Quran daily otherwise one starts to forget it or make errors. It is better not to hifz at all than to hifz the Quran and then forget it. He has taken to bad company in his teenage years and does not recite the Quran. This is a constant source of worry for me." This respondent was particularly devout and at the time of enrolling his son in a madrasa had moved to a new neighborhood in order to ensure that his son gets to hifz Quran with an ʿalim that he respected. If poverty was the primary reason for sending children to madrasas, such fears and the strong sense of obligation felt by the parents to ensure the child remembers the Quran would not be very logical. Taking all these factors into account, it is evident that equating the choice to attend madrasa with poverty skirts the real factors shaping the demand for a madrasa education.

## Choosing a Madrasa: The Religious Argument

My prolonged interviews and group discussions with over 250 parents and 350 students across the socioeconomic and geographical divide establish one fact: religion is a serious matter and the desire to secure the other world is a goal for which some individuals are willing to make serious investment. Islam places great emphasis on acquiring religious knowledge and offers clearly defined rewards to match the level of investment made in securing that knowledge. The first revelation to Mohammad in the Quran starts with the word *Iqra* (read). The practice

2. Most children memorizing the Quran in Pakistan do so without learning the Arabic language, which means that memorization does not itself lead to understanding of the Quran though many may follow the memorization process with reading translations of the Quran.

of hifz[3]—one of the two main routes of religious education followed within the madrasas, the other being the pursuit of higher theological training—in particular is understood to ensure many this-worldly and other-worldly rewards including a guaranteed place in heaven for the hafiz as well as his parents. There was not a single interview with either parents or students that did not include a reference to the statement of the Prophet where he is argued to have promised that "the hafiz would not only enter the heaven on judgment day but would take ten people with him" and that the "parents of the hafiz will have crowns on their head on the judgment day." The importance of these rewards and that of endearing oneself and one's child to God was repeatedly mentioned in the interviews. One of my female respondents from a middle-income neighborhood in Lahore noted, "To be able to recite the Quran properly, you know the rewards of that are so high. When a child does hifz, the whole house benefits. Automatically, the blessings start to come for the entire household from the moment one makes the decision to pursue this route. Memorizing the Quran sharpens the mind and also improves the performance of the child in other subjects." Another very financially and politically affluent individual, one of whose children was becoming a hafiz in a madrasa added, "If I am honest there are so many wrong deeds that one does in life, making my child do hifz is a small investment that one can make to secure the other life. It is at the same time very good for moral grooming of the child."

I found the factors shaping the preference of the parents of children following the theology program, often after completing the process of hifz, to be the same. However, in their case, the choice also shaped the child's profession, namely that of a preacher. Just like the emphasis placed on memorization of the Quran, in the view of all respondents Islam places equal importance on encouraging higher level learning in all areas of Islam,[4] thereby acting as a strong motive for devoting one's child to the pursuit of Islamic education. As noted by one 'alim in Swabi, whose son was now being trained in Islamic theology after completing the hifz program, "The Prophet said that the 'ulama will be the guardians of Islam. These will be the individuals who will protect Islam in all times. Studying Islamic texts with the view to teach them to others is keeping alive the tradition of the Prophet. One is fortunate to be guided into pursuing this direction." In this case,

---

3. There are verses in the Quran that state that God has taken responsibility of protecting the Quran—"We have sent down the Qur'an Ourself, and We Ourself will guard it" (Surah 15: 9). Memorizing the Quran is thus viewed to be facilitating that process.

4. During my fieldwork the 'ulama from the five wafaqs repeatedly argued that Islam does not draw a distinction between this-worldly and other-worldly knowledge. They used this reasoning to argue that they are not against study of secular subjects. They were of the view that Islam itself encourages pursuit of all knowledge be it in the field of medicine or astronomy, as long as the logic deployed to study those fields does not start with denying God's existence.

the pursuit of religious rewards, however, becomes more closely intertwined with this-worldly interests. For instance, for 20 percent of the parents of students heralding from smaller areas, the choice acquired a social significance such as the son becoming an imam at a local mosque on completing his madrasa education. As noted by one of the student respondents, "I came to study in this madrasa because I knew my mother really wants me to become an 'alim. She always told me that there is a need for an imam in our village who can teach the people Islam. I was also inclined toward religion and therefore decided to get trained to become an 'imam. Upon the completion of my education, I will go back to my village. They are all waiting that on return I will lead the prayers and teach the children Quran."

I was repeatedly told that madrasa education is also very good at providing moral training. One of my respondents, who worked as a driver, said: "In regular schools, the children nowadays don't learn any moral education. In fact, after getting school education they refuse to do the jobs their fathers did because they think they are now more qualified than their parents and should be doing better jobs. Instead they waste time because there are no better jobs available. In the process they also become frustrated and rude to their parents. Alternatively, in the madrasas they are taught to respect the parents. Islam places very high emphasis on respect for parents." The students themselves also emphasized the difference in moral training at a madrasa and a regular school. This issue repeatedly came up in discussions about their relationship with teachers and parents. The adult students interviewed noted the respect they feel for their teachers. As put by one male student, "I have studied both in a madrasa and a school, and the relationship and respect I felt toward my teachers in the two contexts was very different. In a madrasa, we used to rush to pick up the shoes of our teacher when he would leave after completing the *dars* because we had so much respect for the knowledge he imparted. He also was so affectionate and cared about every aspect of our life. It is not possible to develop such an attachment with the teachers in secular schools because over there the teachers are not genuinely concerned about the well-being of their students."

Equally strong evidence for high demand for religious rewards in the Pakistani society rests in the mushrooming of private schools since late 1980s, which combine modern and religious education. *Iqra* school chain and the *Roza-tul-Atfal Trust* are two examples of establishments that are running a continuously expanding network of schools across Pakistan targeting the middle- and upper-income groups. Along with the teaching of modern subjects such as English, computer science, and mathematics, these schools—which charge between Rs 700 and Rs 1,000 (US$9–13) per child per month—make the child memorize the Quran in the earlier grades and then impart the teaching of core Islamic principles in the higher grades. The children are admitted from the age of three where at the initial stage they are taught to read the Quran; the emphasis then moves onto memorization of the Quran and in the secondary stages the focus shifts to secular subjects. To ensure the good moral conduct of the child, these schools include separate subjects on *Akhlaqiat* (moral behavior), drawing on Islamic principles. The schools also offer facilities for extracurricular activities, with the result that by the age of sixteen the child becomes not only a *Hafiz-i-Quran* (one who has memorized the Quran), he or she has also secured good grades in matriculation examinations and would be able to secure admission into engineering, medicine, and computer sciences.[5]

The attraction for those families who do not want to commit their child to a madrasa education but want to secure religious rewards is reflected in the first line of the Iqra National Education Trust Brochure: "Along with worldly education in the latest modern areas of knowledge and skills by making the Quran safe in the hearts of your children, make them an asset for the other world." For parents whose children were enrolled in secular schools to now choose school options combining the secular and the religious, supports the argument that there is a genuine demand for religious rewards, one that is not entirely embedded in income deprivation. One of my female respondents, who ran a beauty parlor in a middle-income neighborhood of Karachi, enrolled her son in Iqra school, thus explaining her decision:

> I always wanted one of my children to do hifz but I was not very comfortable with the conditions and the environment that one finds in a madrasa. However, I always thought it would be really nice if he could do hifz. The Qari Sahib who taught me to read Quran, his recitation of the Quran was so good that I used to say that after all he is also someone's son, if only my son could recite the Quran like he did. Therefore, when I heard about Iqra school from some of my female clients whose children were going there, I decided to enroll my youngest son there. He was at that time only four years old. The school combines facilities for hifz and Islamic education while providing equally good education in science and computers. Now he recites so well. It makes me so proud to listen to him. Whenever he recites, my older sons ask him to recite one more time.

This position is supported by Nelson (2006) who based on the result of a survey designed to examine the substantive features of local education demands in a Pakistani district found that 98 percent of the population believes that Islamic

5. Data are difficult to secure but there is widespread recognition within the public that those children who return to secular education after undertaking the hifz process perform very well.

studies should be a "required" part of the curriculum, 60 percent believes that madrasas are an "indispensable" feature of the existing educational landscape, and 40 percent are inclined to identify religious education as their "top educational priority." The key to understanding the demand for a madrasa education rests not in assuming it to be a response to material deprivation but in understanding why individuals value religious rewards; in order to answer this it is important to understand why they value religion itself.

A sensitive listening to the concerns, hopes, and aspirations of the parents and students voiced during the course of interviews and group discussions identifies two primary incentives shaping the demand for religion and both of these are familiar subjects within the literature on the sociology of religion: religion as an answer to the uncertainties of life, whether of an existential nature or those that impact the everyday life, and the pursuit for a meaning of life. When explaining the basis for their religious faith, respondents made repeated references to the temporary nature of this life; for some it invoked philosophical questions about the meaning of life; for others it created a great fear of material loss. According to one respondent, "I am one of those who would like to believe that there is more to human existence than this life given how transient it is. In Islam I find a philosophy that makes me give meaning to life. If I really ask myself whether there is actually going to be a heaven or hell, the truth is that I am not sure. But I am convinced of Islam because what it teaches makes life easier in this world." In the case of rich respondents, the concern with the temporary nature of this world and questions about the meaning or purpose of life were, in particular, the primary basis of faith.

There was additional anxiety about the everyday uncertainties of life among respondents from the middle- and lower-income groups. The failing state structure, the insecurity of income and employment, the lack of health facilities and the spread of public health epidemics like hepatitis, and the poor law and order conditions often set the context in which parents explained their religious faith.[6] In the words of a father of a madrasa student, "This life is so uncertain. Especially in this country, there is such high level of uncertainty. One does not know what will happen the next day. This has made people turn to Islam even more. When you are reminded of death so frequently, you begin to think of investing in the other-world a bit more. Given the efforts we make to secure comforts in this

---

6. Norris and Inglehart (2004: 4) based on data from World Values Survey from 1981–2001 also argue that existential security, "the feeling that survival is secure enough that it can be taken for granted," correlates with lower levels of religious observance and vice versa. They, however, drew different conclusions than those of this chapter as for them "feelings of vulnerability to physical, social, and personal risks" is the sole explanation for religion as opposed to the more complex explanation developed in this chapter.

world, some time and energy committed to religious activities to secure the other world—which deals with the permanent life—is not a bad investment." What I found during the course of these interviews was that, even when religious precepts might not provide a tangible solution to these problems, they do provide an efficient mechanism to psychologically cope with these daily insecurities. Religion enables the individual to carry on with daily life transactions even when the failing state institutions make social, economic, or political exchanges between two or more parties difficult.

The judicial system in Pakistan is extremely weak; litigation proceedings can stretch over decades. Life is insecure on many levels: many of those suffering from serious illnesses do not have the means to purchase health care or, even worse—in the absence of a state regulatory system, those who can afford formal treatment risk contracting other diseases due to unsafe practices in many health clinics and hospitals. These uncertainties marking the everyday existence in Pakistan were captured in an article written by a senior member of the Deobandi wafaq in defense of a madrasa education:

> Today everywhere there is talk of corruption, the courts don't provide justice, in police stations it is not possible to even register a First Information Report (FIR) [official reporting of crime to police] without giving a bribe, in district courts the public seeking justice is exploited, the roads and bridges are made sub-standard, in private schools education has become a big business, in hospitals there is no proper medical treatment, in offices people don't work, politicians indulge in big frauds. Therefore, what is the field or profession that is working on correct principles, where there is no corruption, where poor public's worries are sorted, where the deserving gets his dues, where problems get resolved? (Jalandari 2006)

In such a context, where access to information is limited and there is no security in everyday transactions, the idea of God becomes very appealing, because as soon as one allows for the existence of God one allows oneself to be relieved of the pressure of controlling the outcomes of these transactions.

Central to most religions is the belief that individuals can make the effort for desired ends, but the outcome remains in the hands of God.[7] Within Islamic theology, the relative role of individual will and destiny in shaping outcomes is

7. "No misfortune can happen, either in the earth or in yourselves, that was not set down in writing before." (Surah 57: 22); "He has the keys to the unseen: no one knows them but Him. He knows all that is in the land and sea. No leaf falls without His knowledge, nor is there a single grain in the darkness of the earth, or anything, fresh or withered, that is not written in a clear Record" (Surah 53: 59).

a much debated subject (Iqbal 2009); the dominant understanding among the scholars interviewed was that the individual is required to make the maximum effort to attain good outcomes because even though destiny is determined by God, it is set in proportion to the efforts made by the individual.[8] "Of course, one has to work," said one respondent, "there is no question about it. Islam is very clear that whatever we get comes in proportion to the effort we put into it. However, Islam also makes clear that even after we have made the effort we cannot control the outcome. The outcome is not in our hands. When you think like that the worry goes away. You know you have to work hard, but you know you don't have to worry about the outcome because that cannot be controlled." The Quran encourages human beings to take action, but leave the outcome to God. This emphasis on leaving things to God, after having made the required effort, makes religion a very appealing force in context of everyday uncertainties (Aydar 2006; Gordon 2002).

The consequence of such a psychological position is that it makes decision making easier, thereby reducing the cost of information-gathering and enforcement, which are critical in ensuring any social, economic, or political transactions. *Istikhara,* a prayer often mentioned by my respondents, enables the believer to seek God's guidance on critical decisions where he lacks sufficient information with the understanding that he will be guided to the best outcome. This prayer is based on the very premise that there is a limit to human information-gathering ability:

> O God! In this search, I want your blessing with your knowledge and I ask for strength with your strength, and I ask for your great blessing. The fact is that you have the strength and I don't and you know and I don't know and you are knower of the unseen. O God if you know this work is good for me and for my faith and this world and the other then give me the courage to do it and make it easy for me and if this work is bad for me, my faith or this and the other world then turn it away from me and turn me away from it and give me that where there is goodness for me and make me happy with that choice.

This prayer is recommended whenever one is in doubt about future choices due to inadequate information or is about to make a complex decision. The normal practice is to recite this prayer after *Isha* (the night prayer) and then retire to bed trusting that, if the action for which the guidance is sought is beneficial, then God will facilitate the means to secure it and if it is harmful, God will prevent it

8. "God does not change the condition of a people unless they change what is in themselves" (Surah 13:11).

from happening. One of my female respondents said: "I say this prayer at night whenever there is an important issue on which I have to decide. When saying this prayer, one is advised to keep that issue in mind, say the prayer, and then go to sleep. The philosophy behind this prayer is that one is asking God for advice on an issue on which one has limited information, and in my experience this prayer makes one choose the best alternative. I have seen this work for me repeatedly."

While the *Istikhara* prayer helped overcome the fears emerging from recognizing the limits of human information-gathering ability, and thereby making inefficient transactions, I found the Islamic emphasis on leaving the outcomes of all action to God dramatically reduces the anxiety of entering into a transaction in a context where the enforcement mechanism to punish the violator is absent. I was repeatedly told by my respondents that a basic principle of Islam is that everything that happens is for the best, because in the long term God in his infinite wisdom knows what is best for anyone. The result was that, even if there was suffering due to a specific action, my respondents argued it to be eventually good for the person because in their view either it was meant to contribute to one's spiritual growth and make one stronger or a better alternative awaited in the near future. In the Quran there are repeated references that "if only you knew that this was good for you."[9]

My observations of my respondents make me argue that recognizing the role of religious faith in dealing with the uncertainties of life and daily anxieties should not result in understanding religious faith in purely instrumental terms—a limitation reflected in Norris and Inglehart's (2004) work. Individuals do not consciously start to believe in religion because doing so will help them address information limitations and reduce the uncertainties of life; rather the uncertain context, where life is threatened on a daily basis, triggers questions about the meaning and purpose of life more frequently. In the context of such uncertainties, a genuine appreciation for nonmaterial sources of pleasure is triggered and an active appreciation of life beyond the limits of the material world is developed.

I also noticed that once an individual started to rely on religion, he or she slowly grew to learn more about it and, in the process, often became more convinced of its value. A sister of a famous pop singer in Pakistan, who in recent years has become very expressive of his faith, explained the process of building conviction as gradual, "We all go through phases in life. For me personally the conviction in Islam grew because with time I saw that it provides a very logical philosophy to deal with life. The more I read the Quran with translation the more convinced I became. I have an MBA degree and I teach accounting. In the

---

9. "You may dislike something although it is good for you, or like something although it is bad for you: God knows and you do not" (Surah 2: 216).

evenings, I have also been studying tajweed [rules guiding proper vocalization of the Quranic verses]. I can tell you that tajweed is more difficult than accounting. Understanding the Quran and learning to read it correctly demands commitment." Thus the demand for madrasa education is not the product of a mechanical calculation, where income deprivation causes poor parents to abandon their child in a madrasa; rather, the decision to send a child to a madrasa is embedded either in the individual propensity for seeking a meaning to life or in the external context, where a failed state system makes daily life so uncertain that in learning to cope with this, individuals come to appreciate the value of religious faith. I found that once there is faith then there is also the desire to win religious rewards, and this is where devoting three years of a child's life to memorizing the Quran starts to appear as only a small investment in return for promised rewards.

Thus Manzoor, the son of a daily laborer, or Ahmad, the son of an industrialist, or Shakeel, the son of a junior government clerk, all ended up in the hifz program primarily because of a genuine appreciation for religious rewards and a conscious desire to endear themselves to God. Shakeel's father may have developed this preference due to a genuine propensity for asking spiritual questions, and Mazoor and Ahmad's fathers may have come to develop this appreciation after having experienced the role of religion in addressing the existential and daily uncertainties of life—though interview results make me argue against such assumptions which suggest that the poor cannot be sophisticated enough to have an inner propensity for questioning the meaning of life or having an appreciation for spiritual rewards. However, they all decided to send their children to a madrasa because of a genuine appreciation of Islam and not because of income deprivation. The only serious challenge to an explanation pegged primarily in religious discourse, however, is that if the choice of a madrasa education is the result of a genuine appreciation of religious rewards, even if such appreciation is heightened due to the challenges faced in the external sociopolitical and economic environment, then why is there a higher concentration of students from middle- and lower-middle-income families within the madrasas—especially in the theological courses—rather than an equal representation of the rich?

## Feasibility of the Religious Investment

I have argued so far that the pursuit of religious education is the result of a genuine demand for religious rewards, which can be heightened due to the challenges in the external environment, but cannot be simply attributed to income deprivation. This section further advances this argument to illustrate that this appreciation for religion is not unquestioning, nor does it cause the believer to suddenly ignore all his material preferences; rather the believer is an individual who constantly makes conscious calculations to maximize both his religious and material rewards. The choice to be in a madrasa indicates neither a calculated economic decision nor a blind preference for religious rewards among the economically deprived, as existing work linking madrasa education with preference for jihad tends to suggest. Instead, this decision is evidence of a rational individual's propensity to maximize multiple sources of utility. Islamic texts encourage combining both as Islam does not argue for the complete renunciation of comfort in this world—one of the chapters in the Quran asking the believer to benefit from the comforts provided in this world notes "God wants ease for you, not hardship" (Surah 2: 185). The Quran does not preach monasticism (Surah 57: 27); though the believers are required to remember that the hereafter is more important than the life on earth, they are advised against rejecting appreciation of beauty and bounty of God's creation.[10]

Unless the believer is exceptionally devoted, his or her efforts are aimed at maximizing rewards in this world as well as in the other. I found this to be the reason why children from the rich as well as the poor families focus only on hifz, while those from the middle-income group carry on to study theology. It is the rich who have to pay the highest price if they choose to send their child to pursue such a choice, as this would mean that the child would give up the opportunity to perpetuate the family business. A rich child also has to bear a higher cultural cost where, instead of learning English in elite schools, in which he would otherwise be studying, he will be learning Urdu and Arabic in the madrasa, making him socially unfit for elite circles. My respondent Shakeel was quite conscious of the cost he was paying to become a hafiz. In his words, "Hifz is a very demanding process and the culture in a madrasa is very different than in the school. But, my parents were very keen that I do hifz because in our extended family everyone wants at least one of their children to do hifz. It is a kind of a tradition but of course doing hifz is very demanding and I will have to work very hard to catch up when I return to the regular school." Another respondent from similarly affluent background who had now completed the hifz program noted similar costs:

> To make the child do hifz parents have to invest a lot of energy. I was made to enroll in the hifz program against my will by my father. In my father's family there was a strong tradition to make at least one child

---

10. "Say [Prophet] 'Who has forbidden the adornment and the nourishment God has provided for His servants?' Say, 'They are [allowed] for those who believe during the life of this world…' " (Surah 7: 32).

> a hafiz. He was himself a hafiz. Given the demand of the hifz process, I had to quit the regular school for three years while my siblings and cousins continued within that system. During this period, I lost my command of the English language and felt that my siblings and cousins were gaining a superior education. After completing ten chapters of the Quran, however, my heart got convinced that I wanted to complete the process. At that time I used to think my parents hated me but now I feel proud of having memorized the Quran. I have led the Taraweeh prayer [special night prayer in Ramadan that requires a hafiz to recite from memory large sections from the Quran] in one of the mosques for fourteen years and all people within the family call me hafiz sahib [a term of respect].

For the affluent families, therefore, there are two options: seek their religious rewards by supporting madrasas financially (see chapter 7 for details on equally powerful rewards promised in Islam to those who devote a part of their income to good causes) or enroll their child in a madrasa only for the hifz program. The child is taken out of secular school for two to three years to do hifz, after which he returns to the secular system. In addition, there is widespread impression that doing hifz enhances the child's memory, making him perform better in secular education. Such children are on record as having done very well in matriculation examinations. This benefit of hifz process was repeatedly mentioned in the interviews. Thus, the option of hifz ensures endearment to God with bearable costs to worldly gains. This also explains the dramatic expansion of private schools offering a mixed curriculum, as they bring down the cost of pursuing a religious education for the upper-class families by enabling the children to stay within the secular system while pursuing religious rewards.

For the parents from the middle-income groups, on the other hand, one child devoted to the pursuit of a religious education does not pose a major financial cost. The family size normally increases among the middle-income groups and sending one child to a madrasa becomes a very appealing risk-sharing strategy: this child may never earn as much as the son who becomes a technician or a government clerk—although if he becomes a prominent 'alim his earnings can surpass those of his siblings[11]—but he would at least facilitate the road to salvation, help conduct religious rituals, and bring social respect to the family apart from being economically self-sufficient. It is thus easiest for the middle-income families to maximize both this-worldly and other-worldly rewards by facilitating

11. A senior official of the Ahl-i-Hadith wafaq narrated how he ended up being more financially secure than his brothers and in fact was able to help support some of them as well as his parents.

the way for one of the children to become an ʿalim, and many opt to do precisely that.

In the absolute poor families, children are required to contribute to the family income through labor, which makes the decision to send a child to a madrasa contingent on serious religious commitment. The cultural attributes of such households make such a commitment very taxing for the child: when other children in the household are involved in nonacademic activities and the parents have no educational training, sustaining the motivation to invest in education requires an even higher level of commitment from the child. It is therefore not surprising that many children from poor families also exit the madrasa on completion of the hifz program or even prior to it. In the case of the former, they accept low-ranking jobs within the religious hierarchy that do not require extensive knowledge of the religious texts; in the case of the latter, they end up with odd jobs within the informal economy.

One of my respondents, who was a taxi driver, was forced to take out his first child from madrasa half-way through the hifz process when he faced severe financial problems. He noted, "I had admitted my first child into a madrasa to do hifz but at that point my financial conditions became really tough. I lost my job and my wife passed away. It was a very tough time and I had to take the child out of the madrasa because I needed him to earn. It was a tough time and it was tough on my son too." When his financial conditions became more stable, he was able to enroll his younger son in the hifz program. Family compulsions or an inability to cope with serious academic demands of the study of theology were two of the main reasons quoted in the interviews for the exiting of poor children from the madrasa stream. Those who stay on to do the eight-year fiqh course are normally from lower-middle-income families with an aptitude for hard work.[12]

The reason for sending only one child to a madrasa is also explainable within the same logic of the parents to strike a balance to maximize this-worldly and other-worldly rewards. Given that hifz is difficult, parents want at least one child to undertake this process since one child is promised to take ten adults with him to heaven. The parents therefore prefer the other children to pursue regular fields while one child secures the religious merit for the family: during the interviews parents often elaborated how through the one child undertaking the hifz process the religious influence transmits through the family, making other children and often even the parents more sensitive to religious precepts. A

12. Other studies note similar maximizing behavior of the religious actor. Stark and Finke (2000) found that all members of the Unification Church included in their study were fully aware that membership was very costly and undertook active calculations that justified the costs of the given benefits.

seventeen-year-old hifz student explained: "On the day of judgment there will be crown on the heads of parents of a hafiz. My both brothers are working in an auto-mechanic workshop. They are very happy that I am doing hifz. They love me a lot. My father also likes my *tor tareeka* [way of behaving]. When he hears me recite the Quran he asks me to teach him to recite it the same way too. In the madrasas, the atmosphere is such that you get settled."

The fact that religious choices are based on conscious calculations of the economic costs incurred to secure a specific reward is evident not only in the socioeconomic profile of the students represented within the madrasas but also in the way respondents noted many side benefits—benefits, which in the view of the parents were not the primary reason for sending the child to a madrasa but were still highly valued—of a madrasa education. The rich parents with children enrolled in the hifz program mentioned that religious education enhances the child's memory and makes him more disciplined, which helps him on his return to the secular education system. The poor families acknowledged the guarantee of decent food and boarding facilities and the exposure to urban life as important side benefits of a madrasa education.

Parents from across the economic divide also often mentioned that religious education inculcates the right moral values, including respect for elders and the family, which are fast eroding values due to Western influences. For the lower-income groups in the urban areas, this moral training appeared to play a critical role in preventing the child from falling prey to vices such as drugs or petty crime. A father from a low-income urban settlement in Karachi identified this to be a critical factor that shaped his decision to send all his children to an evening hifz program. In his view, madrasa education built up the moral character of the child to resist drugs and other undesirable habits including petty crime, common among the adolescents in his neighborhood, "There are too many bad influences in today's society. In these urban settlements, we have many problems. We learn to cope with them but the youth get frustrated, they want better quality of life. They however don't have the means and then they start to get involved in wrong things; they go and play cards on the street the whole night. They end up with wrong kind of people and then end up in crime. The madrasa education helps protect the child from all these negative influences."

In order to develop a real understanding of the religious actor it is important not to reduce these calculations of the believer to purely instrumental reasons, as deprivation based theories of religion tend to argue (Glock 1964; Norris and Inglehart 2004); it is impossible not to note parents' genuine appreciation for spiritual rewards when interview after interview reveals parents beaming with pride over the Quranic recitation skills of their children. The level of happiness expressed by some parents on such occasions would match the happiness felt by a family when the father secured a permanent job or a sibling is accepted as a medical student in a prestigious school. Similarly, how can an honest researcher of religious behavior fail to acknowledge a Muslim mother's genuine appreciation of the hifz process when she narrates that she so organized the beds in the house that no one can sleep with their feet toward the daughter who has memorized the Quran "because she has the Quran embedded in her heart."

Thus, there is indeed a genuine appreciation for religious rewards among the believers but, at the same time, this appreciation does not lead to a complete neglect of one's material utility; rather, believers constantly maximize both the religious and spiritual rewards especially when the dominant teachings of Islam place strong emphasis on securing the best of both worlds.

What is important to recognize is that religious faith is neither a product of purely instrumental calculations nor a result of unquestioning obedience to religious authority—rather its explanation rests in recognition of the complexity of human needs. The policy implication of this position is that the more the context changes to make the religious investment more expensive for the parent, the more the demand for a madrasa education will reduce because parents will then shift to less costly options for securing religious rewards, such as making higher donations to religious causes. The demand, however, will never entirely disappear even in the changed context, for some will always have a high preference for religious rewards despite all the material comforts—because it is not just the insecurity of life that leads individuals to seek religion but the rational appeal of religious ideas plays an important role in mobilizing and sustaining a mass following.

## Selection of a Madrasa: Not Free of Constraints

If parental efforts to maximize religious rewards are the result of forward-looking and maximizing calculations, the factors that influence their selection of a particular madrasa reveal equally strategic and rational calculations. This section examines the popular assumption that a madrasa in which a student enrolls is the result of a random selection rather than of conscious choice. I found that the process of selecting a madrasa is quite a strenuous one and parents make many calculations before doing so—in which madrasa a child might land is directly proportional to the child's initial resource endowment, that is the socioeconomic capital of his parents. Even though all madrasas provide free education, the route to entry to a top madrasa is guided mainly by parental income and religious networks; exceptional brilliance is the only other mean to override these two entry criteria.

My fieldwork shows that children from affluent families enter into elite madrasas, suggesting that the initial resource endowment of a child is critical in securing his access to a better madrasa. This resource endowment is marked apparently by wealth, but wealth is a proxy indicator covering a number of other important factors including better information, resourceful networks, and prior investment in education. There are multiple reasons why rich children get admitted to better madrasas: they perform better in competitive entrance examinations because of prior education exposure in good schools; rich parents are better placed to gather information on the madrasa hierarchy and identify a good madrasa and often they are patrons of a big madrasa. Children from poor families, in addition to lacking these advantages, are also often confined due to family obligations to enroll in a madrasa in their local area. The poor parents then have more restrictions on the choice of a madrasa than those economically more affluent. Thus, the madrasa in which a child enrolls is not randomly selected; rather, the selection is a result of a conscious choice, albeit within the given parental resources.

The interviews show that the decision to send a child for hifz is not easy especially among the rich households, given the recognition that hifz is a very demanding process. Rich parents are reluctant to enroll their child in a madrasa for a number of reasons: they do not want their child to benefit from facilities that run on public donations; they do not want their children to mingle too closely with those from very poor households and markedly different socioeconomic status; and they think they are better placed to meet the dietary needs of their child. As expressed by one mother, "For me it was difficult to send my son to a madrasa because madrasas are run on zakat and sadaqa while we are more affluent and are not eligible to benefit from these donations. Further, madrasas get students from a very mixed socioeconomic background. It was therefore difficult for me to decide to send my son to a madrasa. I was also concerned that they might use beating as part of the teaching method." It is because of these perceptions of madrasas that schools offering integrated education, such as Iqra School, have had good reception. These concerns about madrasas were often more severely felt by those middle-income or affluent families who did not have direct contact with the madrasas; my respondents within the affluent families in Karachi who have a tradition of sending at least one child to a madrasa did not express such concerns due to better knowledge of the madrasa hierarchy. In general, within the affluent families I found it was very common to take special care of the child's diet while going through the hifz process because of its physical and mental demands.

Among sensitive parents, even after choosing to send a child to get religious education, there are often doubts. One example of such a respondent was a Pakistani mother, currently based in Jeddah, who had two sons ten years apart in age.

The first took his A Level exams at a British school and then went to the UK for his higher education; the younger was also enrolled in the same school, however by this time the mother had become very keen to get her younger son to do hifz. She talked to her child who was initially reluctant but then agreed primarily to please her. But she was not in favor of putting her child into a madrasa because of the impression she had of beating being associated with madrasa teaching methods, nor did she want to withdraw the child from the school during the process of hifz in case this had a negative impact on the child's psychology. Initially she tried to get a hafiz to come to their home. But it proved difficult for the child to make impressive progress in the memorization process during this hour-long daily tuition, forcing her to look around for madrasa options.

Eventually, she found a madrasa in Jeddah run by a retired military official who explained that he had set up this madrasa, partially because he himself was very frustrated with the existing options when he was trying to get his son to do hifz. Even there she was not fully satisfied as, though there was no beating, the long hours of sitting and memorization was making the child rather depressed. After a year of coping with this, she withdrew the child from that madrasa and at the time of the interview the child was studying with an 'alim who came to their home after school. Throughout the process, she kept discussing the options with her child, even giving him the option to quit the process. At the time of the interview, it was interesting that the child said:

> Initially she felt that I should do it and I was not sure whether I will be able to do it; now she says that maybe I should leave it because it is too demanding, but I say that no I have done half of it and I know that I can do the rest. If others can do it then why can't I? So, I am going to complete the process. I also feel an inner strength due to hifz. At school among my mates, I feel more privileged because I feel I can pray when I am faced with a difficulty, while they can't.

Only a few parents are so conscious of the demands of a religious education on the child, but it is also true that within their limited resources even the lower-middle income and the poor families try to identify the best madrasa for their children. Among the middle class respondents I found families who had relocated to another neighborhood or a city in order to send their son to a madrasa they valued. Eighty percent of respondents mentioned reliance on trusted networks of friends or family within the religious sphere to identify a good madrasa for their child but, among the low-income households, most noticeable was the initiative of the student himself in moving to a better madrasa over time. I found it is very normal among madrasa students to move from one madrasa to another before settling down. For example, one of respondents from a low-income background joined a madrasa in his local village; then, when his family moved to Rawalpindi (a medium-size city), he joined a madrasa on a neighboring street. Once settled in the new city, however, he moved to a central madrasa in Rawalpindi because it offered officially recognized degrees. Now a trained ʿalim teaching in a madrasa, this respondent explained, "In Battagram and Mansehra, the atmosphere is very religious. Majority of the people in the village are inclined toward religion. They also have the option of sending the child to a school but still they send their children to madrasas. I was very keen to study in a madrasa. First, I studied in a madrasa on my street. Then when we shifted to Rawalpindi I had to find a new madrasa. I found a madrasa in my neighborhood which was good but it was not linked to the wafaq. The big madrasa in Raja Bazaar was linked to the wafaq so I then came here. To do hifz is not easy, no one can force someone to do hifz."

It is therefore a combination of resource endowment and personal initiative that determines access to elite madrasas. The choice of madrasa is based on forward-looking calculations, but the outcomes are influenced by the parents' economic and social capital. Children of various economic backgrounds enter madrasas and, while going to the same institution, they tread different paths within it. It is the middle class that stays the longest in the madrasa system and then takes religious education as its profession. These findings bear striking similarities with Gambetta's (1987) work on "push and pull" factors that determine individuals' choices regarding whether to stay in school or leave, and if to stay then how to choose one type of school over another. Countering claims that educational choices are product of traditional values inherited by a specific economic class, Gambetta shows that subjects rationally calculate the various elements, which include economic constraints, personal academic ability, and expected labor market returns when making educational decisions. This process of evaluation takes place based on their personal preferences and life plans, which are partly the result of personal characteristics but which are equally "distorted" by specific class biases. His conclusion to the question, "So were they pushed or did they jump?" helps summarize the findings presented in this chapter: "If anything, they jumped. They jumped as much as they could and as much as they perceived it was worth jumping. The trouble, though, is that not all children can jump to the same extent and the number of pushes they receive in several directions, shaping their opportunities as well as preferences, varies tremendously in society" (Gambetta 1987: 186–87).

Given that normally only one child within a household joins a madrasa, before concluding it might be worth recording the factors shaping that selection. Is it a random decision or a result of forward-looking calculations? In addressing this, it is important to see who takes the decision to enroll a child in the madrasa. In the case of 70 percent of the students surveyed, the decision appeared to be the result of a consultative and accommodative process between parents and the child. Fifteen percent of respondents said it was entirely their own choice, while 10 percent said that it was their parents' choice. I found that the selection of the child was normally based on a combination of his aptitude and his willingness to comply with parental preferences. In my observation the decision was not as instrumentally rational as argued by some—where the handicapped child is sent to a madrasa because he is unfit for other activities (ICG 2002; Singer 2001); rather, the child's selection depends on the starting point of the believer.

It is the gradation of religious faith of the parents—that is, the degree to which they are willing to prioritize investment in pursuing religious rewards irrespective of the costs—that determines which child will be enrolled in a madrasa. The complexity of this choice is reflected in the response of a father who enrolled his daughter in a madrasa, not so much out of his own choice but because of his own father, "My father was a very devout Muslim so he made me send my brightest daughter to the madrasa. She could have done very well in matric examinations and would have secured a position." This respondent himself is a devout Muslim who prays five times a day but because, in his view, hifz is not a compulsory religious obligation, his daughter could have better maximized the benefits in this and the other world if she had followed the secular education system and secured a regular job while practicing Islam in daily life. Thus, though for him, religious rewards were very important and not instrumental, he was willing to make calculations that maximized both his and his daughter's religious and secular interests while for his father the pursuit of religious rewards merited a higher investment.

At the same time, over 70 percent of the surveyed students who had enrolled in a madrasa after secondary school certificate, that is, over sixteen years of age, reported having taken an active part in the decision to join a madrasa often after being inspired by a friend or a cousin. Networks therefore play an important role in shaping preference for religious education. Inner propensity toward otherworldly concerns is another factor.

## Conclusions

In this chapter I have advanced three main propositions, which have implications for the existing assumptions of rational choice theory and the NIE framework. First, in line with advances in behavioral economics, I have argued that nonmaterial sources of utility do have an important bearing on individual choices; the search for religious rewards, and not economic deprivation, is the primary motive driving parents to send children to madrasas. Although the appreciation for ideal rewards is partly shaped by inner propensity, however, the material conditions in a given context play an important role in heightening the appreciation for ideal rewards. The parents send their children to madrasas in search for ideal rewards of a religious nature but in developing that appreciation the insecurity of the day-to-day living plays a critical role in moving people toward exploring these ideal rewards. These uncertainties make exchange, which marks every dimension of human interaction, whether social, economic, or political, very costly as people find it difficult to know or monitor the behavior of other actors, with whom they engage. The notion of God thus becomes a means to deal with these anxieties whether generated due to purely ideal inquiry about the meaning of life or the daily uncertainties of life. Thus, people's inner propensity does play a role in determining their religious faith, but the context of uncertainty and related transaction costs has an important role to play in making individuals gravitate toward religion.

Becker's work (1993, 1996) has noted the importance of including nonmaterial rewards within the utility calculus, so it is legitimate to ask what contribution the above analysis makes. After all, this adjustment to the idea of utility is what enables the rational choice theorists of religion to explain faith in God as rational: the idea of "religious rewards" is central to this literature (Iannaconne 1992; Stark and Finke 2000; Stolz 2006). While sharing their emphasis on the importance of religious rewards for the believer, I have started to map the importance of recognizing the conflicting nature of needs that the two types of rewards, material and ideal, address. This distinction will be fully developed in chapter 7 to establish the importance of understanding the psychological process shaping this interplay if the rationality of religious action is to be understood.

For now, this distinction highlights that it is important not to consider religion on purely instrumental terms. People do not consciously choose religion thinking it will reduce their material uncertainties; rather the appreciation of religious rewards as a response to material scarcity results from actually experiencing them. The main role that material conditions play in developing an appreciation for religion is that the higher uncertainty in the environment raises more questions about the purpose of life; these material conditions however do not themselves lead to conviction in religion. After all not all people exposed to religion become believers.

Finally, I have also argued that the pursuit of religious rewards is not carried out devoid of an assessment of the costs incurred. Parents are constantly trying to maximize both their material and their ideal sources of utility. The reason more children from middle-income groups than from rich or poor enrolled in the higher theology courses was that the parents from the middle class were better able to optimize their ideal and material rewards by committing one child to madrasa education. Further, the factors shaping a child's access to good religious education are the same as those in secular education—the initial resource endowment of the child (parents' socioeconomic profile, their social networks)—as well as his caliber play critical roles in determining which kind of madrasa he will enter. This implies that religious decisions are result of same means-end logic as are decisions within the secular sphere.

The emergence of a demand for religion can, thus, be explained as rational when standard assumptions of rational choice theory are adjusted to account for incomplete information and complexity of the notion of self-interest. The next chapter explores the factors that help rational actors sustain religious conviction over the long term. Many individuals come to believe in religion but not all demonstrate equal conviction in those beliefs, that is not all decide to shape their every action in light of that belief. By studying the factors shaping decisions of Muslim women enrolled in madrasas and members of *Al-Huda,* an Islamic education movement focused on elite women in Pakistan, I analyze the factors that shape conviction in religious beliefs.

6

# LOGIC OF ADAPTIVE PREFERENCE

## Islam and Western Feminism

**You know, our maulvi sahib opened this madrasa because he loved his youngest daughter so much that the thought of sending her off to the big madrasa in Lahore deeply saddened him. This made him lay down the foundation of this madrasa right next to his mosque.**

—Shazia Butt, a twenty-five-year-old teacher and a former student at Jamia-Firdusia, a small female madrasa in a low-income neighborhood in Rawalpindi

**Societal values are deteriorating fast. Because of the Musharraf government one cannot even watch Pakistan Television with a father and a brother; there is too much obscenity on the state television channel. One dreads the time that is to come.**

—Elder sister of a female student enrolled in Iqra model school during a family interview

A conscious move within the ranks of senior ʻulama to address the unmet educational needs of the women in their households was the primary factor to break the nine centuries impasse of exclusive focus on male madrasas and to allow for the emergence of female madrasas in Pakistan. Appearing for the first time in the late 1970s in isolated pockets, these madrasas today are a national phenomenon, located in small villages as well as in large cities. What prompted the ʻulama to expand educational choices for women within their households, and why at a specific point in time? These questions remain unanswered as the widespread existence of female madrasas has not been recognized until recently. This chapter explains the reasons for the birth and dramatic surge in the number of female madrasas in Pakistan. Furthermore, I use these insights as a starting point to address a fundamental debate about Islam within feminist scholarship: namely, what explains Muslim women's preference for Islamic beliefs that restrict their choices and limit their well-being when evaluated against feminist notions of gender equality?[1] This chapter explores factors that help rational actors sustain religious conviction over time.

1. For examples of studies that find Islamic laws to be discriminatory against women, see Azzam (1996); Connors (1996); Karmi (1996); and Ronald (2001). For a review of scholarship depicting

Standard rational choice theory is not concerned with preference formation; it is concerned only with its optimal attainment. Actors' goals are regarded as exogenous to the theory; the emphasis is on the maximization of whatever it is that the actor values. However, critics—New Institutionalists included—argue that an adequate behavioral foundation for economics and social sciences requires more than a mere emphasis on a means and ends rationality (how best to secure the desired goal);[2] what is a rational means to attain the desired end is itself contingent on the context in which the preference is formed (Bowles 2004; Goldthorpe 1998). A large body of literature has emerged to illustrate that preferences are historically and culturally specific and are shaped by the informational and cognitive constraints faced by the actor. Although these works unite in their critique of the neglect of preference formation, they vary in the emphasis they place on why such an engagement is essential.

The dominant critique revolves around concerns that, if preferences are context-specific, then universalist assumptions about the superiority of a specific preference cannot be made (Bowles 2004; Goldthorpe 1998; North 1990). Interestingly, some have used these very limitations of the standard model to argue the reverse: because preferences are context-specific, for the purpose of social choice it is important to pursue certain universalist positions as the preference being exercised may not be optimal. Rather, it may result from an actor's resignation to a suboptimal choice (Bliss 1993; Harsanyi 1982).

This position has been advanced particularly within the feminist literature; Martha Nussbaum (2001) has critiqued the neglect of preference formation on the grounds that, at times, preferences are formed to fit stifling circumstances, the satisfaction of which does not seem to contribute to well-being from a normative perspective. She, in association with Sen (1995), terms this phenomenon "adaptive preference" (Nussbaum 2001). In Nussbaum's view, the assumption that people maximize their utility ignores the possibility of sub-optimal choices that result from a lack of awareness about one's situation or from logical error. Nussbaum has used this argument to urge policy interventions to reform cultural practices in developing and Muslim societies, where she believes women have been so socialized into accepting subordinate status that they have lost any sense of alternatives (Nussbaum 2001, 80), "Sen concludes: 'Quiet acceptance of deprivation and bad fate affects the scale of dissatisfaction generated, and the utilitarian calculus gives sanctity to that distortion.'...this makes utility quite

---

Western feminists' frustration with the choices of Muslim women, who support movements that apparently damage their own interests and agendas, even when they have other options, see Mahmood (2005).

2. For detailed discussion on means-and-ends rationality see Kaplan (1976).

inadequate as a basis of social choice." Nussbaum's work has been criticized for ignoring the agency of women; critics assert that women may exercise particular options not because of a lack of information but rather because they are the most efficient options under the circumstances.[3] This chapter examines the relevance of these alternative justifications—lack of information about alternatives, the sour grapes[4] phenomenon, or optimal strategy in a given context—to understand what best explains female madrasa students' choice to attend madrasas in Pakistan.[5]

## Emergence of a Tradition: Rise of Female Madrasas

For eight centuries the ʿulama in male madrasas, which started to emerge in the Indian subcontinent in the twelfth century, were the dominant players, shaping the rules of the game. In the latter half of the 1970s, a new category of players—female madrasas—entered the field, gradually dotting the madrasa landscape across Pakistan. Three decades later, in terms of total number and student population, female madrasas are steadily catching up with their male counterparts (see table 6.1). In 2006, in the Deobandi wafaq the number of female students

3. Baber (2007) argues that apparently suboptimal decisions by women could be the result of a utility calculation, given their assessment of other options and the probabilities attached to various outcomes. Vasanti, a character used by Nussbaum (2001) to argue for women's socialization into accepting abusive marriages, could in Baber's view make this choice because she recognizes that, given her circumstances, staying in an abusive marriage is her best bet if she wants to have a home and basic necessities. Even though she would obviously prefer not to get beaten, she is prepared to take on that cost in order to avoid her least preferred outcome—homelessness and destitution. Rational choosers do not just consider the desirability of outcomes; they also calculate the probability of achieving them and the opportunity cost of trying to achieve them.

4. Elster (1983) equates adaptive preferences to the sour grapes phenomenon where the actor develops a kind of habituation or resignation regarding a restricted set of feasible options. In this approach, the given preference is neither the result of lack of information nor the best response in the given circumstances; rather it is an unconscious mechanism for reducing cognitive dissonance that takes the form of downgrading inaccessible options so that available options come to be preferred. In this view, if with a change in circumstances, the grapes do come within reach, the fox will jump at them; that is, the preference will change.

5. The arguments developed in this chapter draw on multiple methods used during the eighteen months of fieldwork between October 2006 and December 2008 across selected sites in all four provinces: first, interviews and discussions with 100 parents, 50 teachers, and 200 female students, in the age range of 10 to 25; second, data from 2000 self-administrated questionnaires among thirty female madrasas; third, ethnographic fieldwork in Jamia Hafsa, including group discussions, informal chats, and silent observation of the activities and interactions among its members and those with outside actors while it was in confrontation with the state; and fourth, interviews with the ʿulama of the five wafaqs and those who established the first female madrasas.

**TABLE 6.1** Comparative data on male/female madrasas and students

| | NO. OF REGISTERED MADRASAS | | NO. OF STUDENTS IN REGISTERED MADRASAS | |
|---|---|---|---|---|
| Wafaqs | Male | Female | Male | Female |
| Wafaq-ul-Madaris-al-Arabia (Deobandi) | 6,800 | 1,399 | 1,000,000 | 200,000 |
| Tanzeem-ul- Madaris (Barelvi) | 1,863 | 201 | 75,806 | 7,000 |
| Rabata-ul-Madaris-al-Islamia (Jamaat-i-Islami) | 267 | 106 | 47,183 | 8,730 |
| Wafaq-ul-Madaris-al-Salafia (Ahl-i-Hadith) | 148 | 187 | 15,488 | 16,301 |
| Wafaq-ul Madaris-al-Shia | 337 | 38 | 11,000 | 3,900 |

*Source:* GoP (2006).

registered for examinations at the highest level was twice that of male students: there were 8,615 girls compared to 4,721 boys at the 'Alimiya level and 10,976 girls compared to 6,877 boys at the 'Aliya level (Wafaq-ul-Madaris 2006).[6] In addition, girls on average had a higher pass rate than their male counterparts: the average pass rate for girls across the grades was 88.49 percent compared to 84.47 percent (Wafaq-ul-Madaris 2006). What explains the birth of female madrasas and their rapid expansion? To comprehend the phenomenon, we should reframe the question and first understand why it took eight hundred years for the 'ulama to provide educational facilities for females within their households—especially when a parallel discourse around Muslim women's access to secular education started in the nineteenth century (Minault 1998).

Interviews with the 'ulama show that path dependence, where past choices make investment in new choices a costly option, made further investment in male madrasas an easier option than using financial and human capital to create a parallel set of organizations within the religious hierarchy especially in absence of any strong incentives to make this investment. As explained by a leading scholar from the Ahl-i-Hadith school of thought, "For the 'ulama the main

6. The total number of male madrasas and students is still much higher than female madrasas or students (table 6.1). The data however show that at the higher level, there are more women. A large number of male students enroll for hifz process and many others exit after completing the initial stages of theological studies.

objective of madrasa scholarship has primarily been to produce Islamic scholars who would propagate Islam especially through the platform of the mosque; because women were traditionally excluded from positions of religious authority within the mosque and madrasa in this region, the ʻulama had little incentive to invest in female madrasas." Such investment seemed particularly undesirable because women's access to formal religious education could empower them to reinterpret religious text independently of the male ʻulama, resulting in theory in contestation and competition within the religious hierarchy.[7]

In addition, in the case of Pakistan, the political partition of the subcontinent itself reinforced the need for investment in male madrasas. Areas that boasted premier madrasas during Islamic rule—Delhi, the capital of Muslim empires, and Uttar Pradesh, the stronghold of the Muslim elite—adorned the map of India after partition, leaving the newly created state of Pakistan devoid of premier madrasas and prominent ʻulama. It became a conscious concern for the ʻulama to establish premier madrasas in Pakistan to preserve Islam. Maulana Fazlul Rehman of Jamia Ashrafi, the most prestigious Deobandi madrasa in Lahore, which is not formally part of the Deobandi wafaq because the Jamia's own degrees are recognized by the government, explained: "Mufti Mohammad Hussain Amritsari was running a madrasa in Amritsar at the time of partition, but he migrated to Lahore to establish a madrasa, because there was a need for Islamic scholars in Pakistan. On 15 September 1947, he opened a madrasa in a temporary building given by Moon Chand Trust near *Neela Gumbaad.* Then a thirty-kanal land (15,167 square meters) was secured for Jamia Ashrafi. This is the oldest university in Pakistan and the degrees issued by it are recognized by the government. With time we also opened a section for girls. Today our female wing has students not just from Pakistan but also from Sweden, Norway, and the UK."

Scholars within the leading madrasas in India, for instance Dar-ul-Uloom Deoband, appointed ʻulama from within their ranks to migrate to Pakistan to fill the vacuum. In a volume featuring biographies of Pakistan's leading ʻulama, Maulana Taqi Usmani, a prominent Deobandi scholar, documents how many of these personalities, including his own father, had been sent to Pakistan by senior ʻulama in Deoband because they recognized the need for Islamic scholars in the new state (Usmani 2004). The leading madrasas across the five wafaqs are thus the outcome of conscious efforts on the part of ʻulama in the post-partition

7. An emerging concern where female Islamic preachers argue for mixed prayers, such as the case of Amina Wadud in the United States, whose decision to lead mixed prayer in New York generated great controversy. In most contexts, however, there is little indication that the female preachers emerging in Muslim societies in recent years are challenging the authority of male scholars (Bano and Kalmbach forthcoming).

period; examples from the other four wafaqs include Jamia al-Muntazir (Shia, Lahore), Jamaat-i-Islami Mansura (Lahore), Jamia Salafia (Ahl-i-Hadith, Faisalabad), and Jamia Naeemia (Barelvi, Lahore).

These incentive structures help us understand why for nine hundred years South Asian ‘ulama preserved the tradition of male madrasas rather than shift resources to female madrasas. It becomes more difficult to explain why some ‘ulama eventually did break with tradition and why at a particular point in time. Had the external context of the 1970s changed dramatically, or did internal religious reforms trigger the right incentives to invest in female madrasas? The answer, as argued by senior ‘ulama, rests in the changing context of Pakistani society which, under the forces of globalization, increasingly displayed a mismatch between the claims of modernization and local realities. A senior Deobandi scholar stated, “The ‘ulama are not ignorant of the needs of the society; they have to monitor the changing pulse of the society if they are to stay relevant. Before women were not allowed in the public sphere, however, after partition as opportunities grew for women, the ‘ulama realized that they have to create platforms for women to study Islam if they are not to be swayed by the Western value systems, which eventually destroys the family structure.”

The 1960s and 1970s witnessed an opening up of Pakistani society to global influences. Ayub Khan, the first military ruler of Pakistan, was enamored with the model of Western economic prosperity and shared Western liberal values. Zulfiqar Ali Bhutto, the first elected prime minister of Pakistan, who succeeded Ayub Khan after a brief interlude by Yahya Khan, founded the Pakistan Peoples Party, which was to become the frontrunner of progressive and liberal forces in Pakistan (Mumtaz and Shaheed 1987). Among other measures, Ayub Khan introduced the 1961 Family Laws Ordinance, which discouraged polygamy by making a Muslim’s man religious right to second marriage conditional on securing permission from his first wife. Zulfiqar Ali Bhutto accommodated women in grassroots politics as well as in senior leadership roles, gave them constitutional guarantees including reserved seats in the local government bodies (district government), and appointed women to such key positions as provincial governor, university vice-chancellor, and deputy speaker of the National Assembly. This period also saw the rise of prominent feminist organizations within Pakistan, two of which would shape the discourse on women’s rights: the Aurat Foundation (1976) started by left-wing–oriented university teachers, students and other working women, and Shirkat Gah (1975), established by young women who attended Western universities (Mumtaz and Shaheed 1987).

These enhanced opportunities for women and their increased visibility in the public sphere triggered self-reflection within the ranks of the ‘ulama, of their own initiation as well as from the cajoling of their daughters and sisters who envied the changing opportunities for girls in their neighborhoods. Two concerns came under deliberation: first, as elaborated by Maulana Naeemi, a prominent Barelvi scholar, "the need to ensure that women within religious households are not denied benefits of increased educational opportunities, especially in light of the consensus in Islamic scholarship on the importance of seeking knowledge for both men and women; second, an anxiety to protect their women from the liberal Western values pervading society." As the 'ulama equated women's good moral character to the preservation of family structure, the very conception of the ideal family and society was at stake.

This conception of women's morality as the foundation of a stable family life and a good social order was not unique to the 'ulama; the centrality of women in keeping family together and ensuring the prosperity of future generations remains a widely held belief within the Muslim community in South Asia. The concern was often reiterated during my interviews with religious scholars, female teachers, parents, and students alike. Respondents from each category emphasized the importance of women, especially as mothers, in shaping values within the household. They also reiterated that Islam might assign higher authority within the household to men, but as women enjoy the primary responsibility of rearing children, they in fact directly shape the next generation of men. It was precisely this recognition that had led some men from elite Muslim families to initiate the first movement to educate Muslim women in the nineteenth century, resulting in the establishment of the first Muslim Women's College at Aligarh (India).[8] These men were concerned that in the rapidly changing external environment under colonial rule, Muslim women would fail to relate to the men of their families who had to adapt to the changing societal realities and would be unable to rear children to meet the demands of the time. They therefore created a curriculum that combined secular and religious subjects to enable these women to situate themselves in a changing context without losing their traditional values.

A century later, the 'ulama in Pakistan were to respond to a similar challenge—to prepare their women to relate to changes in the external environment while retaining their traditional values. The difference was that while the nineteenth-century movement aimed at equipping Muslim women to engage with an increasingly secular context through participation in modern educational institutions, the twentieth-century madrasa-based movement was more inclined to confront secular society. The efforts of these men, albeit motivated by the same concerns, led to different outcomes partly because of their different ideological orientations: the men leading the nineteenth-century movement, such as Sir Syed

8. For a detailed analysis of this movement, see Minault (1998).

Ahmad Khan, often classified as reformist scholars within the Islamic tradition (Moaddel and Talatoff 2000), wanted to retain Islamic values by adapting them to the demands of institutions introduced by the British; the 'ulama introducing the female madrasas in Pakistan in the twentieth century felt little need to accommodate Western value systems.

However, an equally important factor was the pace of change in the external environment; with increasing access to television across Pakistan and the rise of feminist movements in the West, the clash between Western cultural influences and traditional value systems was not only starker, its influence was more pervasive and spread across all sections of society. Female madrasas thus emerged from an ideological move to preserve traditional value structures in light of threats from the growing liberalization of society.

Mapping the growth of female madrasas since the first few emerged in the late 1970s shows that despite the apparent appeal of equipping women within the religious household to deal with a changing external context, not many 'ulama—even those among the senior ranks—were keen adopters. The emphasis on preserving women's piety, which was central to the establishment of female madrasas, posed the main obstacle to their establishment. If a female student boarding at a madrasa were to be implicated in an illicit affair, whether by force or willing compliance, it could "tarnish the 'alim's reputation." "For the 'alim," according to a scholar from the Alh-i-Hadith school of thought, "his reputation is the most valuable asset; he works very hard to build credibility within his group of followers, once lost a reputation is very difficult to rebuild. To be responsible for young girls was thus not an easy option for the 'ulama when any mishap with even a single female student could have dire consequences for the image of the 'alim. Only very senior 'ulama could therefore afford to take this risk at the beginning; also given the novelty of the idea at that stage, only these senior 'ulama who had strong following stood a chance of mobilizing parents to send their daughters to boarding facilities." The role of prominent 'ulama in establishing the tradition of female madrasas is traceable by looking at profiles of some of the 'ulama who initiated the first female madrasas. Such an analysis reveals that those who were willing to take this risk were prominent personalities with the intellectual caliber and financial independence to innovate and a reputation strong enough to withstand possible scandal: Jamia Naeemia and Jamia Khair-ul-Madaris, both established by prominent 'ulama, were among the first madrasas to establish a female section.

The initiation of the model by elite 'ulama, therefore, was not in itself enough to trigger the massive spread of female madrasas. It took more than a decade from the birth of the first female madrasa in the late 1970s to the dramatic expansion starting in the late 1980s. According to a Deobandi scholar, "it took ten years for the pioneering 'ulama to establish that female students could be provided boarding facilities without risk to the 'alim's reputation." An equally if not more important factor in winning converts was the unpredicted dividends of the investment in female education, which came to the surface only gradually. As graduating students from the madrasas returned to their homes after four years of Islamic education, they became instrumental in spreading religious teaching in their broader community. In the words of Maulana Mohsin, a senior scholar from the Ahl-i-Shia school of thought in Islamabad:

> We wanted to open a female madrasa ourselves but could not do so because of a lack of female teachers but then one female madrasa opened and it became possible to get female teachers. The reason female madrasas have spread so fast is that the eastern girls are normally within the four walls of the house and until they get married they are sitting idle at home so with opening of female madrasas they now have a good opportunity to use this time to gain education. Once provided with this opportunity they did very well because girls generally give more attention than boys to their studies and learn well. Finally, girls speak more than men. With time we saw that they spread Islamic principles to more people in the house and in their immediate community than men. With girls you teach them for three to four months and then the information starts spreading.

Unlike in male madrasas, parents of girls attending female madrasas paid fees, providing the potential of turning the latter into economically profitable ventures. These multiple incentives made an appealing option for the 'ulama, whether motivated by religious or by material incentives. From the 1990s on, the phenomenon multiplied dramatically; it became a customary practice for an 'alim operating a male madrasa to open a female madrasa in a separate building. Jamaat-i-Islami established its first female madrasa in the late 1980s, and was the last wafaq to do so; by now it has an extensive female madrasa network under the wing of the Jamiat ul Mohsinat Trust. The model had to be first recognized as a success before it could initiate large-scale conversions.

The birth of the female madrasas and their rapid expansion lends support to Liebowitz and Margolis's (1995) critique of the dominant view that finds path dependence an irreversible process.[9] It indicates that actors will invest the required resources to reverse path dependence provided the pay-offs are significant. What we see in the case of the 'ulama is that, once the changing external context established strong enough incentives to invest in female madrasas, some

9. For a review of key positions in the path dependence literature, see Pierson (2000).

did so, and the increasing visibility of these incentives over time engendered a herd mentality. The analysis also illustrates, as we saw in the rise of Oxford and the elite madrasas in South Asia, that the tactical knowledge of elite players and their ability to maximize in a changing context was central to the rise of female madrasas. Another analytically gripping aspect of the ascent of female madrasas is its ability to elucidate how elite players within a hierarchy co-opt interests of other players with their own in order to avoid competition.

Leadership within female madrasas remains in the hands of female family members of the 'ulama, normally wives or daughters-in-law; these female madrasas function as sister organizations of the male madrasas. Teaching in the higher classes is done by male 'ulama. For instance, within Jamaat-i-Islami the highest qualification, namely that of Daura-i-Hadith, makes it obligatory for all students to spend forty days at the headquarters in Mansura (Lahore) attending lectures by senior 'ulama. In the three decades since their inception, female madrasas have expanded at a dramatic pace and the daughters-in-law and wives of the 'ulama who act as principals are in full control of the everyday operations; however, curriculum authority rests in the hands of male 'ulama.

During my interviews and visits to madrasas, it was very clear that these women exercised full control over the everyday working of the madrasas; all were confident of their roles as teachers and managers. During field visits they were always busy either attending meetings or teaching. They were often seen flanked by groups of former students who had stopped by to pay respect and have a chat. The atmosphere was relaxed and jovial, and the affinity and informality (within respectful limits) between these women and students was obvious. During one of my visits to the female branch of Jamia Naeemia, the leading Barelvi madrasa in Lahore, in the office of the principal who was the daughter-in-law of the main 'alim, I met three former students who were now teaching at Punjab University, the main government-funded university in Lahore. The warmth marking the interaction among these former students and the principal and the teachers was striking; everyone seemed happy just as a family is when children who have left home to pursue their professions return to visit. Discussions with them revealed that these students routinely visited the madrasa. One of the students explained:

> The bonds we have cultivated with [the principal] Madam Nabila and other teachers here can never be severed. It is not like a school system where the teacher only covers the assigned text and never really gets to know the real life challenges of the students; the teachers here become involved in all aspects of our lives, they give us advice on personal, spiritual, as well as professional matters. Even when it comes to marriage

> proposals, we seek their advice on suitability of the prospective proposals as these are sensitive matters.

Such gatherings around principals or teachers of the female madrasas were a routine occurrence during my visits. Yet, despite this respect from their students, the principals and teachers in the madrasas I surveyed were highly deferential toward the male ʿulama. Again, their conversations as well as their relaxed mannerism suggested that this deference was a product of conviction rather than compulsion.

By keeping the madrasa management in the hands of female family members and idealizing the women's role as family-makers within the madrasa curriculum, the ʿulama have introduced new organizations within the religious hierarchy, which effectively compete with rival organizations in the secular world, namely secular government and private schools and colleges. The new players, because of family ties, financial dependence, and most important, weak technological skills—here interpreted as knowledge of religious text—have no incentives to challenge the elite players. Financial and technological dependence is one way of aligning interests within a hierarchy. Another method as illustrated by Miller (1992) is through creation of nonmaterial incentives such as ideology. The ʿulama have relied on both to create incentives that keep interests of scholars within female madrasas in line with their male counterparts. In the words of the principal of Jamia-Naeemia:

> Female madrasas need the senior ʿulama because even experienced female teachers cannot match their grasp of the complex texts taught in the higher grades. The female teachers fail to build that extensive knowledge base because once outside the madrasa, they have limited venues to continue higher learning; especially after marriage, family obligations limit their ability to pursue formal religious scholarship while for the aspiring male graduates, pursuit of religious education remains a lifelong process.

Principals of female madrasas from across the five wafaqs repeatedly advanced similar arguments. A female teacher in a madrasa in Multan explained, "The more difficult books are read by men because by the time girls reach that stage they get married."

This difference in emphasis was also reflected in the condensed curriculum taught in female madrasas, which ranges from four to six years of education as opposed to the eight-year course of Daura-i-Hadith in the male madrasas. It is clear that the leading male madrasas emphasize producing leading religious scholars of the future, while for female madrasas the primary objective is to groom honorable women who become productive members of society by safeguarding their traditional roles. As more graduating students establish their own madrasas free from family ties, perhaps they may seek to reinterpret religious text; however, as I saw in the behavior of the current female leadership and in repeated discussions with students, there appears to be no sign of any simmering tension. These women, like many Muslim women exposed to Western lifestyles, see a genuine appeal in orthodox Islamic precepts.

## Parental Demand: Reducing Intergenerational Transaction Costs

The expansion in the number of madrasas was not simply a product of strategic calculations on the part of the ‘ulama. Equally important were demand side factors. The expanding student base was no longer confined to the ‘ulama's own relatives but drew on an increasingly heterogeneous population of female students from across income and geographical divides: across the thirty madrasas surveyed, 60 percent of the students came from smaller neighboring cities or rural areas. Two characteristics of female madrasas help rule out any claims that rapidly expanding demand primarily resulted from economic deprivation. First, most female madrasas, unlike their male counterparts, charge between Rs 400 to Rs 1,500 (US$5–19) per month, which is comparable to the tuition fees of a respectable private secular educational institution in Pakistan;[10] second, a high percentage of students in female madrasas is between the ages of sixteen and twenty-one, entering the madrasas after completing their matriculation or FA—equivalent to a high-school diploma in the United States—in regular government and private schools. In the Jamaat-i-Islami madrasas, for instance, the matriculation certificate is a compulsory condition for admission. Whereas access to prior secular education indicates some financial stability, the switch to madrasa education implies a conscious preference for religious education over secular options. What factors explain the shaping of parents' and students' decisions?

Analysis of the factors shaping parental preferences across the four provinces, despite rural/urban and sectarian divides, reveals a striking commonality. At the heart of parental preference for female madrasas rest the same concerns that motivated the ‘ulama to establish female madrasas: an anxiety to preserve traditional values, and thereby the family structure, in a fast changing environment.

10. Private secular schools charge a fee of as low as Rs 100 per month (about US $1.40) (Andrabi et al. 2006).

The most repeated claim in my interviews with parents was along the lines, "the time has become very bad" and the "society has become very bad." Interviews showed that parental choices are based on a calculation that girls trained in Islamic texts will imbibe religious values so that they will voluntarily, rather than by compulsion, choose in favor of tradition. The difference between the choices of the parents and the 'ulama, however, is that the parents' reversion to tradition—where mothers who did not study in madrasas send their daughters to attend them—is not a result of pure ideological commitment. Rather, it is primarily a calculated response to the threat they face to their material well-being if their daughters take inspiration from Western cultural influences and deviate from societal expectations.

Scholarship, especially within sociology and anthropology, is cognizant of the uncomfortable interface between modernity and tradition. However, precisely how global forces have an impact at national, sub-national, and local village levels, and how the formal institutions of the state play a critical role in determining the specific nature of this interface, is still a nascent field of inquiry. The study of female madrasas highlights the heightened probability of a reassertion of tradition in societies where the state fails to put in place formal institutions to reap the benefits of modernization. Indeed, it reveals the challenges of engaging with global influences when there is a mismatch in society's ability to engage with processes of economic modernization and those of cultural modernization. Economic modernization in Pakistan led to public appreciation of Western living standards, increased demand for formal sector jobs, and recognition of the benefits of investment in education. Space also opened up for women to seek higher education and employment in the formal economy. With the spread of media and an increasing involvement of western aid agencies in implementing development programs, ideas of material prosperity spread from cities to rural areas. Public expectations were raised, but the mechanisms required to gain access to this economic prosperity were never institutionalized; rather, access to modernity was contingent on the initial resource endowment of each individual family. The state education system did not improve, jobs in the formal sector did not expand—and especially not in proportion with the increase in population.[11] Middle-income groups, even when willing to invest in private education, could afford only low-performing schools

11. Only half of the population is literate. The political domination of the feudal and military elites has resulted in low investment in education: maintaining the historical trend, education got 2 percent of the annual GDP in 2004 whereas military spending got 4 percent (Word Bank 2007a, 2007b). The unemployment rate was 6 percent in 2006 (Asian Development Bank 2008) and the underemployment rate is much higher; in addition, 68 percent of the population resides in rural areas and is largely reliant on informal economic activity. With a population growth rate of 2.1 percent, the current population of 150 million is estimated to double in twenty years.

whose students ultimately could not compete with graduates from elite educational institutions in the employment market.

This uneven distribution of the benefits of economic modernization might not have triggered a reaction on its own, but economic changes were being outpaced by a parallel process of cultural modernization, whose spread, unlike economic development, was not contingent on the state developing a level playing field for all. Central was the role of the media, where a revolution in information technology has made cable TV, the Internet, and mobile phones accessible to the poorest income groups even in rural areas of Pakistan.[12] The TV cable network in particular has become the most economical form of entertainment for families; it, however, also poses the most serious threat to traditional values. Interviewees repeatedly emphasized the negative influence of the media. As one parent said, "the trends on the media and cable are not at all healthy"; another parent added, "these channels promote values which encourage promiscuous behavior in the society and disrespect for traditional values."

The most-watched channels on the cable network air Indian movies and soap operas. These give girls ideas of an economically empowered lifestyle and promote fanciful notions of romantic love affairs outside the institution of marriage. At the same time they implant the idea of the right to choose one's own partner. Interviews with parents illustrate that for them, especially those within the middle-income group, this mismatch in the pace of economic and of cultural modernity creates an unsettling sense of lost control. Many feel unable to regulate these new forces. Hopeful of reaping benefits from economic modernization, these parents enter their girls in secular educational institutions, but the government schools and colleges that they can afford provide no guarantee of employment.

The choice of madrasa education for girls is partially a product of this clash between cultural and economic modernization, as was noted in countless interviews. One parent told me, "The television creates the biggest *fassad* [mayhem]. On TV all inappropriate behavior is shown. The government thinks this is *roshan khayali* [progressive thinking]. Our respect is in our own hands. If you are standing at the bus stop and know that boys will tease you then it is best you cover yourself. Something that is precious is better kept hidden. Seeing the girls in the madrasas, there is a *sakoon* [peace]. See how many cricketers and artists like Junaid Jamshaid are going toward religion."

The principal of the largest female Jamaat-i-Islami madrasa in Karachi added, "The influence of girls is everywhere now. Their role is increasing in every field

12. Cable TV network can be secured for a monthly payment of US $5; Internet cafes allow one hour of access for less than half a dollar; and mobile calls cost less than twenty cents for domestic calls of three minutes' duration.

now. Even in the O level exams, girls' share is rising. This influx of Western values supported by the state is having a reaction. We never saw so many girls with hijabs in the Karachi University. We also never had hijab garment shops like we have now in the Rabi Center in Karachi. There is a clash between the *hukamran* [the rulers] and the public."

Maulana Charag-uddin, a Deobandi scholar leading a large madrasa in the Satellite Town area of Rawalpindi and a chain of related madrasas in the Khyber Pakhtunkhwa and Hazara region, added, "The female madrasas are popular because they provide better services. In the colleges and universities you have to spend more money, and still the result is not very good. After sixteen years of education there is little learning. In madrasas, the girls at least learn *akhlaq* [cordial conduct] and *adab* [respect]. The result is good. Then when they leave the madrasa they start to teach in their area. In most of the girls' madrasas, female teachers are teaching."

These issues, raised during the interviews, suggest a new reality for girls within middle-income families: after acquiring their bachelor qualifications in secular colleges, they return to the confines of their home, waiting for their sole prospect of upward mobility, namely a good marriage. The difference, however, is that unlike their mothers, these girls have studied, have been exposed to the latest fashion trends, have learned the significance of Valentine's Day, and have acquired fanciful notions of romantic relationships with happy endings, drawn from Indian soap operas and movies. In a context where the marriageable age is rising, and cheap access to mobile phones and Internet has made it possible to meet new people and sustain prolonged interaction without leaving the confines of the home, the fear that girls could entertain ideas of having affairs has become a real and constant concern for their families. The objection to such affairs is not simply moral; the real fear is a failed relationship, where girls get drawn into intimate contact by men who have no intention of marriage, thereby ruining their prospects of a suitable match. As one father noted, "The Western style women's rights groups that we see emerging in Pakistan accuse us of repressing our daughters if we try to protect them from negative influences. However, we protect them and restrict certain liberties for their own good. Who will marry a girl with a reputation of a pre-marital affair? Our religious values are therefore meant to protect the interest of the girl."

The massive demand for female madrasas is the result of increased access to what liberal theorists understand as negative freedom (the absence of external obstacles to self-guided choice and action, whether imposed by the state, corporations, or private individuals) as opposed to positive freedom (the capacity to realize an autonomous will only generally fashioned in accord with the dictates of "universal reason" or "self-interest" and hence unencumbered by the weight of custom, transcendental will, and tradition).[13] This in turn is due to the failure of the state to develop institutionalized structures to provide equal opportunities for all to engage with economic modernization. This situation illustrates, like many studies in the institutional literature, that when formal institutions fail, informal institutions—which are more responsive to local needs—become dominant (Helmke and Levitsky 2004). The dramatic spread of the informal institution of Islamic beliefs, as manifest in the popularity of female madrasas, is thus a direct result of the failure of the formal institutions of the state to develop an equal opportunity for all.

During my interviews, respondents repeatedly voiced concerns about secular colleges, where in their view girls not only had affairs but some even indulged in prostitution to make money for their frivolous material needs.[14] Moreover, constant exposure to the latest fashion trends caused girls to add to their parents' economic burdens by making demands for clothes and accessories. Seventy percent of madrasa students defended madrasa education on the grounds that it encourages simplicity, which not only relieves girls of the pressures to follow changing trends but makes them more productive members of their families. In the words of one of the students who entered a madrasa after completing her FA in a secular college:

> In the college, the atmosphere is very much about material aspirations. Girls are taught to prioritize their careers over building a family. Also, girls are encouraged to exercise more freedom over their future choices even in matters of marriage. The result is that girls in colleges celebrate Valentine's Day and take pride in having a boyfriend; they are also so much into fashion and acquisition of new clothes and accessories. But such aspirations also lead to heightened frustrations as not all can afford them. Also, these are not our values; they should not be encouraged.

Madrasa education not only becomes a means for securing women's piety but also provides more comprehensive moral training in which girls learn to cope with existing circumstances in the role of daughter, sister, wife, and future mother, rather than acquire expectations that aggravate the economic burden on the male members of the family. As noted in a newsletter issued by one of the female madrasas from the Jamaat-i-Islami school of thought, "This institution wants to create such a group of students, which in light of the instructions of Quran and Sunna, will provide the society, best women in

13. For discussion of negative and positive freedoms in liberal theory, see Mahmood (2005).

14. Such rumors were making the rounds, even within secular families, during the time of my fieldwork.

the form of good mothers, virtuous wives, and loving sisters. A woman who will make her home heaven while directing everyone in that home to follow the righteous path."

This in turn makes a madrasa education an important signal in the marriage market. It indicates the likelihood that a girl is pious, family-oriented, and less demanding of material comforts. The fear about how the times have gone bad[15] also repeatedly emerges in the publications of madrasas and other Islamic organizations: "The conditions of the society have taken such a shape that every serious person appears worried. In this media-exposed society, every individual wants to send his child to a place where the child can acquire proper knowledge, proper guidance, and a neat and clean environment. Where the company is also good, environment is also good, and the children learn about religion as well as the world...At the Quran Foundation [which runs 250 schools in Pakistan], along with modern subjects, Quranic education is also imparted, which can help solve current day problems."[16]

The age at which female students enroll in the madrasas, as opposed to the age of their male counterparts, suggests the emphasis on moral training; the majority of female students are above the age of sixteen and enter the madrasas after having already completed matriculation or bachelor's degree. Further, they enroll for the four-year fiqh (Islamic jurisprudence) course, which imparts knowledge of basic Islamic principles to shape everyday behavior, rather than hifz (memorization of the Quran), which is popular among male madrasa students. In the Deoband wafaq's higher grades the number of female students dramatically exceeded the male students, but in hifz the boys far outnumber the girls—in 2006, only 12,125 girls were enrolled for hifz in registered Deobandi madrasas as opposed to 42,925 boys (Wafaq-ul-Madaris 2006). The high concentration of students from middle-income groups in female madrasas also supports this reasoning, because this is the group most confronted with the challenges sketched out above. These girls have been through secular schools and the college system, but neither the quality of education nor the job market conditions ensure productive employment, thereby leading to more frustrated expectations. Girls from upper-income families gain education in elite organizations

15. The rise of Islamic movements as a response to perceived secularization has been noted by others: Mahmood (2005) found that members of the mosque movement in Egypt repeatedly described the rise of this thirty-year-old movement as a response to secularization or Westernization, which was defined as a historical process that has reduced Islamic knowledge to an abstract system of beliefs with no direct bearing on the practicalities of life. Like the female madrasas, the movement was not just concerned with the knowledge of Islamic rituals but focused on how to organize daily conduct with principles of Islamic piety.

16. Advertisement in Al-Mohsinat Trust newsletter (2007).

and so have access to dynamic careers in all fields and, due to financial affluence, can afford access to multiple recreational activities. Many also travel overseas to study in Western universities; in addition, a strong family background also promises better marriage prospects.

Among the poor income groups, girls of this age are engaged in the informal economy, normally working as domestic helpers, making concern about morality a luxury. It is thus the middle-income group where females are most vulnerable to the unsettling influences of the disjuncture between the pace of economic and cultural modernity, and it is girls from these very families that register a high presence within the madrasas. It is important to acknowledge that, while the extended demand for female madrasas within middle-income groups is a response to the unsettling influences of modernity, technological and infrastructural developments have also stimulated the demand for and facilitated access to madrasa education. The introduction of the Varan bus service, which ensured secure travel between the twin cities of Islamabad and Rawalpindi, was critical in facilitating access for some of my respondents to the Al-Huda school (a new Islamic education movement primarily aimed at women from upper-income groups); and widespread access to cable TV, while promoting Indian soap operas, also led to the mushroom growth of Islamic channels, which for 40 percent of my respondents had played an important role in stimulating interest in Islamic education. As noted by one respondent in Rawalpindi, "My education in Al-Huda school in Islamabad was made possible by the Varan bus service. I had wanted to pursue Islamic education for some time but we did not have private transport and the daily fare for the taxi would get too high. That year the Varan bus service started a route that had a stop in front of our house and another outside the Al-Huda campus in Islamabad. This enabled me to pursue the one-year Islamic education degree at Al-Huda."

The theoretical insights from this analysis are significant: religious beliefs, by aligning the incentives of girls from the middle-income families with those of their parents minimize the cost of monitoring and enforcement, thereby making them the most efficient means of reducing the cost of intergenerational transactions. This directly supports the transactional cost approach in the New Institutional Economics (North 1990), which maintains that institutions arise as a means to reduce transaction costs between two parties. The logic of the parental preference for madrasa education is thus clear, namely a desire to inculcate their children with their own values. But what process convinces the girls to constrain their choices in line with Islamic beliefs? Mere exposure to text does not guarantee an automatic assimilation of information by a rational actor. The answer rests in both the practical relevance of the religious beliefs and their intrinsic appeal.

## Students' Acceptance: Maximizing Gains within Constraints

Parents may send their daughters to madrasas in the hopes of retaining parental control over their daughters' choices by aligning the girls' interests with their own, but my interviews with the girls show that the factors shaping their beliefs have different dynamics. The results from a survey of the socio-economic profile and future aspirations of female students, and interviews with students across the four provinces of Pakistan, reveal a genuine desire among a large number of students to enhance their grasp of Islamic beliefs—70 percent of respondents gave their wish to learn about Islam as the primary motive for enrolling in a madrasa. At the same time, the results highlighted how the socioeconomic and psychological relevance of religious beliefs in the girls' everyday lives built conviction in those beliefs. Interviews with the girls, and observations of their mutual interactions within the madrasas, suggest that the pay-offs of madrasa education range from simple material gains to a complex set of psychological and social rewards.

One rudimentary benefit of madrasa education is that, compared with regular colleges, it provides a more efficient means of acquiring both secular and religious education. All madrasas encourage their students to secure secular degrees up to bachelor's level[17] if they do not already have them at the time of admission to a madrasa. As boarding facilities with strict disciplinary guidelines, madrasas provide a conducive learning environment, where girls organize themselves into small study groups in the evenings, to prepare themselves for examinations for secular degrees as private candidates. These qualifications make the students eligible to seek entry into a master's program at regular universities, which can become a route for securing permanent teaching positions within the universities—an option 30 percent of respondents had successfully exercised. At the most basic level, madrasa education thus allows girls to receive a religious education without necessarily foreclosing their secular educational options. That the 'ulama themselves are conscious of the appeal of combining secular or vocational education with religious studies is reflected in advertisements of the madrasas of Jamaat-i-Islami: "Where girls along with the Quran, Hadith and Fiqh gain specialization in computer, calligraphy, fabric painting, glass painting, sewing, and many other household activities" (Al-Mohsinat Trust 2007).

Furthermore, madrasa life itself is socially empowering. For the course of study, girls leave their homes to live in madrasas, which involves travel—large madrasas being a big city phenomenon draw over 60 percent of the students

17. This confirms that neither the parents nor the 'ulama oppose secular subjects; rather, they resist the liberal environment in secular educational institutions.

from rural areas—and an opportunity to live with girls from different socioeconomic backgrounds and cultural settings. The result is the acquisition of a wealth of social networks and contacts, which these girls would have never acquired in their hometowns. My fieldwork in the Jamaat-i-Islami madrasa in Mardan gave me a sense of the strong bonds and friendships the girls form within the madrasas. Late night conversations, praying together in early morning as well as at *tahajjud* (night prayer), early morning chats while sipping tea, studying together until late in the evening in small study circles, and then converting the same space into a sleeping area by using traditional floor bedding—all made it easy to understand why these students, mostly from northern areas, the tribal belt, and other remote areas of Khyber Pakhtunkhwa, enjoyed collective living in the madrasas more than their routine lives at home.

These instrumental benefits of madrasa education are most apparent and significant for students from remote areas and poor economic background. For 40 percent of these girls, madrasas are their sole means of access to basic education: "When admitted to the madrasa I did not know how to read or write Urdu as we speak only Balochi at home so when I first wrote a letter to my mother in Urdu she was so excited that she did not believe that I had written it myself; I had to write it in front of her when I next saw her to make her believe it."[18]

Such benefits are peripheral to the real dividends that girls accrue from a madrasa education, which ensures important routes for social, economic, and psychological empowerment. In a society where religion matters, these girls on returning home become an asset to the community. They become an authoritative voice to answer religious questions regarding the everyday matters of concern for local women; they are requested to conduct religious rituals and lead prayers at religious gatherings hosted within the households;[19] they acquire social respect and recognition by teaching the Quran to neighborhood children free of charge. In my visits to small towns, I often stopped to visit madrasas established by students from the bigger female madrasas I had included in my formal survey. I visited three madrasas established by former students of Jamia Hafsa, one each in Mianwali, Multan, and Sahiwal. All three had been established two to three years earlier and had a student population of thirty to sixty students from within the city or surrounding areas. I also managed to visit students of the bigger madrasas who were now informally preaching to other women in the neighborhood

---

18. Arzu, a student in the Jamaat-i-Islami madrasa in Quetta, who comes from a remote village in rural Baluchistan, the province with lowest development indicators.

19. It is common within Pakistani society to organize many forms of religious gatherings at home; these can involve the collective recitation of the Holy Quran or a lecture on a specific Islamic precept.

by holding a weekly session at their home or in the home of a neighbor who had more space. In addition, I also had a chance to attend a number of religious ceremonies, such as *Quran Kuwani* (collective reading of the entire Quran in one sitting), in the upper income groups, where students from female madrasas were invited to lead the closing prayers. In case of these requests, the host made some payment to the madrasa for providing these services.

Interviews across all five wafaqs, and the brochures of these madrasas, show the emphasis placed by the ‘ulama on spreading knowledge acquired during studies at the madrasas. As I saw in my fieldwork, this aim has a serious impact on students’ aspirations: all respondents planned to engage in activities that would help them spread the message of Islam when they returned home. The ‘ulama’s claim that women spread ideas faster than men and across more extensive social networks seems to be true. As one ‘alim argued, “You can consult the ‘ulama mainly when you come to the mosque, while women go into the community, and reach those who won’t come to the mosque. The reach of the women is thus much wider.” These female graduates now parallel the *Tablighi Jamaat*—a movement that operates within communities to initiate internal reform among Muslims—in their effectiveness in spreading Islamic beliefs at grassroots level.

Madrasa education not only makes the girls socially influential, it can also contribute to their economic prosperity. It is common practice among female students, especially those from rural areas and smaller cities, to open a madrasa of their own on their return home: 60 percent of the survey respondents stated that they would like to establish their own madrasas. Given that female madrasas charge monthly tuition fees, though such charges are routinely waived to accommodate students from poor income groups, they can be profitable sources of income. A madrasa education thus provides opportunities for women with entrepreneurial skills, opportunities that students of secular schools and colleges can rarely exercise. The primary reason for this difference is that starting a madrasa, which can begin in one room at the teacher’s house, is less cost-intensive than establishing a secular school, where parents prefer a separate, dedicated building. Since 2002, truly entrepreneurial students can even enter national politics: the policy of reserving 20 percent of seats in the national parliament for women allows women from madrasas to seek reserved seats through the platform of religious political parties.

Arguably the most significant factor in sustaining girls’ conviction in Islamic beliefs, is the strong psychological incentives provided by madrasa education. My interviews and discussions with students reveal that religious beliefs help reduce the importance of material aspirations, making the girls more content with their circumstances, in addition to giving them confidence that they are a positive force in the society. All of madrasa education is tuned to making the girls feel worthy by eulogizing their critical role in society as mother, sister, daughter, and wife. This is captured in a brochure of the Jamaat-i-Islami madrasa: "Half of the responsibility for the promotion and development of an Islamic Society is shouldered by women. Unfortunately, today's Muslim women are steeped in ignorance and have wandered far from the role they were born to play. To have a positive reformatory impact on society, women with *taqwa* [faith] and high moral values are needed." The brochure goes on to state the mission of the madrasas as: "to groom practicing Muslim girl students equipped with modern education who present themselves as role models for the betterment of society." That the teachings of Islamic texts had added to their confidence and given them a sense of purpose was a recurrent theme during the interviews and group discussions with the girls.

In addition to assigning great social significance to the roles that girls play as members of the family, madrasa education also empowers them by removing their fears of individuals or social structures. The basic premise of Islamic teaching is, because all good or bad that comes to an individual rests in the will of God, no one can harm anyone else unless this is so willed by Allah. This message, for girls who are exposed to numerous pressures especially when living in joint families in the initial years of their marriage, is psychologically empowering. I interviewed three sisters who had all followed a year-long Islamic education course at a neighborhood madrasa. The two younger sisters noted of their elder sister, who had started this course after she was already married, "We have seen the difference it made in her dealings with her in-laws; it gave her a lot of positive confidence, and peace of mind in dealing with her mother-in-law who is quite domineering. She still remains respectful toward her but after receiving Islamic education, she acquired confidence that no one can harm you without the will of Allah, so she was no longer living in fear of her." Students routinely noted in interviews that to know the rights that Islam has bestowed on them as wives and daughters-in-law makes them confident of their place within the household, besides enabling them to resolve tensions more amicably by using religious discourse.

Another Islamic precept that pays significant dividends in generating a sense of contentment within madrasa graduates is the virtue of simplicity: to be grateful for whatever one has. Islam encourages the believer to strive for material prosperity but also highlights the virtues of being content with little; the Prophet's life is an example of simplicity. Madrasa education repeatedly draws on incidents from the Prophet's life, and those of his daughters, to empower the girls to deal with material scarcity. Whereas girls within colleges face peer pressure to follow the latest fashion trends and have an eligible suitor on Valentine's Day,[20] girls in

---

20. Based on interviews with girls from regular colleges.

the madrasa system have been repeatedly exposed to the virtues of simplicity and piety. Seventy percent of the students saw such desires as frivolous. Because 80 percent of these students come to the madrasa after studying in the secular educational system, at least half of them appeared to genuinely find this moral position more rewarding than their prior experience of pursuing aspirations, which as interviews indicate were out of reach.[21] Thus, madrasa education continues to make the girls' desires and demands match the practical realities of their lives, thereby reducing the disappointment of unmet expectations and relieving pressure on the parents.

These psychological mechanisms for ensuring a sense of purpose are significant when compared with the benefits of a secular education system that determines a student's worth in terms of future employability—opportunities for which are very limited. A madrasa education is able to convince girls of Islamic beliefs because these beliefs provide psychological means to deal with practical challenges, which have either no material solutions or solutions available only to a few. Psychological incentives in the rise of institutions (analyzed in detail in chapter 7) are central to explaining the rationality of the materially irrational choices often associated with religious behavior. More generally, analysis of the factors building students' conviction in religious beliefs shows that demand is heightened when well matched with practical realities, in other words when the costs of investment in religious commitment are at their lowest. The importance of tangible, this-worldly rewards from God in generating and sustaining faith is also noted within the rational choice sociology of religion (Stark and Finke 2000), and during the interviews with parents and students in the male madrasas. Eighty percent of the parents narrated how changes that they saw in their children after they began religious education had reinforced their own religious conviction: "All my children inherited my limitation; they could not remember the mathematical tables. But my one son whom I had enrolled for hifz process was able to recite all the thirty tables in one go." To this respondent, this was a miracle of religious learning.

Madrasa education thus helps align the incentives of parents and students, limiting the need for external checks. This claim supports Miller's (1992) work who counters the traditional emphasis on economic incentives to argue for the importance of nonmaterial incentives in the effective working of hierarchy. It

---

21. This indicates that Elster's (1983) sour grapes phenomenon does contribute to mobilizing demand for madrasa education and, as per Elster's predictions, students who are primarily driven to religious education because of a lack of opportunities within secular society are likely to move toward the secular system if circumstances allow. However, this does not rule out that many students are genuinely committed to religious education because they find the Islamic way of life more meaningful.

also highlights the role of psychological incentives in shaping individual choices. The question, however, is: Are these forms of psychological and material empowerment meaningful when they restrict the choices of these women—the necessity to cover their bodies and hair, the emphasis on the role of the mother, the strict restrictions on sexual activity prior to marriage—in ways that appear sub-optimal from normative standards of gender equality in the West?

The next section of this chapter presents the perspectives of teachers and students not only from the madrasas but also from Al-Huda to understand why despite their restrictions, Islamic beliefs continue to mobilize a mass following among Muslim women. I include their voices because these women, unlike their counterparts in madrasas, are often exposed to Western educational institutions and clearly were not driven to weekly Al-Huda meetings held at luxury hotels as a response to material scarcity. Why do women from affluent segments of society voluntarily follow Islamic principles?

## Adaptive Preference: Correct Interpretation

That Islamic beliefs inculcated within the madrasas are orthodox is undisputable: in repeated interviews and group discussions, exploring Islamic injunctions concerning women, students and teachers across the five sects emphasized literal interpretations of the Quran. Throughout the five wafaqs, there was a consensus on women's obligation to observe *purdah* (veiling); similarly, all praised woman's primary role as home-maker and defended the strict prohibition on sexual liberty, noting the importance of preserving women's piety. The Ahl-i-Shia wafaq, more progressive in its interpretation on many issues and a bit cynical of orthodox Sunni practices such as the emphasis on memorizing the Quran, expressed no significant difference of opinion when it came to issue of purdah. All the female madrasas from the Ahl-i-Shia wafaq that I visited across the country observed a level of purdah similar to what I witnessed in the female madrasas associated with Sunni wafaqs.

Despite differences on many other doctrinal issues, on the subject of veiling, and the gender division of labor proposed in Islam all were largely in unison. Repeatedly in individual and group interviews, students within the madrasas and at Al-Huda defended these precepts, at times for their practical relevance but primarily because for them these precepts held a logical appeal. The instrumental reason for wearing the hijab revolved mainly around issues of security in a society where weak law and order makes women from middle-income families, who rely on public transport, vulnerable to male harassment; the *niqab* (facial covering) was similarly seen as beneficial, helping to protect girls' identity by making it difficult for men to recognize them; and the *jilbab* (full-length religious-dress), by covering the clothes, was argued to reduce excessive spending.

Though these instrumental benefits of religious belief were acknowledged by all respondents, they were recorded as side benefits.[22] The primary debate revolved around the superiority of Islamic beliefs for women's well-being. For my respondents, Islam provided a vision of gender equality more viable than Western feminism. For these women it was absolutely clear that, in terms of equality, Islam placed men and women on the same pedestal; the difference rested mainly in the role designed for them to optimize their respective biological strengths. In their reasoning, the denial of biological difference was unrealistic and thereby counterproductive, because it placed an additional burden on women and threatened the family structure; both developments, in their view, were detrimental to women's interests. "Why would women want to compete with men or rival them when rationally it is in everyone's individual as well as societal interest for the two genders to cooperate and build on their respective strengths?" was a very common retort when I asked if excessive emphasis on women's maternal role neglected the benefits of economic independence.

For these women, the dividends associated with women's economic empowerment were deceptive, because such an approach neglected additional burden on women. In the words of one respondent, "it leads to a societal structure where collective expectations are so developed that for a woman, the choice to be at home with her children becomes a nonoption." For 90 percent of respondents, this economic independence was the cause of the breakdown of the family structure in the West. In their view, where there is no natural reason for interdependence between partners, family unity is automatically threatened: "If I am earning as much as my husband it is only natural I will be less inclined to heed to my husband. This will automatically reduce the tolerance level within the household, threatening its unity." Placing the responsibility of economic security squarely on the shoulders of men while giving women the freedom to pursue professional activities as a matter of choice, Islam provided a more viable model to these women.

On the subject of sexual liberty, they were quick to counter arguments advanced in Western discourse. For them the natural instinct of woman is to restrain her sexuality; they argued that the sexual liberation of women was actually of greater benefit to men who, in their view, were more prone to seeking sexual gratification than women who, by their very nature, seek emotionally secure and stable relationships. For these women, sex outside of marriage was wrong

---

22. Similar functionalist interpretations of women's recourse to Islamic beliefs have been adopted to explain the popularity of veiling in many studies on Muslim women (El Guindi 1999; Hoffman-Ladd 1987; MacLeod 1991; Zuhur 1992).

because it marginalized the rights of any child conceived outside a relationship that had no social or legal recognition; at the same time, abstinence from sexual experience until marriage gives a special meaning to the marital relationship. "When women change partners frequently, they only reduce the charm of the ultimate relationship because it is very natural that they will always be comparing; therefore I say, why follow a route which is bound to leave you dissatisfied?" argued one Western-educated respondent. "Why live with the baggage of failed relationships?" she added.

Another woman of similar profile noted how disappointed she was when, during a year-long stay in the United States, she ended up accompanying her host family to a wedding ceremony where the bride already had two children fathered by two different men. "I am liberal by Muslim standards. I don't wear hijab and work with male colleagues but this kind of liberty leaves me unimpressed," she noted. These women were also of the view that early exposure to sexual relations made women vulnerable to sexual impulses, which rushed them into unstable relationships. Further, they argued, the emphasis on sexual liberty was all the more disadvantageous to women as they progressed through the life cycle: "During her twenties and thirties a woman might have equal chances of drawing attention of men, but it is more difficult for her to find a good husband as she progresses beyond forty; for men age is hardly a constraint. It is therefore in a woman's own interest to be in a binding relationship than to seek short-term interactions."[23] These women believed that because of their very biological and emotional make-up, the institution of marriage and family was more in their interest than that of men. Consequently, when women made adjustments in the short term to safeguard the interests of their family, they did so not as an act of sacrifice or exploitation but as a rational move to protect their own long-term interest. As to extreme segregation between genders, they argued that human nature is prone to be tempted by vice and therefore to avert an undesirable action it was best to avoid temptation; discouraging free mixing of the sexes limits opportunities for casual relationships.

Comparing these perspectives with those of Western feminists presents an interesting contradiction; those from the rational, Western world draw on notions of female equality based on ideal moral standards whereas the latter, who are associated with an orthodox moral worldview, base their conception of gender roles on rational calculations of what is biologically possible and practically feasible. These women's choices and decision-making processes employ a means-ends rationality. They have a clear idea of a desirable end and calculate

---

23. Over 8 percent of respondents shared this view expressed by a middle-age woman from an affluent background.

back from it: multiple premarital relationships and economic independence will logically make it more difficult for them to adjust to the demands of establishing a stable family, so why pursue those options when it is in the woman's long-term interest to be in a stable family? Western feminism is also criticized for its "materialistic" aspirations. Excessive emphasis on women's engagement in economic activity at the cost of time for family was in general viewed to be a likely outcome of Western feminism, which was found lacking in appeal.

One striking aspect of my fieldwork was the frequency with which these women made references to what they viewed as the outcomes of the Western feminist model—high divorce rates in Western societies, single motherhood, and the tendency to leave parents in nursing homes. Whether women acquire these views about Western society through the media, Islamic textbooks, or a conscious propaganda campaign by the 'ulama is unclear, but even in the smallest madrasas in remote areas, girls were quick to refer to what they viewed as the failure of Western society. The modernity of the West has thus, it appears, become proof for these women of the wisdom of embracing tradition. One of the bluntest statements in defense of the Islamic way of life came from a senior Shia scholar in Islamabad:

> No we are *bunyad parast* [followers of fundamental rules], and *nizam parast* [followers of the system], and *a'yian parsat* [followers of the constitution]. A Muslim is one who is *bunyad parast* and wants to follow the *Qanoon* [constitution]. Our problem is that our rulers are not *bunyad parast.* It is because we are *bunyad parast* that our next generation is still on the right track; in our society there is still a section for *valadat* [name of the father] on an application form. Our homes are still intact because of this.

The debates, in summary, challenge universalist assumptions within liberal Western feminism on three accounts: first, they argue for acknowledging the different biological and emotional needs of men and women; second, they highlight the importance of sexual self-restraint to enable women to have more stable and gratifying relationships; third, they prefer the family's interest over those of the individual, not because they prioritize the family over themselves, but because they feel that their own interest is best protected in a stable family system. These positions, especially those surrounding the relations between individual and family, are starkly opposed to Nussbaum's liberal position (1999, 2001) and highlight the limitations of universalist positions.[24]

24. A similar critique of individual liberty has been presented in the past by blacks and other ethnic groups who argued that the family actually protected women's interests (Mahmood 2005).

In terms of insights into the processes of preference formation, these debates support the New Institutionalists' position that preferences bear strong influences from history and culture; thus it is important to engage with the substance of preference and not just with its attainment. The existence of instrumental reasons for following some Islamic precepts also lends support to theories of the sour grapes phenomenon, where a choice can be defended because the alternative is inaccessible.[25] However what this analysis contradicts is the notion of adaptive preference as promoted by Nussbaum; Muslim women's apparently suboptimal choices are in fact the result of conscious choice. These choices are preferred either for their practical relevance under given constraints or for their appeal to reason, and not because the women have become so used to the inferior equilibrium that they have either no sense of superior alternatives or have become averse to questioning. Preferences are indeed adapted to context, but this adaptation is a result of conscious calculation and not a product of submissive rule-obeying behavior. It is important to understand the incentives inherent in a given context if the optimality of preference is to be assessed. Strategic calculation, not habitual behavior, is the basis of adaptive preference.

## Conclusions

The choices and decisions of actors involved in female madrasas lend support to many positions within strategic theories of institutional change. Elite players can be motivated to invest in reversing path dependence if they can see tangible pay-off in the immediate or longer term. Both material and ideological incentives are significant in aligning the interests of subordinate actors within the religious hierarchy. The rise of female madrasas demonstrates that the maximizing behavior of elite players (those who have tacit knowledge) in response to incentives present in the external environment is central to the rise of new organizations.

As for the central question raised in this chapter, how religious beliefs win widespread appeal over time, the demand for female madrasas suggests that the answer rests in both the practical relevance of these beliefs and their logical appeal. Out of the two positions on preference formation identified at the outset, the evidence discredits the idea that individuals can be indoctrinated to

25. The fact that not all Muslim women support these beliefs, or at least not their strict interpretation, illustrates the role of the individual cognitive structure of each actor in the process of preference formation (North 1990).

prefer inferior alternatives over the long term. Rather, people consciously adapt to inferior alternatives because in the given circumstances those alternatives are the optimal if not the ideal options; the optimality of the choice may not be obvious to outsiders because choices are historically and culturally determined, and are shaped by information and cognitive constraints faced by the actor.

For parents, madrasa education helps reduce intergenerational transaction costs by aligning the interests of parents and daughters. In a fast changing external context, where parents feel a sense of loss of control over their children's choices, they find it much more cost-effective to invest in the religious education of their daughters, which by building girls' conviction in religious beliefs constrains their choices to suit those of the parents; this reduces the pressure on parents to monitor and regulate their daughter's actions. As for the students, Islamic beliefs are more efficient than secular education in equipping them to meet the practical challenges of life, thus becoming instrumentally useful. Equally important, these beliefs present a conception of the good life, which has genuine appeal for an overwhelming number of Muslim women even outside the madrasas—highlighting the cultural and historical specificity of a preference. My fieldwork illustrates that religious preference is neither entirely instrumental (shaped by exogenous factors) nor entirely ideological (shaped by factors endogenous to the institution). Rather, it is a product of incentives that emerge from the interaction of the two; the more the ideological appeal of a religious idea is reinforced, the more it becomes meaningful in people's daily lives.

Finally, I have documented the importance of psychological incentives in shaping religious action. That rational actors maximize not only their material utility but many forms of nonmaterial utility is now fully embraced within the standard rational choice model; what, however, remain under-explored are the conditions under which ideal rewards take precedence over material rewards and vice versa.

Chapters 5 and 6 have explained the determinants of demand for religious beliefs, that is, why beliefs come to shape individual preferences. Chapter 5 identified the appreciation of spiritual rewards as well as the uncertainties of material existence and the resulting transaction costs as the two main factors creating a demand for religious beliefs. Chapter 6 further demonstrated that religious beliefs that take hold over individual preferences are those that have a logical appeal and demonstrate a relevance to believers' everyday existence. Neither chapter supported claims of blind adherence to beliefs. Rather, both chapters showed a believer's conscious engagement with the religious beliefs, and attempts to balance the demands of religious beliefs and those of material existence. The two chapters thus illustrate the significance of transaction costs in understanding demand for informal institutions, and the significance of the context in which a preference is shaped in order to determine its optimality. The final part of the book now looks at actual mechanisms that allow religious beliefs, and thereby informal institutions, to overcome the anxieties created by recognizable limits of the material world. In doing so, I also show why informal institutions often facilitate collective action not easily mobilized through formal institutions.

# Part III

# INFORMAL INSTITUTIONS AND COLLECTIVE OUTCOMES

**Unlike Marxian analysis, the economic approach I refer to does not assume that individuals are motivated solely by selfishness or material gain. It is a *method* of analysis, not an assumption about particular motivations. Along with others, I have tried to pry economists away from narrow assumptions about self-interest. Behavior is driven by a much richer set of values and preferences.**

—Gary S. Becker, *Nobel Lecture: The Economic Way of Looking at Behavior* (1993: 385)

**I do not mean to imply that there are not occasions in which people are willing to engage in substantial sacrifices for their ideas and ideals; indeed, the degree to which people feel strongly about their ideological views may frequently lead them to engage in very substantial sacrifices, and such sacrifices have played a major role throughout history. . . . improved understanding of institutional change requires greater understanding than we now possess of just what makes ideas and ideologies catch hold. Therefore, we are still at something of a loss to define, in very precise terms, the interplay between changes in relative prices, the ideas and ideologies that form people's perceptions, and the roles that the two play in inducing changes in institutions.**

—Douglass C. North, *Institutions, Institutional Change and Economic Performance* (1990: 85–86)

7

# THE MISSING FREE-RIDER

## Religious Rewards and Collective Action

**If the Maulvi in the mosque has the zeal he will start to teach students from his area and slowly a madrasa will emerge alongside the mosque. The community can feed one 'alim very comfortably.**

—Jameel Anwar, an Islamabad-based lawyer, educated in a madrasa in Rawalpindi

**Madrasas run with cooperation of the people. People see if the imam of the madrasa has kept the *hasab-keetab* [accounts] properly; they see how many students are graduating from here every year. Some people contribute on regular basis; some give more as zakat during Ramadan.**

—Maulana Charag-uddin-Shah, adviser on religious affairs to one of the prominent political parties in Pakistan, runs a number of madrasas in Khyber Pakhtunkhwa and Punjab

True to the image of a developing country, the cities of Pakistan are crowded places where the streets are routinely jammed with traffic. But every Friday, for two hours around noon, they become a commuter's heaven as the crowds move from the roads to the mosques. Friday prayer has a special significance among Muslims: all five daily prayers offer higher religious merit to the believer if said within a mosque, but attending the Friday prayer in congregation and listening to the sermon is mandatory for men. The presiding imam does not charge individuals for use of the mosque's services, but voluntary contributions are expected. Mosques, as well as the madrasas where the imams are trained to carry out these roles, are thus a precious public good in Muslim societies—because the consumption of their services cannot be restricted to those who contribute to their production. The fact that enough individuals do contribute for these institutions to survive raises a significant question: Why would a rational believer contribute to the production costs of mosques and madrasas when their services can be availed of for nothing? This question becomes more pertinent when it is recognized that there is no religious injunction that the believer should contribute to the production of the service, and that the decision is entirely voluntary.

Since the publication of Olson's *Logic of Collective Action* (1971) and Hardin's *Tragedy of the Commons* (1968), it is now widely recognized that a good whose consumption cannot be regulated will be under-produced as rational individuals will try to take maximum benefit from it without making a contribution to its production cost—that is, they will prefer to free-ride. The resulting social dilemma, whereby individually rational action leads to collectively irrational outcomes, has become central to theoretical debates on collective action. Ostrom (1990, 2003) and Wade (1998) have helped develop our understanding of the factors that help check free-riding: Ostrom draws attention to "the rich interplay between the nature of the good, the property-right-regimes in place, the governance system used for making new rules and the resulting payoff structure" (2003: 262) as determining the probability of collective action, while Wade identifies the severity of the need as an important check on free-riding. In addition to accounts concerned with the external factors shaping the agent's decision, a related theme in the literature has focused on explanations that are internal to the individual.

In this approach, individuals are held to have a complex utility set that allows for other-regarding or materially sacrificing preferences; the analysis assumes that individuals maximize welfare as they conceive it whether they be selfish, altruistic, loyal, spiteful, or masochistic (Becker 1993: 386). Here, it is predicted that individuals with a high preference for ideal pursuits will seek to enhance their utility by pursuing goals that come at a material cost. Seen through this lens, the decision to contribute to the production of a religiously valued public good falls comfortably within the purview of rational action. Iannaccone (1992: 273), grappling with the puzzle of voluntary material sacrifice in pursuit of religious reward, asks: "How can burnt offerings and their analogues survive in religious markets when self-interest and competitive pressures bar them from most other markets?" Most authors explain such sacrifices as a search for "compensators"—that is, "the belief that a reward will be obtained in the distant future or in some other context which cannot be immediately verified" (Stark and Bainbridge 1985: 6). Religiously inspired sacrifices are thus seen as an investment in pursuit of other-worldly rewards. In the rational choice studies of religion, the emphasis thus shifts from studying external factors in favor of studying the individual's personal preferences. I propose two correctives to this approach.

First, I show the significance of both internally driven psychological processes and factors external to the individual in shaping religiously inspired collective action. While the willingness to contribute to mosque and madrasa is inspired by search for religious rewards, elite madrasas emerge because of the greater ability of imams of these madrasas to check free-riding. Second, I argue that disaggregating utility alone does not help understand religious behavior. In line with recent advances in behavioral economics (see Bowles 2004 for a detailed review), I show that there is a need for developing much better understanding of why certain utility sets are valued, and what are the psychological mechanisms that ensure that ideal utility sought through religious commitment often comes at the cost of material sacrifice. I argue that in understanding religious behavior, the central puzzle is *not* why a believer contributes to the cost of production of mosques and madrasas when rational individuals try to utilize the benefits at the least possible cost; rather, the puzzle is why most religious rituals promising spiritual rewards involve material or bodily sacrifice. I draw on interviews with a hundred participants in the mosque–madrasa network in Pakistan, drawn from across the eight districts covered in this study, my own observations and narratives of the ʻulama, to prove that making believers experience material and bodily sacrifices is the only way to make the believer overcome fear of material loss: it is thus the benefits the believer sees of religion in this world, and not just the "future investment," that is key to understanding the rationality of religious conviction and the material sacrifices associated with it.

## Madrasas as Producers of a Public Good

In common perception, a madrasa is a platform to provide free education to poor children; in reality its role is more fundamental. Madrasas produce the public good of "trained imams" who perform religious rituals valued and utilized by all members of society irrespective of whether or not they contribute to the production of trained imams.[1] To fully understand the public good value of trained imams, it is important to understand the significance of the services they provide in Muslim societies. Islam places high value on saying prayers five times daily within the mosque, so that a prayer said in a mosque behind an imam renders ten times higher reward than that for a similar prayer said at home. In addition, saying the weekly Friday prayers and the Eid prayers in the mosque is obligatory for all male Muslims. The mosques and the trained imams leading these mosques are thus a valued public good in a Muslim society. The mosques fulfill the need of the believer to carry out prayer in a congregation; and the madrasas meet the need to produce imams to lead these prayers. The services that they collectively provide are free and nonexcludable.

In addition, the imams provide another critical public service—issuing fatwas (religious verdicts on matters not explicitly addressed in the Quran or Sunna). The Sunni ʻulama devote a significant amount of their time accommodating public requests for fatwas; in Shia scholarship this authority is, however, restricted to the *mujtahid*. The imams provide fatwas free of charge, and all believers, not

1. It is these madrasas, and not the state-funded schools of theology, which ensure the production of religious scholars and teachers to fill positions within the mosques in Pakistan.

just the one inquiring, are free to benefit from these rulings. My interview with a prominent 'alim from the Barelvi school, who agreed to meet me on the understanding that I let him follow his daily chores while we spoke, was repeatedly interrupted by telephone calls seeking advice on religious matters. The callers, women as well as men, sought Islamic interpretations of diverse issues ranging from the legitimacy of the military operations in the tribal belts to verification of a particular food item as halal. No payment was ever mentioned regarding these services.

The production of these public goods,[2] however, has costs: mosque construction, maintenance, the imam's salary, and the costs of the madrasa where the imam was originally trained have to be covered to ensure continued production of the public good. The users of public good are expected to contribute to this cost through responding to the calls for contributions occasionally made by the imam at the end of the prayers, by leaving donations in the box close to the exit point in most mosques, and by making financial contributions to the madrasa. The imams of the madrasas I surveyed always cited public donations as their most important source of funding.

During my visits to madrasas, while waiting to meet with the head, I often saw individuals come in to make a donation. In large madrasas, where the imam himself was not the one collecting these donations, the donors were issued a receipt. In smaller madrasas, where donors gave money directly to the imam, I rarely saw such a provision. The most noticeable aspect of these donations was their prescriptive nature: a black goat to be sacrificed, food to be distributed among the children in the madrasa, money for the maintenance of a mosque or a madrasa, and so on. The other noticeable aspect was a clear linking of each objective with specific categories of giving in Islam. Individuals donating for sacrifice of a goat or distribution of food among madrasa children marked their donations as sadaqa, while those contributing toward maintenance often classified it as kheerat. Zakat, another form of Islamic giving, which unlike sadaqa and kheerat is compulsory on all Muslims of a certain wealth, was the prominent form of donation during the month of Ramadan. The crucial question, therefore, is: If believers can have these services free, and their contribution, or lack of it, can go unnoticed—visibility of the contribution being one important criterion for checking free-riding (Olson 1971; Ostrom 1990)—why do they donate? It should

2. As well as public goods, mosques and madrasas also provide some private goods. The mosques often hold evening Quranic classes for children from the neighboring community; students from the madrasas teach children in their homes; and the imams conduct the Islamic rituals of birth and death. These services constitute private goods because only those who ask for them benefit, and because the recipient of the service normally pays for it.

further be noted that while the Islamic texts place great emphasis on giving,[3] there is no compulsion on the believer to pay for the services provided by mosques or madrasas; thus someone free-riding on the production of the mosque space is not even liable to have a guilty conscience.[4] The crucial question, then, is what is it that checks free-riding in the production of mosques and madrasas on a sufficiently large scale to ensure continued supply of this free good.[5]

## Whether or Not to Free-Ride? Motives of the Believers

My attempt to understand the inner motives shaping the decisions of donors to the 110 surveyed madrasas did broadly support the utility-maximizing thesis advanced in rational choice approaches to the study of religion: however, I found the working of ideal and material utility to be much more complex than is recognized in the literature. I identified four dominant modes of mobilization of resources for the mosque–madrasa network. It is worth noting that the four processes of resource mobilization I document also illustrate the weakness of current policy debates, which see the expansion of the mosque–madrasa nexus in Pakistan as the result of external funding. As noted in chapter 4, elite madrasas have access to religious and financial networks in the Gulf; however, I found no such evidence with regard to the ordinary madrasas. Although the wife of a senior official of the Ahl-i-Hadith wafaq did gift me a pack of dates from the Kingdom of Saudi Arabia, while the daughter-in-law of the imam of a prestigious Deobandi madrasa in Karachi mentioned how blessed she was to have had her marriage ceremony performed in Mecca by the Imam of Khanna Kaba; such references never came up in discussions in the ordinary madrasas whether medium or small. The madrasas at the bottom of the pyramid, which constitute 60 percent of the total madrasas, rarely have access to such funding. Further, even for the elite madrasas, patrons in the Gulf are just one of the sources of funds.

---

3. "You who believe, give charitably from the good things you have acquired and that We have produced for you from the earth." (Surah 2: 267); "Those who give, out of their own possessions, by night and by day, in private and in public, will have their reward with their Lord: no fear for them, nor will they grieve." (Surah 2: 274).

4. The dominant conception within Islam is that mosques are centers for the worship of God, therefore, nobody should be forbidden access. The Quran states "Places of worship are for God alone" (Surah 72: 19). This verse is interpreted as indicating that mosques are the property of God alone, and thus that no one may prevent anybody from entering for the purpose of worship.

5. It is clear that at any one point in the prayer there are free-riders—for example, occasional visitors to a mosque who do not contribute to the service. Yet it is also clear that a sufficiently large number of individuals consciously choose *not* to free-ride.

Contrary to the allegations of overseas support, the evolution of a madrasa is in fact a very organic and grassroots-led process.

In 80 percent of the cases surveyed in rural communities or new urban settlements in major cities, members of the community had volunteered to bear the cost of establishing a mosque so as to offer congregational prayers, and a madrasa had gradually evolved alongside it to ensure Quranic educational opportunities for neighborhood children. In such cases there was often a mosque or madrasa committee in place. In a low-income settlement I visited in Karachi, a madrasa had evolved within three years of the establishment of a mosque, whose foundation had been laid by the community once a few households had settled. As one member of the committee noted: "A mosque, followed by a madrasa, is normally one of the first communal projects a community undertakes when it organizes itself. Every community wants to have a neighborhood mosque that is easily accessible. The mosque comes first and once an imam is appointed, slowly a madrasa evolves."

The narrative of the rise of the local mosque and its attached madrasa in a small village in the scenic hills of Murree provides a similar insight. Until a few years ago the village had no mosque or madrasa, and for any special prayers the men had to travel long distances to another village. This long commute became particularly problematic during Ramadan, when many men had to travel every night to the neighboring village to perform their *Taraweeh* prayer. As explained by a committee member who supervised the new madrasa: "It was the women of the village who argued for pooling resources to establish our own mosque. Fearing for their own security at night when they were left alone at home and that of the men from their families undertaking late night commutes, women from the area convinced the men within their families to work toward establishing a mosque in their own village." The challenge, however, was to find a trained imam because there were none in the village, and a related challenge was to mobilize the resources to cover his salary. Recognizing the severity of the need, the community members agreed to contribute in proportion to their income under the supervision of a local committee, and a qualified imam was selected from the city. Once the mosque was established, the madrasa followed, and the imam started to give lessons in Quranic reading and memorization to village children.

The story of the origin of another madrasa in a small village in Abottabad region was not much different. Like Murree, Abottabad consists of small hills that host many small villages which are not easily accessible. Many of the individuals from this area go to work in nearby cities. As more men migrated away, there was an increase in surplus income that led the community collectively consider engaging an imam to run a village mosque. In the absence of a properly trained madrasa graduate in the village, an imam had to be recruited from the city. Once appointed, the imam started to respond to requests to provide hifz facilities for the local children, laying the foundation for a one-room madrasa next to the mosque.

My conversations with senior scholars and imams of the madrasas also made it clear that the imam of a mosque has an interest in establishing a madrasa. As one senior scholar noted: "A madrasa establishes the stature of the imam of the mosque, it also becomes a source of income." Children who board at a madrasa are taught free of charge, but those who come for afternoon Quranic classes pay a fee. Further, the presence of children in the madrasa helps mobilize donations. The scholar added: "When people see children in a madrasa, they are more encouraged to make a donation because they think they have proof that the donation is being used for a right cause." Thus, once a community is affluent enough to collectively support an imam for the local mosque, there is high probability that a madrasa will follow.

The five medium-size madrasas I surveyed in rural areas or in low-income urban settlements revealed two additional sources of funding: support from individuals or families from the locality who had moved overseas; and, support from a religious political party, especially Jamaat-i-'Ulama.[6] These two sources of donations were the main cause of the rise of bigger madrasas or mosques in the rural areas. One respondent was clearly taking pains to ensure smooth running of the madrasa he had funded in his home village, and was also keen to ensure its long-term sustainability. He noted, "I was fortunate to move to the Gulf two decades ago. The job I secured there greatly improved my income. I now have some surplus income, which I want to invest in a good cause. I therefore decided to open a madrasa in my home village as there is no provision for securing proper Islamic education in that village." Although now based in a city, he travels to the village twice a week to monitor the performance of the two teachers he had appointed. He was also in the process of registering the madrasa as a waqf property to ensure his children did not have any claim to the land on which the madrasa is located.

These smaller and medium madrasas (i.e., Ibtida'iya and Khasa) constitute close to 60 percent of the total madrasas in Pakistan; for the remaining 40 percent, local mosque and madrasa committees are less important than independent donors, some of whom might utilize the religious services provided, while others donate without using them.[7] There are donors of all sizes, but it is the rich patrons who are key to sustaining the elite madrasas, who exert great influence on

6. Jamaat-i-'Ulama is one of the main Islamic political parties in Pakistan and is affiliated with the Deobandi school of thought. The party's base is in Khyber Pakhtunkhwa.

7. Such as a believer benefiting from the fatwa or scholarly work of the imam of a big madrasa in another city.

shaping debates within their school of thought. For the elite madrasas of Karachi and other big cities, these patrons are central to covering core monthly costs. Although such donors make up only 30 percent of the total pool of donors for large madrasas in my survey, they contributed 60 percent of the total donations. For the leader of any madrasa, there is a strong incentive to seek the support of such independent donors. In the earlier stages of a young imam's career, while he is not known in the community, a committee-based system is convenient because it provides financial security. But as the imam gains confidence and respect, it is in his best interest to move beyond the security of the committee and opt for independent donors.

Closer examination of a number of cases of the two types revealed that this shift in authority is contingent on the imam's ability to become less dependent on the financial contributions of the committee members by mobilizing greater contributions from the independent donors (Bano 2007a). In 20 percent of the cases, the shift occurred after the death of the core board members who established the mosque or madrasa. After their death, the imam, rather than descendants of the board members, was better placed to take the lead. In remaining 80 percent, the change happened within the lifetime of the core committee members: for instance, in one case, the imam was able to gain relative independence from the committee when he built a strong case for extension of the mosque-madrasa complex. The committee members, being unable to financially support the extension, gave him the liberty to plan as he wished if he could mobilize the required funds (Bano 2007a). In the elite madrasas, however, it is clear that being founded by reputed scholars, the ʿulama behind the madrasa were in full control from the start.

Donations from expatriate Pakistanis or in some cases Islamic political parties and donations from large patrons provided the main sources of funds for the madrasas I surveyed (see table 7.1); the survey identified state officials as another source of mobilizing resources. In many cases, a madrasa is able to gain concessions from the government through the use of discretionary powers by state officials sympathetic to Islamic causes. The most critical resource here is the approval to use state land. For the head of a small madrasa built on public land without state approval—and thus liable at any time to be demolished—the support of an official can be crucial. As noted by one ʿalim at a small madrasa:

> Without contact with the government, the madrasas cannot run. Madrasas get regular visitors from the neighboring police stations. They assess whether a madrasa is teaching or is involved in politics. A madrasa has to register with the government. However, there are also *naik* [pious] people, in the government who are considerate toward the needs of the madrasas. At one point, the local government authorities were going to

> demolish my madrasa, but I sought help from the brigadier who used to come to say prayers at my mosque. I knew he is very appreciative of my *Qira'at* [recitation] of the Quran. He intervened and stopped the demolition.

During the interviews with the donors from all categories, it was clear that the search for religious rewards was central to their actions. Islam places emphasis on the sharing of wealth and promises great rewards for the act of giving—not only in the other world, but also in this. Zakat is one of the five pillars of Islam and a compulsory tax on all affluent Muslims.[8] Occurring 32 times in the Quran, the word zakat is twenty-seven times conjoined with the command to offer prayer, the second key pillar of Islam.[9] There are other headings under which charity should be offered, such as sadaqa (voluntary alms) (Surah 2: 280; Surah 4: 92; Surah 5: 45).[10] In terms of incentives, zakat saves the believer from the fire of hell and purifies the income while sadaqa acts as an expiation of sins; it is recommended that sadaqa be given immediately following any transgression and as a protection against evil. Sadaqa is also encouraged as a means of increasing wealth in this world, where the giver gets many times more than he gave—also characteristic of kheerat. There are verses in the Quran that ask: "Who will give God a good loan, which He will increase for him many times?" (Surah 2: 245).

**TABLE 7.1** Patterns of resource mobilization

| LEVEL OF MADRASA | MOSQUE/MADRASA COMMITTEE (%) | INDEPENDENT DONORS (%) | LARGE PATRONS (%) |
|---|---|---|---|
| Elite madrasas | 5 | 35 | 60 |
| Level 4: 'Alimiya | 5 | 35 | 60 |
| Level 3: 'Aliya | 20 | 50 | 30 |
| Level 2: Khasa | 40 | 55 | 5 |
| Level 1: Ibtida'iya | 70 | 30 | Only in exceptional cases |

*Source:* Based on the fieldwork (2006–2008).

8. "In order to cleanse and purify them [Prophet], take alms out of their property and pray for them—..." (Surah 9:103).

9. "though all they were ordered to do was worship God alone, sincerely devoting their religion to Him as people of true faith, keep up the prayer, and pay the prescribed alms, for that is the true religion." (Surah 98: 5); "We have truly given abundance to you [Prophet]—so pray to your Lord and make your sacrifice to Him alone" (Surah 108: 1–2).

10. There is also a concept of *sadaqa-i-jariya* (permanent alms), referring to a gift or deed that will benefit others over a period of time. The giver or doer is promised a reward for as long as the gift or deed continues to serve others. Kheerat is essentially an extension of the notion of social responsibility established through zakat and sadaqa. It entails giving away as much of one's wealth as one can for public welfare or to the poor and the needy.

My interviewees repeatedly cited endearing oneself to God, saving oneself from punishment and torture in the hereafter, and gaining a place among the believers in heaven, as the key incentive for giving. As the imam who narrated the story of the brigadier who helped stop the demolition of the madrasa noted, "Afterward when I saw him, he said 'I did this work entirely for the Quran.'" Thus, religion and the associated religious rewards, matter to the individuals, and this leads to a willingness to invest in the production of religiously valued public goods. For Muslims, mosques and madrasas perform the central functions of Islam, and contributing toward maintenances of this system helps secure religious rewards. Pursuit of religious rewards is thus clearly central to the mechanisms for checking free-riding in religion.

Such findings apparently fit comfortably with the existing rational choice theory literature concerned with religion. The motive is utility maximization: though individuals have preferences for different kind of rewards, all seek to maximize what they value (Becker 1993). Thus, mosques and madrasas are able to check free-riding not because believers are more moral and honest than their counterparts in the economic market, but because religion establishes demands for certain rewards that can be attained only through *participating* in production of religious goods. Free-riding is thus simply not an option. The fact that these donations increase dramatically during the month of Ramadan, when the rewards of any religious giving is promised to be increased a hundredfold, further proves that it is the desire to secure God's goodwill and accumulate spiritual rewards that drives people to give—and not because they feel responsible for providing for the public good that they all use.

However, my observations suggest that what is central to shaping behavior in these cases is not the promise of distant rewards in heaven or the search for "compensators" in the other world, but rather the rewards the individual experiences in this world: the conviction regarding the reality of other-worldly rewards actually rests on experiencing the benefits of religious conviction in this world. My respondents noted the importance of securing other-worldly rewards, but they also noted that religious conviction is critical to making this life better. The key to understanding why religion can check free-riding is therefore to understand the psychological impact that the material and bodily sacrifices associated with religious rituals have on building conviction in religion.

## Material Sacrifice and Religious Rewards

That religious rewards are often contingent on making a material sacrifice is specific not just to Islam, but is an attribute shared by most religions. Many religions promise spiritual growth and rewards in exchange for activities or an approach to life, which checks the pursuit of excessive material (financial as well as bodily) pleasures. Some demand extreme sacrifice and encourage living a very simple life (for example, Buddhism), but Islam encourages leading a comfortable life in this world while teaching that material sacrifice remains critical to faith. The Quran repeatedly encourages the believer to attempt to excel in this world and make the best of this world's pleasures: however, to acquire religious merit the believer must dispense with some of his wealth or material comfort. This emphasis on material sacrifice, not just monetary but also bodily, is reflected in the very conception of the five pillars of Islam: *tauheed* (belief in oneness of God), *namaz* (daily five-time prayers), *roza* (fasting), *hajj* (pilgrimage to Mecca), *zakat* (Islamic alms)—as well as jihad, which is another important principle. More important, a closer examination of the prerequisites for following these principles and the incentive structures within them suggests that they are designed to address the fears emerging from existential concerns and uncertainties of life.

*Tauheed,* the statement that God is one and Mohammad is his last Messenger, belief in which is the first condition of being a Muslim, requires acknowledging the presence of one God and that he is the all-knower and all-doer. The practical implication of this belief is that the believer is made to acknowledge the limits of human will and appreciate the existence of a superior authority capable of addressing concerns beyond his capability. *Namaz* taxes the believer's time and physical energy by requiring the believer to bow down to the authority of God five times a day irrespective of any worldly engagements. The believer has to interrupt his activities to say his prayers, and in the process is reminded of the temporary nature of life and the need to invest in the life to come. The practical impact of the prayer is that the believer can relieve himself of the daily stresses of life by learning to leave things to God.[11] *Zakat* teaches one to check one's love of material accumulation and develop the inner strength to part with one's wealth. *Roza* similarly requires bodily sacrifice; the believer has to resist bodily pleasures (food, as well as any form of sexual intimacy), in return for experiencing the pleasure of closeness to God. *Hajj,* the holy pilgrimage to Mecca, is similarly a physically—and for many also financially—taxing exercise, while jihad, whether interpreted to mean the actual act of waging war against the nonbeliever or the broader concept of fighting one's *nafs* (negative self, ego), demands resistance to material pleasures and even the sacrifice of life itself.

The question, then, is why the material and bodily sacrifices—those very sacrifices that make a religious actor look irrational to the wealth-maximizing actor—are so critical to faith. The answer is suggested by the considerations in chapter 5 about the role of the life's uncertainties and everyday stresses in raising questions about the meaning of life. Religion is a response to human concerns

11. The sense of *sakoon* (peace of mind) is what most respondents aimed to achieve through the act of prayer.

about the uncertainty of life whether rising from an intellectual curiosity or the stresses caused by the pursuit of this-worldly aspirations; the way religion addresses these concerns is by downplaying the significance of material reward. Thus, all religions guide believers to check traits that create anxiety—such as the pursuit of money, excessive competition, obsession with bodily pleasures, pride, and the stress caused by thinking of the transience of life. The way religions achieve such an end is by creating a genuine appreciation of spiritual rewards. This transaction cannot be instrumental, whereby the believer begins to believe in God because it will help relieve stress: the believer has actually to experience and feel spiritual rewards, as invoked by these sacrificial acts, because only then can the believer secure the psychological comfort that is the real reward being sought through religious faith. Thus we need to not only disaggregate utility and recognize the tension between ideal and material utility, but also to attempt to identify the reasons for this inverse relationship.

Emphasis on this-worldly rewards of material sacrifice in the name of religion was a recurrent theme in my discussions with those contributing to the running of a mosque or a madrasa; it was also a recurrent theme in explaining faith in religion itself. "We do so much for this world, why not do something for the other-world," a respondent in Quetta, while noting the value of other-worldly rewards, also emphasized how his conviction in these rewards developed from the benefits he has seen stem from religious conviction in this world. He further added, "Who can deny the inner harmony one achieves when one cares to offer the *tahajjud* prayer [optional prayer said in the middle of the night]." I repeatedly encountered respondents who vouched that they had seen their income grow manifold in proportion to what they donated. I also often had responses from parents of hafiz that they became convinced of the power of the Quran by seeing how well their child now performances in secular school. As explained by one father, "It is the miracle of the Quran that we see that children who are taken out of school at grade five to memorize the Quran in the madrasa, cope very well when they return to the secular education system in grade seven on completion of the hifz program. These children always perform very well in matriculation examinations." Similarly, respondents who knew girls from madrasas noted how they were convinced of the power of Islamic principles in leading a good life by witnessing the positive change Islamic education brought in the mannerism of these girls. Thus, conviction in the value of the other-worldly rewards developed out of having experienced this-worldly benefits.

All religions make a serious investment in convincing the believer of the other life and its related rewards. The Quran makes repeated references to heaven and provides descriptive accounts of the comforts that await the believer in heaven, while frequently referring to the temporary nature of this life and this world.

There is a particular emphasis on *dua*, the act of asking God for help in all matters, at the end of each prayer. It is the actual ability of these religious rituals and the religious texts to teach the believer the appreciation of ideal rewards, and make her feel emotionally, psychologically, and spiritually elevated, that in the long term retains the faith of the believer. It is therefore important to understand this complex interplay between material and nonmaterial rewards if one is to understand the rationality of religious action. It is also important to recognize that it is the benefits of religious rituals that the believer sees in this world, rather than simply the promise of heaven, which helps the believer develop religious conviction.

Theoretically, this demands that we recognize the dual notion of utility and the dual forms of pleasures that human beings have the capability to appreciate. Unless we recognize this duality, and the opposing pull of the two forms of utility, the relative power of the material and nonmaterial incentives for a specific context cannot be accurately predicted. The result is that policy interventions aimed at enhancing freely undertaken cooperative action by introducing material incentives often end up breaking down that cooperation, because the introduction of material incentives crowds out the nonmaterial sources of utility, which until then had acted as incentives for participation (Alkire and Deneulin 2002; Frey 1994; Titmuss 1970). Religion thus tries to inculcate a dual notion of utility: ideal and material. It does not advise against the pursuit of material prosperity, but it primarily devotes itself to inculcating a sense of spiritual prosperity, psychological and emotive in nature, that helps address the fear and anxieties emerging from the limits of the material world—the most tangible fear being that of death.

My position differs from Gary Becker's (1993), who argues that we should expand the notion of utility to include all behavior, even that which is self-sacrificing. By failing to emphasize the inverse relationship between material and ideal utility, Becker's view ignores the need to study the interaction between the two forms, and prevents us from recognizing that ideal rewards often come at the cost of the material. My position also differs from that of North (1990) and Bowles (2004), who argue for multiple motivations. Rather, I argue that the motive for action is unitary; that is, utility maximization. What constitutes utility is, however, more complex than the pursuit of material interest. Developing such a distinction is important if we are to develop a better understanding of the rise of and change in institutions (especially informal institutions)—and if critiques that label Becker's expanded notion of utility tautological are to be circumvented.[12] Else as Goldthorpe (1998: 178) notes: "in the face of action that evidently

12. "Correspondingly, pursuing one's interests can cover—to the point of tautology—all human action while it will more usefully designate a specific manner or style of conduct, known variously as 'rational' or as 'instrumental' action" (Hirschman 1985).

does not conform to the criteria of rationality that are imposed, one response is simply that of postulating hitherto unrecognized features of the situation—unobservable 'psychic' income or costs seem a favourite option . . . —which, once taken into account, render the action rational after all. Thus, rather than the theory stimulating further research of any kind, it is in effect 'closed.'" The adequate response to such a critique can come only by developing a disaggregated notion of utility where the features of the ideal and material rewards, the differing human needs they serve and the precise nature of interaction between the two is clearly defined. Only such an analysis can ensure that the expanded notion of utility is not in some instances taken to account for all altruistic and moral action and at other points reduced simply to pursuit of pure material interest. The progress in behavioral economics to better study factors shaping formation of a specific utility set is thus very welcome. As Bowles (2004: 96) notes, "Within behavioral economics, in response to violation of self-interest axiom, economists have attempted to reformulate a utility function. . . . There now exist a number of utility functions. The basic ingredients of the proposed utility functions are self-interest, altruism, spite, fair-mindedness, and reciprocity. The functions differ in the way that these components are combined and the types of behaviors the authors wish to stress." Fehr and Schmidt (1999) propose a utility function that takes into account both self-interest and what they term "inequality aversion." Akerlof and Kranton (2010) similarly argue for better recognizing the role of identity within the utility calculus. The findings of this chapter lend further support to refining our understanding of complex forces shaping people's sense of utility and the tension within these forces.

I now move to address the pull factors—those that are external to the individual in shaping collective action to produce mosques and madrasas. The most critical external factors shaping the believer's decision to contribute to a madrasa is the characteristics of the 'alim. In analyzing these factors, I explain two important questions, raised in chapter four, regarding the working of religious hierarchy: Why the practical deeds of the 'alim, and not just his knowledge, are important in reaching the ranks of the elite 'ulama? and Why are the elite within the religious hierarchy at times able to convert competition into deference.

## Reigning in Free-Riding: The Decision to Support a Madrasa

In explaining the two dominant modes through which individuals come forward to contribute to mosques and madrasas, namely through the formation of mosque committees and individual donations, I argued that most imams of mosques and madrasas want to transcend their dependence on the committee members and increase the number of independent donors. In order to achieve this end, the imam needs to be able to check free-riding by developing mechanisms that compel users of the mosque facilities to contribute toward its running. This calls for an analysis of the characteristics of the imam, which act as the pull factors in attracting followers who donate to mosques and madrasas. Interviews with donors suggest that the decision to donate is guided by the search for religious rewards, but the selection of a particular mosque and madrasa is contingent on the respect the believer has for the knowledge and the personality of the imam. Believers do not go to just any mosque to say their prayers, except when in unfamiliar settings; rather, they make a conscious selection out of the available options in the accessible geographical radius, based on the intellectual caliber and personal commitment of the imam to Islamic beliefs. Thus the impulse to give for the production of religious goods is internally driven, but its expression is shaped by the characteristics of the imam leading the mosque.

Interviews with donors as well as with the ʻulama indicate that, in order to check free-riding, the imam has to ensure that he impresses the believers with his knowledge and builds trust that he will spend the money collected properly and not on himself. All types of donors use similar mechanisms to monitor the imams; however, the big donors, due to the higher investment, are more stringent about checking the criteria. The quality of the teaching and the caliber of the imam are critical in people's choice of madrasa. The imam who heads the madrasa is part of the community, present in people's lives during all the important life-cycle ceremonies, including birth and death, and many of his senior students teach the Quran to children in neighboring houses. I found respondents judge an imam by the quality of his *khutbah* (sermon), and by watching whether he practices what he preaches. People also consult the imam on religious issues influencing daily life, and some also ask for fatwas. In the words of one respondent: "One gets to know a lot about the capacity and capability of the imam through that." Further, as was also discovered in the study of the rise of the elite madrasas, the personal traits of the ʻulama, especially those exemplifying the life of simplicity and material sacrifice, are critical in building respect for them. During the interviews the givers often referred to the humble life of the imam of the mosque they supported. The importance of this simple living was also noted by the ʻulama themselves in mobilizing donations; as the head of a medium-size madrasa noted, "The maluvi's living is within the public. The public surrounds him from all four sides. The maluvi goes to their homes; people come to his house. They keep getting to know where their money is being spent. They can see the mosque and the madrasa. If I change cars every day they will question it in their minds."

That the imam's indifference to material pleasures was important in attracting believers to make donations was also visible in the fact that most donors noted that they were irritated by imams who repeatedly asked for donations or who sent children from the madrasas to beg for donations. People respect those imams who show restraint in asking for donations. During the interviews, most imams were keen to highlight that they do not send people out to collect money, calling this a disrespectful practice. Explaining his fundraising mechanisms, an 'alim in a madrasa in Balochistan emphasized with pride that "Unlike Punjab, you will never see 'ulama from the madrasas in Balochistan go around randomly begging for money. The 'ulama from Balochistan make an annual visit to businessmen in Karachi to collect donations but they go only to those businessmen who they know; they don't go knocking on every door."

Other measures, which help people test the commitment of the imams, include the visibility of the work undertaken. The madrasas with a large number of students naturally attract more attention, as the bigger number reflects the imam's academic popularity as well as his administrative ability to manage a large establishment. A female donor emphasized how her donations were based on the efficiency and commitment of the imam: "I do occasionally make a small donation to the smaller madrasa in the area. I know that the imam of that madrasa lacks proper training and his commitment to his work appears questionable, especially when he sends out messengers with sorrowful stories to collect donations. But the fact that God's name is being recited in that place and relatively poor children are studying there makes me feel that I should donate at least a small amount to it. However, I give my main donation to the big madrasa because I know the imam there is knowledgeable and ensures a very high quality of education for his students."

The emphasis on selecting the right recipient becomes all the more clear during the interviews with big donors—those who are key to the expansion of a madrasa. The bigger donations normally come from the religiously inclined, who—due to their interest in religious education—make active efforts to identify good madrasas. In their case, giving is not tied to the madrasa in the area: these are people who will contribute to a mosque or madrasas not because it is in their locality, but because they have the knowledge to compare the efficiency and performance of various madrasas and determine which ones are superior. One donor said that it was the reputation—built on numerous criteria—of a particular madrasa that determined whether he supported it. The imam's Friday sermons, and his publications as well as those of other scholars associated with a madrasa, are two obvious means of building that reputation. Participation in gatherings of religious scholars, the monthly newsletter produced by the wafaq, the scholarly work of the graduates, and other such networks also help establish a madrasa's good reputation.

Potential donors explore various madrasas, meet like-minded people with shared interests, attend public ceremonies, read the imam's published work, and make informed decisions about the institution's efficiency. These individuals thus become part of a network through which the reputation of a good madrasa gets established, and big donors often come from this group. These people also become connectors, as they inform other people in their social networks about good madrasas. Many respondents who themselves had limited knowledge about the madrasas outside their area mentioned that they gave to a specific madrasa on the recommendation of a relative who was known to be very religious and knowledgeable about religious institutions. Thus, whether a believer makes large or small contributions to a mosque or a madrasa, he takes into account the caliber and the personality traits of the 'alim. These findings raise two important questions. First, if the believer mainly contributes to the production of the mosque and madrasa in order to seek the religious rewards promised for the act of giving, as has been argued here, then why does the believer make such a conscious effort to identify a deserving imam? Second, why does the believer judge the imam not just by his religious knowledge but also by his level of adherence to religious beliefs as reflected in his day-to-day living? The answer rests in the dynamic interplay between material and nonmaterial rewards.

The reason the believer makes a conscious effort to identify a deserving imam is that, as part of the promises made to the believer for the act of giving, Islam requires the believer to act responsibly in identifying the beneficiary of that donation. As discussed above, Islam gives detailed guidelines regarding the dispensation of all forms of religious giving, and the Quran also advises believers to be careful in their selection of the one they support. During the interviews it became clear that, apart from the religious injunction to be careful in one's giving, the desire that their hard-earned money was actually going toward improving mosque and madrasa services was another incentive to make the believers seriously evaluate the capacity and commitment of various imams. The fact that believers do not take serious pains to trace the specific utilization of their donations, however, highlights the stronger significance of the religious injunctions in explaining their action. In explaining the efforts believers make to ensure identification of a deserving mosque and madrasa, often a respondent concluded with the following note: "You cannot investigate too much. Eventually, God knows that we gave that money with the right *neeyat* [intention], if the imam misuses it then it is between him and his God."

To understand the emphasis placed on the personal traits of the imam, the nature of nonmaterial incentives and their interplay with material reward is again important. As has already been argued, religion is a response to the limits of this world, or an inner compulsion to seek a meaning to life; the way it does this is by reducing the significance of this life and its material pleasures for the believer. Developing a genuine appreciation for these nonmaterial forms of utility, however, requires greater discipline and training compared to indulging in the pleasures of the material world. Therefore, the believer needs to be convinced of their value, and the imam's own appreciation for these ideal rewards—the imam being the representative of the religion—becomes the test for establishing the appeal of the religious incentives themselves. A simple lifestyle and good moral character on the part of the imam demonstrates the power of the ideal rewards to believers; the imam's own conviction in the religion shows the follower that these incentives can actually be rewarding—because he himself has devoted his life to it. It is also due to the believer's recognition of the difficulty of developing an appreciation for these ideal rewards that the elite 'ulama who live simply and humbly are often able to convert competition in the religious hierarchy into deference. I found that believers and fellow 'ulama know the difficulty of developing an appreciation of ideal and spiritual rewards, and recognize and respect those who manifest the strength to resist material pleasures. Thus, recognizing the duality of utility and rewards is critical in understanding how the same rational actor, using the same logic, makes different choices in the economic market and in the religious sphere.

## Conclusions

The analysis in this chapter supports existing work within institutional and behavioral economics (Bowles 2004; Greif 2006; North 1990) on the importance of nonmaterial incentives in facilitating the rise of institutional mechanisms that support collective action. However, while I recognize the importance of nonmaterial incentives, I also note that the emphasis placed by these authors on accounting for other-regarding preferences is less important. Instead I argue that the motive for action is unitary—utility maximization—but that there are two types of utility: ideal and material. Though some individuals have a greater inner propensity toward ideal rewards, for most the appreciation for ideal utility develops from recognizing the limits of material utility—a limit that is inherent in the temporary nature of life itself.

The way religion overcomes the anxiety caused by the transience of material utility is through reducing the importance of material things and instead developing an appreciation for ideal rewards. This appreciation is, however, not instrumental; rather, individuals have to actually experience the inner glow and the sense of enhanced well-being through the acts of material sacrifice inherent in religious rituals to build their conviction in religion. What this suggests is that human nature has appreciation for both material and ideal utility, though the latter calls for higher self-discipline, leading most individuals to strategize in order to maximize both forms of utility at least cost. This in turn means that individuals consciously engage in activities that reduce their material well-being—such as the decision to part with one's money to support the mosque and madrasa instead of free-riding on their services—in order to improve their ideal well-being.

It is this dynamic interplay between ideal and material utility that helps explain many aspects of the working of informal institutions including their higher stickiness (chapter 3), the informal elite's ability to overcome competition (chapter 4), and the role of informal institutions in mobilizing collective action. It is due to the recognition of the stronger pull of material rewards that once an 'alim convincingly demonstrates that he is actually living according to what he preaches, and thereby leading a materially sacrificing life, he is able to covert competition into deference. Similarly, informal institutions are sticker because they rely on ideal rewards to motivate individuals to comply with institutional rules; thus the appeal of these ideal rewards enables such an institution to survive for a long time even once it no longer offers the most efficient means of utility-maximization. Further, the nature of ideal rewards is such that their attainment lies in participation, with the result that free-riding is simply not an option.

Throughout this research we have seen that people act strategically to maximize both their material and ideal utility. They want to have the best of this world, but also want to hedge against its uncertainties, or to seek a meaning to life, and in the process they develop an appreciation for ideal rewards. If such an analysis of interaction between ideal and material utility is indeed valid, then the question is: What explains the rise of extreme or exclusionary preferences for ideal utility, as seen in case of the decision to participate in militant jihad? Could it actually be that the biggest material sacrifice—of life itself—is actually driven by promise of rewards, which are very spiritual in nature? The Quran might promise "seventy-two black-eyed virgins" to the martyr, but there is no promise that in heaven people will be resurrected in their bodily forms: heaven in the view of some Islamic philosophers is a purely spiritual realm (Hope and Young 1994; Leaman 1999; Smith and Haddad 2002). The next chapter turns to the issue for which Pakistani madrasas are most in the picture, namely the links between madrasas and violent jihad, and the relative role of text and context in promoting militancy.

# 8

# EXCLUSIONARY INSTITUTIONAL PREFERENCE

## The Logic of Jihad

> **When you cannot fight the giant on his terms, the art is to bring him down to the fool's level. This is what Osama [bin Laden] has done so successfully; the United States is crumbling economically, the war has been won.**
>
> —Ahmed, a supporter of jihadist groups

> **Our view is that the system has collapsed and people are not getting any relief. If the government gives relief then only an elite *tabqa* [class] gets it. The system needs change and we are going to change this system. This system has collapsed and this is also the viewpoint of our students. We say that this system has to go. When this system will go at least something new will come. Our demand is that we want to introduce the Islamic system.**
>
> —Abdul Rasheed Ghazi, one of the two leaders of the Red Mosque and Jamia Hafsa resistance who died on 10 July 2007 in the military operation designed to crush the movement

Ahmed, who admires Osama bin Laden's ability to take on the world's superpower, belongs to the liberal elite of Islamabad and is a wine-drinking and party-loving son of an influential bureaucrat. He came around to support jihad after repeated sittings with what he refers to as "true jihadists," who introduced him to Western literature detailing the politics of oil and the geopolitics of U.S. foreign policies. Jamia Hafsa represented the elite of the girls' madrasas in Pakistan where, in line with the analysis developed in chapter 4, the majority of the students came from middle-income groups rather than the absolute poor. Yet these students chose to take up arms against General Musharraf's regime for its unconditional support of the U.S. war on terror; the Red Mosque 'ulama were not leading a group of poor adolescents easily swayable for the promise of the other world. Farah, yet another category of respondents supporting jihad that I encountered in the field, was born and raised within a liberal household in the UK. She followed the Western lifestyle until exposure to some teachings in a mosque in London got her hooked onto a serious study of Islamic movements. Later married to her

Dubai-based cousin, a flight steward by profession, she encouraged him to quit because of the professional obligation to serve alcohol. On moving to Pakistan, she encouraged her husband to join the jihad. Now, with three children, she still prefers the vulnerable living as a jihadist and the irregular income over reversion to her former Western lifestyle.

Not one of these three categories of respondents fits the imagery of a jihadist promoted in the literature on Pakistani madrasas and jihad (ICG 2002; Singer 2001; Stern 2000), where economically and socially marginalized madrasa students are seen to be susceptible to religious indoctrination—yet they all joined the jihad and formed an exclusionary institutional identity.[1] A believer, whether in the role of an ‘alim, parent, donor, or student, constantly weighs economic costs of pursuing a religious action—eventually exercising the option that best maximizes both his material and ideal utility, whereby if one source of attaining ideal utility becomes too costly the actor pragmatically chooses an alternative course. Such behavior does not reflect an instrumental use of religion; Islamic thought encourages the believer to be flexible in such calculations and make the best of both worlds, as long as the given action does not deviate from the basic principles of faith.[2] Why then, in the case of militant Islam, do we see the exercise of extreme religious preference?

The literature on militant Islam identifies two dominant explanations for jihad: a flaw inherent in the scripture or a rational response to the socioeconomic or political marginalization faced by the Muslim youth. The two differ in their emphasis, the former highlighting the supremacy of the text and an unquestioning acceptance of religious authority, the latter highlighting the socioeconomic and political context of the Muslim societies where economic deprivation, social marginalization, and unrepresentative political regimes create an environment conducive to harboring reactionary sentiments. The problem, however, as argued by Euben (1999) is that both streams of literature present radical Islam as a response of the frustrated youth that gravitates toward Islamic militancy due to unfavorable material conditions. Euben (1999) instead argues for taking into account the moral appeal of Islamic ideas and the alternative notion of modernity advanced by religious discourse, and not just the material conditions, in

1. As Sen (2006) argues, individuals do not have one but multiple identities. The question thus becomes: What makes one identity, as seen in case of jihad or ethnic violence, crowd out association to other identities?

2. The Quran carries numerous references to ease in following the religion such as "God wants ease for you, not hardship" (Surah 2: 185); "while those who believed and did good deeds will have the best of rewards: we shall command them to do what is easy for them" (Surah 18: 88); "He has chosen you and placed no hardship in your religion" (Surah 22: 78); "We have made it easy to learn lessons from the Qur'an"' (Surah 54: 17).

explaining radical Islam. In this chapter I draw on interviews with fifty jihadists and group discussions with ʿulama, teachers, and students of Jamia Hafsa to identify which of these alternative theories best helps understand their decision to support Islamic militancy.[3] I focus on two questions: What motivates individuals to join the jihad and form an exclusionary religious identity or institutional preference, a preference that seems to be formed irrespective of the magnitude of material costs incurred? and How do individuals decide to join one jihadist organization over another? In addition, I identify factors that help militant groups win mass public support in Muslim countries.[4]

The need to understand the basis of popular appeal of any militant resistance is noted in studies on rebel groups (Collier and Hoeffler 2000). As Tessler and Robbins (2007: 305) note, "Organizations involved in civil wars require at least a passive supportive society in which to hide and from which to obtain the resources necessary for survival." I therefore explore the decision-making processes of four groups: leaders (who lead a jihadist group), jihadists (who join the group as fighters), supporters (who contribute to the group through funds or publishing newspapers or magazines on the activities of these groups), and sympathizers (people within the general public who express moral support for these groups).

## Why Exclusionary Identity? Existing Theories

What leads individuals to form exclusionary identity—or in other words an exclusionary institutional preference—is a puzzle that is not specific to jihad but is applicable to much of ethnic and sectarian violence. Such exclusionary preferences are an exception to human behavior, where, as widely noted within political economy literature, choice at any point in time is not a product of one institution but that of the interdependent web of an institutional matrix (Alt and Shepsle 1990; Bates 1990). What makes the analysis of Islamic jihad all the more complex is that

3. Suicide missions are extreme manifestations of this exclusionary identity. For detailed discussion on the differences between the two, see Gambetta (2006). Here the focus remains on jihad where the joiner does not have a 100 percent guarantee of death but the material sacrifice involved is still significant.

4. As noted in the cover story of the first issue of *Newsweek* after September 11: "Why else is America's response to the terror attacks so deeply constrained by fears of an 'Islamic backlash' on the streets? Pakistan will dare not allow Washington the use of its bases. Saudi Arabia trembles at the thought of having to help us publicly. Egypt pleads that our strikes be as limited as possible. The problem is not that Osama bin Laden believes that this is a religious war against America. It's that millions of people across the Islamic world seem to agree" (Zakaria 2001). Even as late as 2007, an opinion poll in Pakistan showed that Osama bin Laden was more popular than General Musharraf.

unlike the act of mob violence often associated with ethnic and sectarian tensions, which might be spontaneous, in the case of jihadist groups this exclusionary preference is not based on momentary impulse but is taken under normal life circumstances and has a certain level of stability.[5] Although not all Islamic jihadists go to the extreme of suicide bombing, they do choose a life of high risk and sustain their motivation over a long period of time—given the time lapse involved in the initial decision to join a jihadist group, recruitment to one, acquisition of militant training, and actual deployment in the field. The stability of the decision for significant periods of time—even if some jihadists do withdraw after being in the field for a year or two—puts into question the assumption that such a choice is a result of simple indoctrination, especially when religion promises them the same rewards without incurring intense costs: the Quran promises heaven for much less costly actions, such as making one's child memorize the Quran. Gambetta's (2006: 149) questioning of stability of preference of a suicide bomber is thus equally applicable to that of jihadists stationed in the field, "On the spur of the moment, many people may feel committed enough to a cause to volunteer to die for it, but not so many will wake up the next morning with the same fierce determination."

It is important to trace the origin of militant Islam in Pakistan (Cohen 2003; Grare 2006a; Hussain 2007; Nasr 2000, 2002; Schoflield and Zekulin 2007). For a country created in the name of Islam, it is not surprising that from its very inception in 1947 an array of Islamic groups aimed to influence the national policy agenda despite the country's leadership resting in the hands of relatively secular political elite (Ahmed 1997; Ali 1970; Haqqani 2005; Zaidi 2003). Until the late 1970s, apart from India's complaints about Pakistan's role in instigating Islamic militancy in the Indian-held Kashmir (Akhtar 1993; Schofield 2003), there were no serious concerns around religious militancy within Pakistan. In 2001, when September 11 happened, Pakistan was, however, the frontline state accused of providing protection to the Taliban and Al-Qaida (Dorronsoro 2002; Roy 2002). Moreover, despite having been acknowledged since then as a partner in the U.S.-led war on terror, the country is still viewed as the focal point for the gathering of Islamic militants from across the world.[6] What is the explanation for this institutional shift in Islam in Pakistan, where sections within the society moved from observance of routine religious rituals to expression of highly militant behavior? In order to understand this, it is necessary to analyze the different strands of Islamic militancy present in modern-day Pakistan.

---

5. Gambetta (2006) draws similar distinction between those who plan suicide attacks and those who actually execute them.

6. The titles of cover stories for the *Economist* ("Pakistan: The World's Most Dangerous Place") and *Newsweek* ("Pakistan: The Most Dangerous Place") published in 2008 are revealing.

The first conceptual distinction for understanding the working of jihad in Pakistan is to appreciate the difference between cross-border and within-border jihad. Pakistan's involvement in jihad is as old as the country's history, where the decision of the maharaja of Kashmir to accede to India at the time of partition caused a group of Pakistani fighters to gravitate toward Kashmir to arguably protect the Muslim majority population from Indian aggression (Ganguly 1986). Whether or not the Pakistani state sponsored this initial group of fighters (Behera 2001), with the Kashmir dispute remaining unresolved even after the passage of a UN resolution in 1948 asking for a plebiscite, the Pakistani state developed stakes in supporting Muslim resistance within Kashmir (Bahl 2007; Haqqani 2003; Shibli 2009). The Pakistani support for Islamic militancy in Kashmir remained largely informal until the 1980s, drawing on individuals rather than organized jihadist groups (Behera 2001).

The Soviet invasion of Afghanistan was the key factor to mark the formalization of jihad in Pakistan (Weaver 2002). With support from the CIA and the Saudi intelligence agency, Pakistan's Inter-Services Intelligence (ISI), facilitated the rise of formal jihadist organizations that mobilized ordinary Pakistanis to join the jihad in Afghanistan (Clements 2003). The Zia-ul-Haq government mobilized support for this jihad by calling on the public to support their Muslim brothers in Afghanistan; it also created fears of Soviet invasion if not defeated in Afghanistan (Hilali 2005). Thereby began a state-sponsored process of recruiting Muslim fighters within Pakistan, commonly referred to as mujahedeen, to fight the Soviets (Hussain 2005). The state—with the support from the United States and Saudi Arabia—funded the jihad, but the actual recruitment and organization were realized through the platform of jihadist organizations, thereby establishing close links between the leaders of these organizations and the Pakistani intelligence agencies (Abbas 2005). For the Pakistani government, and arguably even for the leaders of these organizations, strategic rather than religious motives shaped this engagement. However, for the ordinary Pakistanis who risked their lives on the battlefields in Afghanistan, the primary concern was "the Muslim brother." Until this time, the Islamic sentiment played out in a foreign context, thereby being a cross-border jihad, one that happened outside Pakistan's own boundaries. Once Soviet army was defeated, the jihadist organizations and ISI stayed engaged in Afghanistan and developed close ties with the Taliban when the latter came to power (Rashid 2001). Conversely, some jihadist organizations directed their attention to Kashmir.

The nature of Pakistani jihad changed dramatically in the post–September 11 era, when jihad moved within Pakistani borders (Grare 2006b; Rabasa 2004). During the Afghan-Soviet war, the tribal belt on the border between Pakistan and Afghanistan became a nesting ground for a great number of mujahedeen as well as for many of the Afghan refugees who were free to cross the Pakistani border. Some of the orphaned Afghani children came to reside in Pakistani madrasas (Noor 2008) located within the tribal belt and further inland in the Khyber Pakhtunkhwa province, leading to the emergence of the Taliban in Pakistan (Rashid 2001). During the war, many foreign fighters who had come to fight in Afghanistan married into local tribes in the tribal belt, integrating into the local community. As the allied forces faced steady resistance in Afghanistan, the U.S. government argued that Al-Qaida members and Taliban leaders were finding refuge in Pakistan's tribal belt. Starting in 2004, under pressure from the Bush administration, the Pakistani military started to carry out military operations in the tribal belt (Buckley and Fawn 2003; Meher 2004). These operations extended to the settled areas of Khyber Pakhtunkhwa in 2007. Over 70,000 Pakistani troops continue to be deployed in Khyber Pakhtunkhwa. The resistance against the military operations has resulted in fierce clashes between the Islamic militants and the Pakistani armed forces. The high number of casualties on both sides has on more than three occasions led to signing of peace accords between the two sides.

More important, the resistance has moved beyond the tribal belt. Suicide attacks in Pakistani cities, unheard of prior to September 11, have become a routine occurrence. The most forceful evidence of the growing resistance to the Pakistani government's support for the war on terror came in early 2007, when the central mosque of Islamabad and its associated seminary took up arms against the government (Fair 2008; Markey 2008). This switch from cross-border to within-border jihad has implications: the fighters of today are not necessarily the same as the fighters of yesterday nor are necessarily their motives. Those joining cross-border jihad cannot arguably be driven by nationalist sentiments, while those engaged in within-border jihad could have very nationalist and territorial concerns in mind. Within-border jihad targets fellow Muslim brothers in the Pakistani army as opposed to the Soviets in Afghanistan or Hindus in Kashmir.

The other complication worth recognizing in understanding jihad in Pakistan is the difference between religious organizations engaged in Islamic jihad and those engaged in sectarian violence (Kukreja 2003; Martin 2006). Both resort to arms in the name of Islam. Authors often do not analytically differentiate between the two though the two differentiate between themselves and receive different levels of support from the public. During the fieldwork for this research, representatives of the jihadist groups were keen to differentiate themselves from the sectarian groups; the latter, however, were often keen to claim jihadist affiliation. I found public perceptions of these groups also reflecting this distinction; where the former was seen to stand for a cause, the latter was viewed as the result of religious bigotry and a cause for public concern.

Whether it is the study of cross-border or within-border jihad or a comparison of Islamic militancy or sectarian violence, current literature is quick to attribute its cause to religious training imparted in the Pakistani madrasas. Madrasas are argued to brainwash young Muslim men into joining the jihad.[7] The International Crisis Group (ICG 2002) argues that the madrasas produce graduates who have a narrow worldview, lack modern civic education and, due to living in poverty, become a destabilizing factor in society whereby they are susceptible to romantic notions of sectarian and international jihad, which promises instant salvation. Most studies draw on anecdotal evidence and make such sweeping claims based on limited data that their findings do not stand up to serious scrutiny (ICG 2002; Singer 2002; Stern 2001). The discourse on Islamic militancy in Pakistan remains focused on madrasas and religious indoctrination, despite the fact that in other contexts such claims have been seriously questioned.

## Madrasas and Militancy: Widening the Net

Any serious academic scholarship aiming to make claims about the sources of Islamic militancy must acknowledge the difficulty of making such claims when it is impossible to establish the total pool of militants. When the total number of militants and their backgrounds are not known, generalizations based on few anecdotes can be grossly misleading. Studies profiling militants in other contexts have already discredited the deprivation thesis: the profiling of members of Al-Qaida[8] or other Islamic groups operating in other contexts such as Palestine (Ricolfi 2006) shows the presence not of poor madrasa students but socially well-placed Muslim men from secular educational system. In scholarship on Islamic militancy in Pakistan, however, madrasas remain the focus of attention. It is true that students from some Pakistani madrasas went for jihad in Afghanistan. Taqi Usmani (2004), who heads a leading Deobandi seminary in Karachi, for instance, pens in one of his book with great pride the departure of some of his students to join the jihad in Afghanistan. Other leading Deobandi madrasas, especially in Khyber Pakhtunkhwa, educated Afghan children who later joined the Taliban; further, 'ulama from these madrasas supported their students' decision to join

7. Such statements mostly appear in studies claiming madrasas to be result of poverty and failure of the state schooling system. Jihad thus becomes a natural response of the deprived and marginalized.

8. Based on educational biographies for nearly 300 known members of violent Islamist groups from thirty countries, Gambetta and Hertog (2006) show that vast majority—69 percent—had attended college. Of those with clear areas of study, nearly half had pursued engineering.

the ranks of the Taliban in times of need. To date, however, evidence to support claims that madrasas provide military training remains very weak.

Moreover, such claims fail to analyze whether the students opted to join the jihad in Afghanistan on their own initiative or were guided into this action by the ʻulama. It became clear to me during the course of this research that in order to understand the recruitment process it is more important to identify the route, which facilitated the actual movement of these students from the Pakistani madrasas to Afghanistan, and identify the actors that provided them with training and ammunition. It is here that it becomes important to draw a clear distinction between madrasas and jihadist organizations.[9] The Pakistanis who fought in Afghanistan or Kashmir moved there through established jihadist organizations, which exist outside the madrasas.[10] During the Afghan-Soviet war, six such organizations played a prominent role (Rashid 1999; 2001). The members of these organizations came from madrasas, but a large number of them came from universities in Pakistan as well as in the West, and many had no formal education. Hizb-ul-Mujahidin, the jihadist splinter group of the Jamaat-i-Islami, which was most active in Afghan jihad and even today has an active presence in Indian-held Kashmir, recruits mainly from Pakistani colleges and universities, not madrasas. Its leader (at the time of the interview in 2007) had a master's degree in political science. Lashkar-i-Taiba, another important jihadist organization, was established by professors from a prominent engineering university in Lahore.

The profile of the fifty respondents interviewed for this study also does not support the claim that madrasas are the primary ground for recruiting militants: out of the pool of fifty jihadists I was able to trace, only five had a madrasa education. Sixty percent[11] of respondents belonged to economically and socially affluent circles and had studied in regular schools and universities, 30 percent of whom had even studied overseas. The leaders of the post–September 11 resistance in the tribal belt also did not come primarily from madrasas: Beitullah Mesud, who posed tough resistance to the Pakistani army in 2008, for instance, was not a madrasa graduate. In the list of missing people—those held by the Pakistani intelligence agencies on suspicion of involvement in acts of Islamic

9. The jihadists organizations have a clear command structure but operate in terms of loose networks as most jihadists are not formally employed.

10. The Red Mosque was the first case of a mosque leadership staging an armed resistance; prior to this all resistance has come through the platforms of the jihadist organizations.

11. This should not be interpreted as a representation of the ratio of total jihadists in Pakistan. Given the difficulty of identifying jihadists willing to talk to researchers, the sample relied on the snowball sampling technique and thus had a bias toward jihadists from affluent groups as this was the group in which I had the relevant social networks to gain access. This sample was also important to tap given that the existing literature on jihad in Pakistan continues to link this phenomenon to economic deprivation.

militancy—only 20 percent were madrasa students. Eighty percent of the people on this list came from non-madrasa background and included software engineers, businessmen, an MBA graduate from IBA (a leading Pakistani University), a hardware expert, a male nurse, a computer engineer, and a taxi driver.[12]

Thus, militants come from much more diverse backgrounds than from just madrasas. This supports Granovetter's (1973) analysis that it is "weak ties" that are more important in expanding an actor's networks; it is the jihadist organizations that draw on the diverse pool of members as opposed to madrasas, where students form close ties due to their communal living, that are actually at the center of planning and recruitment for Islamic jihad. 'Ulama within the madrasas repeatedly reiterated this point in our discussions. "These madrasas existed prior to these jihadist organizations and there was no militancy," said a senior 'alim. "The militancy we see in Pakistan today is a reaction to wrong policies of the Western and Pakistani governments. It is channeled through jihadist organizations, who recruit fighters from all different income groups, and educational backgrounds. No madrasa has the institutional set up to train individuals for jihad," he added.

The Red Mosque resistance coming from the platform of a madrasa, and the ensuing resistance in Swat, did lend support to the alleged links between militancy and madrasas. A closer look at the Red Mosque resistance, however, reveals an interesting fact: of the two 'ulama (who were brothers) leading the resistance, the one who fought until his death held a master's degree in history from Quaid-i-Azam University, a leading state university, and had once also worked with a UN agency. Conversely, the elder brother, who was a trained 'alim, attempted to escape from the madrasa when it came under siege, hiding under a burqa. The profile of the 'alim who resisted until his death reveals that he was not trained in the madrasa tradition but was by nature prone to support ideological causes. He had fought in Afghanistan and had played a central role in organizing the campaign for missing people.

The other important point to note is that Jamia Hafsa, the female madrasa run by the Red Mosque, was the most prestigious of the female madrasas within the Deobandi wafaq. Jamia Hafsa housed students from middle-income background who had completed some degree of secular education. It was not a madrasa full of poverty-stricken and deprived students and given the students' exposure to secular schools, chances of them being swayed by religious propaganda alone were comparatively slim. The legitimate question to ask, thus, is not why madrasas breed militancy but what factors motivate individuals, whether from madrasas or from

12. Data are based on the list of missing people issued by the Supreme Court of Pakistan.

other places, to join the jihad? Or in other words, what develops an exclusionary preference for Islamic identity making people relinquish all other associations?

## Formation of Exclusionary Affiliations

My interviews with fifty respondents including those who fought in Afghanistan or Kashmir (cross-border jihad) and those involved in current resistance within Pakistan (within-border jihad), make it clear that it is not the pursuit of religious rewards that moves individuals to acquire exclusionary identities; it is the strong sense of injustice among those who think about these issues that stirs them into action. I found this sense of injustice to be linked to a concern about collective identity of Muslims in the global world and not to be the result of socioeconomic deprivation of the individual jihadists. In arguing this it is very important to clarify that here I am making no judgment about the legitimacy of these conceptions of injustice nor am I arguing that this sense of injustice is supported in Islamic texts. Rather I am emphasizing that a perceived sense of political injustice was at the heart of the actions of the jihadists I interviewed.

I found that religion does play a role in reducing the high personal costs (time, money, and ultimately life) of this ideological resistance by providing for otherworldly rewards and also promising success to the jihadists in this world. The religious texts help rationalize fighting a force, which is much greater in might, as the end result of the struggle is viewed to be in God's hands. The Quran makes repeated references to the support Allah provides to the believers.[13] However, I found that although religion helps sustain support for jihad, the primary factor in mobilizing the jihadists is a strong sense of political injustice. Interviews with the jihadists and students of Jamia Hafsa show that without a strong sense of political injustice, the promise of "seventy-two black-eyed virgins" in heaven is not a sufficiently strong incentive for individuals to join the jihad.

My deliberations with the jihadists, across the economic, ethnic, or gender divide, show that political events and not Islamic teachings motivated them. The jihadists repeatedly raised concerns about U.S. biases toward the Muslim world. All respondents were politically informed, 60 percent were avid newspaper readers, and all were quick to quote actual facts and figures to assert their claim that

---

13. "If you are steadfast and mindful of God, your Lord will reinforce you with five thousand swooping angels if the enemy should suddenly attack you! And God arranged it so, as a message of hope for you [believers] to put your hearts at rest" (Surah 3: 125–126); "Those who have been attacked are permitted to take up arms because they have been wronged—God has the power to help them—those who have been driven unjustly from their homes" (Surah 22: 39).

the United States was biased against the Muslim world. In such discussions the situation in Palestine was always the central reference followed by the U.S. invasion of Afghanistan and Iraq. One of respondents interrupted the interview to bring a stack of books from his reading room that he argued convinced him of the biased Western policies. He was introduced to these books (all written by Western authors) by individuals he referred to as "senior jihadists." The books covered themes such as the U.S. support of Israel, U.S. oil interests in the Muslim world, and the cost of the war on terror and its negative consequences for the U.S. economy.

The discussions around post-2004 shift of jihad within Pakistan's borders reflected even stronger sense of injustice. The jihadists I interviewed explained the resistance against the Pakistani military in the tribal belt and the introduction of suicide attacks within Pakistan as a natural response to the Musharraf government's strategy to align with the United States. All maintained that the military operations by the Pakistani army and the U.S. drone attacks were unjust and that these harmed innocent civilians. To support their position, a couple of respondents referred to the 2006 U.S. drone attack on the madrasa in Bajour, which resulted in the death of eight-two students. Commenting on this incident and the suicide attack, which allegedly took place in retaliation to this operation one respondent argued, "If a Muslim youth confronts a *zalim* [tyrant] and *jabar* [oppressor] that is called jihad. There are very few people who have the *jazba* [courage] for jihad; it is a God-gifted courage. The grave injustice that was witnessed in case of Bajour was bound to provoke a reaction."

Here it is important to note that none of my respondents described the scenario of Islamic militants fighting the Pakistani army as desirable. As noted by a respondent affiliated with a prominent jihadist group in Lahore, "My organization does not believe in fighting the government because we think it will weaken Pakistan against its enemies and cause internal strife. It is because of this that we are not involved in the resistance in the tribal belt even when we think what is happening there is unjust." But in the context where the Musharraf regime was seen to have become an uncritical ally of the U.S. war on terror for perpetuation of its military rule, most respondents found retaliation to be the only option. Thus, even if a few jihadist groups tried to officially stay away from the resistance in the tribal belt, not all members abided.

A general consequence of this emphasis on the discourse of injustice in explaining jihad, was that all interviewed jihadists held "genuine jihadists"[14] in high esteem because to them these were people driven by ideological issues and had the courage to stand up to resist injustices. In the words of one respondent,

14. There was a recognition that much of jihad has been tampered with by the state, thus, the emphasis on genuine jihadists during the interviews.

"The real jihadists are people of exceptionally strong character; they are people who can take pain. There are few who are willing to go for a protest, there are even fewer who are willing to face tear gas, and then there is an even smaller number who is actually willing to go to jail. Those in the last category have the maximum level of tolerance and it is these people who go to jihad. They fight for principles; they react to injustices."

My fieldwork within the Red Mosque and Jamia Hafsa during the period of resistance revealed a similar emphasis on the sense of injustice as a primary trigger for mobilizing jihadist sentiment. Students who joined me in group discussions recorded the immorality of the ongoing military operations in the tribal belt, which in their view had caused the death of innocent people. They raised concerns about the missing people. The fact that the Pakistani law enforcement and intelligence agencies had been handing over suspects to the United States without a trial in their own country, often in return for financial compensation had become a very emotive concern.[15] According to one student, "What is the sense of loyalty left for a country where we know that our own leaders are selling our people to the United States in return for money? We used to say that the Pakistani army is God's army because it is defending a Muslim country. However, the current army is selling its own people. How can we not protest?"

The presence of a large number of students from Khyber Pakhtunkhwa and the tribal belt had made these concerns sound very real to fellow students and teachers. In discussions respondents from the tribal belt gave very personalized accounts of life and material losses incurred by the local population during these military operations, while the other students listened very attentively. These narratives reflected a sense of strong injustice built overtime. In these discussions, the concerns about the military operations in the tribal belt, the missing people, the poor state of law and order, economic unemployment—all were linked to one root cause, an unaccountable government, which was now also viewed to be selling national sovereignty to strengthen itself.

Umme Hassan, the principal of Jamia Hafsa, referred to multiple grievances against the state to build rhetoric of injustice. During the interviews she routinely linked the perceived injustices of the war on terror with the poor functioning of the state in delivering justice to the ordinary public:

> When someone comes and attacks you, you will do something. You will have to resist. It is so disheartening when you see that the country was built for Islam and what is happening now. Outside forces are

15. General Musharraf recorded in his biography that the CIA handsomely compensated his regime for every suspect handed over to the United States (Cohen and Chollet 2007).

> being given priority. Islamic fighters in the tribal belt or Afghanistan are involved in *dafi* [defensive] jihad; we have however now decided to start this *akdami* [reformatory] jihad to seek justice for the ordinary people, because the state system is running without any rules. Economic survival for an ordinary person is getting harder while government officials keep accumulating more. For the poor public, there is no access to justice. They are after me so now they are harassing my old parents, who have nothing to do with this resistance. They have an FIR against my brother in law. That is why we are against this system, and want to raise a voice. There is no expectation of justice from this government. The courage to face death is with no one other than Muslims.

Abdul Rasheed Ghazi similarly noted multiple grievances in his interviews:

> The rich is getting richer while the poor is getting poorer. Our judge is making decisions to please the government. When you take the nation to such extreme in the name of war on terror, what do you expect from people whose parents or young sons or daughters are being kidnapped by the country's own agencies and sold to the United States? These people are not even given a trial in their own country and are thus denied the basic right to defend themselves. When the law fails to protect you what do you do? There is not even a single madrasa where jihad training is imparted. But yes when it comes to teaching Islamic principles of jihad, we teach them. Our students come and say that there is so much wrong in this society, and ask us to give them permission to react to it. I say, no I cannot give you that permission. We ask the government not to push us to the limit where we have to give our students such permission.

The campaign for missing people, led by the wife of one of the victims, had resulted in production of a list of people who had been detained by Pakistani and U.S. intelligence agencies, often in very inhumane conditions. These people were denied access to the judicial system, and were not allowed to contact their relatives. The presence of the relatives of the people, with photographs of their missing family members, at protest rallies in Islamabad led to a heightened sense of injustice among those present at these rallies against the policies of the war on terror.[16]

I found that the evidence on missing people and accounts of students from the tribal belt played a critical role in convincing Jamia Hafsa students to support

---

16. During interviews, Amna Janjua, wife of one of the victims who has led the campaign for the release of "missing people" repeatedly emphasized Ghazi's role in strengthening this moment: "After returning from a day-long protest, he used to be the one to push us and say we now must write press-releases."

the Red Mosque 'ulama. Whatever the real motives of the 'ulama in staging the resistance (some accused them of being funded by intelligence agencies), their ability to mobilize the students to support the resistance rested in building a discourse pegged entirely in the conception of justice. The 'ulama and Umme Hassan had successfully convinced the students that those who wanted to live by Islamic way of life were being persecuted. In fact, the justification for the very demand for imposition of Shari'a law was presented as a demand for justice. It was argued that Islam promises all individuals equal rights, a guarantee that the secular Pakistani state with a weak judiciary was failing to provide. In one of my interviews with Abdul Rasheed Ghazi, he noted with a strong sense of remorse:

> In this country the *jagirdari nizam* [feudal system] and *jirga* [tribal justice] system persist where inappropriate decisions against the poor people take place. Nobody says that they are running a parallel system. If this system is allowed to function parallel to the state's legal apparatus, whereby the poor are exploited by the bigger landlords who control the jirga system, why should we be stopped for arguing for a Shari'a Court that promises equality to all. My family comes from an area where such jirgas take place;[17] the *sardars* [the feudal or tribal elders] are so powerful that no one is allowed to sit with them at their level, people have to sit at their feet.

I found that the ability to demonstrate that ordinary Pakistanis and Muslims as a collective are faced with gross injustices at the hands of their own states as well as global forces and that the jihadists are fighting to establish a more just social and political order within the Muslim states and globally is central to the ability of the jihadist leaders to mobilize mujahedeen, supporters, and sympathizers.

That such a sense of injustice is important in mobilizing fighters was also visible in the consciousness I found among all respondents about the strict principles Islam has for what is valid jihad, who has the authority to declare it, and who can be a legitimate target of jihad. Respondents were in general conscious of present-day theological critiques of contemporary jihad: it targets civilians; carries out killings when no Muslim authority has declared war; and, chooses a method of attack—namely suicide, which is unlawful in Islam. The way respondents justified jihad and their involvement was by drawing a distinction between aggressive and defensive jihad: aggressive jihad was defined as one launched by

17. Interview, 14 March 2008, Lal Masjid, Islamabad.

a Muslim authority to promote Islam, while defensive jihad was viewed as self-defense when attacked. As elaborated by one respondent:

> If a Muslim land is under siege by foreign troops then it is obligatory on Muslims to undertake jihad against the aggressor. This is *dafi* [defensive] jihad. In this case, there is no need to wait for an approval from the established state or religious authority. The *akdami* [reformatory or aggressive] jihad is optional, which is taken to correct an unfair system or expand an already established Muslim state. Here it is important to seek the leader's approval before declaring jihad.

During the interviews, my respondents justified their involvement in jihad arguing that it is the aggressive jihad that requires permission from the Muslim leader; the latter, in the view of these groups, is an inevitable obligation for all believers as, when under siege, one is required to resist irrespective of the decision of the central authority. Jihad was also justified through staging a critique of the undemocratically elected authoritarian regimes in the Muslim world, where leaders are unwilling to resist Western forces who exploit Muslims due to their personal vested interests. Repeatedly, my respondents argued that whether it be Afghanistan, Kashmir, Iraq, or the ongoing resistance within Pakistan, it was all retaliatory rather than aggressive. One respondent stated, "It is the United States that has invaded Muslim lands; it is the U.S. troops who are launching attacks on the Muslim armies and ordinary citizens. How can the Muslims not react? But even when we are reacting only to defend ourselves we are labeled as terrorists." He concluded by adding, "We are so caught up in defensive jihad, we have not yet moved toward aggressive jihad."

Respondents within the Red Mosque echoed similar arguments; they defended resistance as a defensive measure against a state that had sold its loyalty to the United States and where the very practice of Islam was at threat. The reactionary nature of some of the major suicide attacks is visible in their timings and targets: the bombing of the madrasa in Bajour was followed by the first serious suicide attack on a military training camp in the tribal belt with the death toll reaching forty; the government itself acknowledged this as a reaction to the attack on the madrasa in Bajour. The Red Mosque operation led to a number of suicide attacks on security targets, the most lethal of which was carried out on the highly protected military facility hosting the military brigade that had carried out the military operation on the Red Mosque.

Although all respondents were driven by the perceived injustices of the Western world and their own governments, careful analysis of the interviews helps identify three additional contributing factors that moved jihadists from the general pool of sympathizers to an active mode. The first noticeable characteristic of the jihadists I interviewed was that they seemed to have a higher preference for ideal rewards, and the way they rationalized the sacrifice of material comfort and the risk they posed to their lives was by questioning the very meaning and purpose of life. The temporary nature of this life was often mentioned in these interviews to further the argument that because life is bound to end anyway, why not end it for a purpose. One respondent from a financially affluent background said, "The ultimate truth is that eventually everyone has to die. For some the idea of dying for a cause gives much more meaning to life itself." Such fighters, as noted in Gambetta (2006), are often individuals who feel excited in doing something different and want to leave a mark; they demonstrate a higher preference for ideal utility. The excitement of leaving a legacy clearly appeals to jihadists. Abdul Rasheed Ghazi was thinking about the legacy he was leaving behind; he was very conscious of the implication of his struggle for the broader Islamic resistance. In one of his last telephone interviews with a cable TV channel, Ghazi stated: "I want to save my life and that of the students but after the way the government humiliated my brother, it is not just the issue of our lives, it is the issue of the reputation of all Islamic movements."

Thirty percent of respondents noted the specific dynamics of youth, and the sense of excitement and adventure as additional mobilizing factors for teenagers and those in their early twenties. As another respondent from an affluent background argued, "It is a combination of that youthful age and excitement. My brother and I volunteered because in those days there were not many other distractions. Today there are too many gadgets and other attractions to keep the young preoccupied that not many people will go for jihad." Gambetta (2006) in the edited volume on suicide mission also notes that those placed close to places of entertainment had a greater chance of being swayed away from the suicide mission. Finally, for another 10 percent failure to achieve material prosperity could at times be a cause of gravitation toward jihadist groups as a means to acquire a sense of personal worth. "We must also acknowledge that some people gravitate toward jihad because of their inability to excel in the worldly pursuits, jihad then becomes a way of striving for that extraordinary status," said one respondent. "However, this does not mean that they are doing it without a commitment. The primary drive is the sense of injustice, and the recognition of the need to respond to that. Failure to excel in this world can for some create great commitment to excel in this ideal pursuit," he added.

In addition to these contextual factors, I found that where Islamic texts play an important role in mobilizing jihadists is in developing the psychological courage required to risk one's life in pursuit of ideal utility. The religious texts play this role in a number of ways: by giving a sense of courage to take on an enemy through constant references in the Quran that the outcomes are in God's hands;

by giving the sense of being special to have the will to fight for the Islamic cause; and, by creating a personal incentive for making the material sacrifice for the promised endearment to God. As the leader of Hizb-ul- Mujahedeen stated, "People gravitate toward jihadist groups due to political injustices but there is always the question: What does the one sacrificing his life gets out of it? It is here that faith becomes important in sustaining the jihadist sentiment."

Another way I found Islam helps develop psychological strength to undertake jihad is through building pride in the Muslim past. Islamic history provides the Muslims with a conception of their grand past, and encourages them to be rulers instead of the subjugated. Islamic texts also inspire the believer not to accept any one's hegemony but only that of God. Religious belief thus removes or at least reduces the fear of taking on a more forceful enemy. Evidently, not all Muslims interpret this to mean taking up of armed resistance against perceived sources of aggression. However, the texts do lend themselves to such interpretations in the hands of those who are aiming to fight a political struggle in which they have come to believe. Those who have viewed jihad in Pakistan as the result of economic marginalization and religious indoctrination have, therefore, been doubly wrong: it is not a sense of material deprivation, and thereby a heightened appreciation for other-worldly rewards, but a sense of courage and pride that the jihadists draw from the religious texts.

In addition to the incentives provided by the Islamic ideology to stand firm on certain causes, the other critical factor in sustaining commitment to jihad is the existence of morally supportive networks. What makes the initial idea of joining a jihadist group translate into action—becoming convinced that one wants to physically contribute to the struggle, identifying the platform to fight from, and staying undeterred when confronted with the harsh realities of jihad—is the ability to identify the right networks. Even in the case of the Red Mosque, the moral support that the girls received from being with each other was critical in sustaining the struggle despite losses. During my fieldwork, an activity day organized in the central court of the Jamia Hafsa, where a group of senior students entertained over 3,000 students with skits designed to ridicule the government and valorize the movement, demonstrated the role of group support in reinforcing one's commitment. The girls were dressed in men's attire mimicking prominent ministers, who had been appearing on TV talk shows to explain the government's position on the Red Mosque. The skits referred to specific interviews or comments by these ministers where they had recognized their inability to squash this movement. Many of the skits represented the ministers as being very fearful of the idea of actually facing the bamboo-stick holding students of Jamia Hafsa.

Thus I found that the factors moving individuals from being passive sympathizers to active jihadists are linked to the perceived injustices of the formal institutions and the absence of legitimate means to resist the perceived aggressor. This leads some to adopt nonstate means to secure justice. In this progression from feeling the need to react and actually reacting, where Islamic texts play an important role is in building psychological courage to stay committed to jihad at the times of weakness by providing for other-worldly rewards; the religious texts themselves are not the primary motive for joining the jihad. What this shows is that, though individuals often adjust their action to reduce the cost of ideological commitment, when the cause of ideological commitment is seriously threatened individuals can forego pursuit of material well-being in favor of ideal rewards.

The above findings are in line with results from a growing number of recent studies on the phenomenon of militant Islam. Tessler and Robbins's (2007) representative national surveys in Algeria and Jordan on popular basis of support for terrorism yield similar results. They show that religious orientation, judgments about Western culture, or economic circumstances do not account for variance in approval of terrorist acts against U.S.-based targets. Rather, approval of terrorism against the United States is likely more among men and women with negative judgments about their own government and about U.S. foreign policy. More important, in line with the argument developed in this chapter, they contend that the decision to support jihad results not from a sense of personal injustice but from the perception of who is responsible for the situations of the Muslims, "What can be concluded from this interpretation is that support for terrorism against the United States does not flow directly from discontent with personal or even societal circumstances but rather from perceptions about who or what is responsible for the status quo and that this is the case among younger persons in particular" (Tessler and Robbins 2007: 324).

Similarly, Krueger (2007) argues that education and income have no discernible impact on public support for terrorism. One reason, he argues, why greater income might not lead to lower support for suicide bombing is that wealthier individuals are more likely to be ideologically extreme and committed because they have more time to dedicate to ideological pursuits. Drawing an analogy with voting, he argues that just as we find that those who incur a high opportunity cost for voting—that is individuals who are better educated and have high-paying jobs actually tend to vote—so is the case with the terrorists. He argues that in case of voting, it is these people who care about influencing the outcome and consider themselves sufficiently well-informed to express their opinion, in the case of Islamic terrorism it is those who hold strong political views and are confident enough to impose their vision by violent means rather than the poor who become terrorists. My argument about the collective sense of injustice rather than individual economic deprivation being the primary motive for joining the jihad is also in line with Krueger's proposition, "It is possible that members of the elites become terrorists because they are outraged by the economic conditions of their fellow countrymen" (2007: 6).

Based on a survey in six predominately Muslim countries that have experienced suicide bombings—Indonesia, Jordan, Lebanon, Morocco, Pakistan, and Turkey—Shafiq and Sinno (2010) further support Krueger's (2007) argument. They show that those politically dissatisfied with domestic policies are more likely to approve of suicide bombings. Further, they show that educational attainment rather than income increases the likelihood of being politically dissatisfied. In addition, their comparative research highlights the complexity of the phenomenon by showing that effect of educational attainment and income on support for suicide bombings varies across countries and targets. They also show that respondents with primary education in Pakistan were more likely to be politically dissatisfied than those without primary education.

In addition, an edited volume on suicide missions which covers five different contexts including four secular contexts, notes similar outcomes (Gambetta 2006). The volume editor notes that the willingness to lay down one's life for a cause depends on the strength of one's conviction, and forced recruitment is not compatible with the degree of commitment and self-discipline required by suicide attackers. Other factors noted as being important in mobilizing suicide attackers included peer pressure and psychological pressure such as a feeling of guilt toward other pilots in case of the Japanese kamikaze and the clustering of Palestine suicide volunteers in a few towns to provide peer support. Additional factors were the desire to be well thought of by others; vanity; desire for fame; the search for glory; the desire to transcend death by living on in the grateful or admiring memory of others; and revenge, as in the case of Palestine and Chechnya. The study on Palestinian suicide bombers published in this volume also supports the findings of this chapter by showing that the income and the education of suicide bombers tended to be higher than that of the general population and that religion is a form of consolation or a bonus rather than a motivation for such missions. As one of the contributors notes: "Like the knowledge that one's relatives will be financially taken care of after one is dead, the belief in some kind of afterlife may attenuate the psychological costs of commitment…, rather than offering a positive motivation, the religious and financial expectation might have the disinhibitory effect of lifting some of the normative constraints against SMs (suicide missions)" (Elster 2006: 243).

## Whom to Join?

Given the well-acknowledged role of the intelligence agencies in recruiting fighters, an important question to ask about the decision-making processes of the jihadists is how they select a specific organization or platform. Some studies estimate the existence of over fifty-five jihadist organizations in Pakistan (Jaffrelot 2002), out of which ten were quite active at the time of my fieldwork. For the believer, selecting an organization to join presents the same dilemma as selecting a madrasa for donation but on a much-amplified scale. Whereas a giver has to trust his money with an 'alim, a jihadist has an even bigger challenge—that of trusting his life with the head of an organization. The consequences of wrong selection are dire, not only because of the fear of being exploited but, more important, because suicide is a punishable sin in Islam. What factors then make people choose one jihadist group over another? Interviews with jihadists reveal that, just as in the case of choosing a madrasa to make one's donation, there is constant questioning of the motives, caliber, and the method adopted by the leaders of a particular organization.

One of the most important factors in shaping the choice of an organization is each jihadist's individual networks. I found that prior to joining an organization most respondents went through an exploratory path, where information secured about these organizations through networking with other individuals was critical in coming to the final decision. One respondent explained:

> When you get inclined to go for jihad it is quite normal that you start seeking relevant literature on jihadist organizations. In fact, often you get inclined after reading such literature. In selecting an organization, the sectarian affiliation also matters. Because I belong to Ahl-i-Hadith school of thought, for me it was natural to be attracted by Lashkar-i-Taiba, which belongs to this school of thought. This enables me to better assess the theological legitimacy of the leader's justifications for jihad. This is, however, just one of the criteria. The most critical criteria are the history of the achievements of the organization and the reputation of its leader. If the leader is known to be involved in money matters, there are often suspicions about his intentions.

For madrasa students such information is easily available within the current student body and the alumni, but this information is quite readily available even for individuals outside the madrasas. Apart from friends and acquaintances already involved in such activities, the large variety of publications produced by Islamic groups, ranging from dailies, weeklies, and monthlies, are an important source of information for potential joiners.

In selection of an organization, the individual's sectarian affiliations also play some role: all the prominent jihadist organizations are categorized by the jihadists in line with the sectarian affiliations of its leader even if the organization itself is willing to recruit irrespective of the candidate's sectarian affiliation. For example,

Lashkar-i-Taiba was always identified as belonging to the Ahl-i-Hadith school of thought, Hizb-ul-Mujahidin was associated with Jamaat-i-Islami, and Jaisha-i-Mohammad was viewed to be one of the prominent jihadist groups inspired by the Deobandi school of thought. The question is this: If the primary motivation for jihad rests in political injustices, then why are the theological positions of these jihadist organizations important to their identity? For most jihadists, the answer is linked to the importance of being convinced that the fight is actually in pursuit of securing collective justice for the Muslims and is being fought on legitimate Islamic grounds.

All jihadists interviewed were very concerned with the validity of the method of jihad pursued by a group's leader. This, as the leader of Hizb-ul-Mujahidin explained, requires the leaders of these organizations to be sufficiently conversant with the theological texts on jihad in order to justify the selected method and the need for jihad in the given context. I found respondents had different levels of tolerance toward using violence: some were very clear that civilians should be targeted under no conditions; others justified such a practice on the grounds that U.S. attacks also affect the civilians. In general, most recognized the need to avoid extreme measures such as suicide missions. The dominant justification for adopting extreme measures such as suicide missions was that these were the only means to resist a financially and militarily much stronger enemy when states in the Muslim countries were failing to respond.

Most respondents were of the view, that if the United Nations could not act as a neutral platform, if the Pakistani government refused to address these issues because of privileges it wanted to secure from the United States—then as with the case of the Palestinians pitted against a sophisticatedly armed Israeli army—how could Muslims seek justice without gravitating to these Islamic groups. Even in the case of the Red Mosque, the extreme measure of physically staging a resistance against the state gradually gained legitimacy in the eyes of the students when in their view the peaceful methods of protest adopted by the 'ulama—such as issuance of a fatwa against military operations in the tribal belt; working through civil society organizations to stage protest rallies; and, filing petitions with government officials to produce the missing people—failed to have an impact. As noted by a jihadist who was not linked to the Red Mosque, "First in the tribal area and now after the Red Mosque operation, the *foj* [military] has become a term of abuse in Pakistan. Now the public is unprotected in our country and the armies of the enemy are protected."

Here it is important to note that this is by no means being argued to be the preferred response in Islamic theology or the dominant response within Muslim communities. The use of Islamic texts by these groups to justify jihad has been contested by Islamic scholars just as many Muslims share the perceived sense of political injustice faced by the Muslims in global political arena but do not approve of armed resistance as a logical or morally appropriate way forward. The emphasis here is only on identifying the major factors shaping the discourse and decisions of people to join the jihad. A comparative work looking at those Muslims who might share the injustice but do not join the jihad can be useful subject of investigation for a future study.

I found these concerns, regarding the validity of the method and the legitimacy of the jihad, were also visible in the discomfort felt by the leaders and members of the jihadist groups on the shifting of jihad from cross-border to within-border. A Muslim causing the death of another Muslim, which was the case when they were pitted against the Pakistani army, was an undesirable outcome—a concern reiterated by the leader of Hizb-ul-Mujahidin during the interview while Lashkar-i-Taiba as a policy does not fight against the state. In the words of a member of Lashkar-i-Taiba, "We are not active in the tribal belt, we are not fighting against the Pakistani army because we have a clear position that we won't fight the Pakistani army because Muslims should not fight each other. However, when the state becomes aggressive then it becomes difficult to make all the members of the group adhere to these policies." It is therefore not surprising that the militancy in the tribal belts has been led by local Pashtun leaders, for example Beitullah Mesud in 2007 and 2008, rather than the established jihadist organizations—though even Mesud in press statements referred to ongoing clashes with the Pakistani military as undesirable because "this strengthens the non-Muslims."

Finally, I found that in joining a jihadist organization, a potential fighter makes an assessment of the probability of the success of the organization's strategy—before risking their lives, most jihadists want some reassurance of chances of success of the strategy and the benefits of their contribution. As noted by one respondent, "a clearly losing battle strategy fails to retain people." The interviews, however, also show that what is considered to be a success strategy varies according to the individual's cognitive constraints and the context. This is where the mind-set, that when you cannot fight the enemy head-on then bring it down to the fool's level, becomes relevant. The strategy of attacking a few Western targets, which in turn have made many Muslim countries vulnerable to military attacks from the United States, might not appear very effective to most Muslims but for the jihadists it is an efficient choice because it puts a huge financial burden on the U.S. economy and creates a sense of insecurity in the Western world for not that high a cost for these groups. For them the strategy is therefore not irrational. The perception of following a strategy, which has chances of success, also played a critical role in sustaining the resistance at the Red Mosque.

During the group discussions and the skits presented on the activity day organized at a time when the resistance was at its peak, girls made repeated references to the numerous concessions that the movement's leaders had been able to win from the government since the launch of the resistance. These small successes were critical in sustaining the morale to carry on the fight. Thus, a shared perception of injustice, the morality of the method, and the effectiveness of the strategy, along with supporting networks, were critical factors in shaping each individual's decision to join a particular organization. Ostrom's (1990) position that institutional change is best understood as an incremental and self-transforming process is fully supported by the study of mobilization for jihad in Pakistan. Writing about institutional change in managing common pool resources, she noted "The investment in institutional change was not made in a single step. Rather, the process of institutional change in all basins involved many small steps that had low initial costs. Because the process was incremental and sequential and early successes were achieved, intermediate benefits from the initial investments were realized before anyone needed to make larger investments. Each institutional change transformed the structure of incentives within which future strategic decisions would be made" (Ostrom 1990: 137).

## The Becoming of Popular Jihad: The Sympathizers

So far I have analyzed the factors shaping the decision of those who join the jihadist organizations; based on interviews with the general public and an observation of the public response to the Red Mosque operation, I now explore the decision-making processes shaping mass public support for these Islamic groups. I found the factors enabling these groups to win popular support to be the same as in the case of the jihadists: the sense of political injustice, the moral and religious legitimacy of the method, and the chances of success of the strategy.

In informal discussions with respondents from different socioeconomic backgrounds I found that the individuals harboring sympathy for the resistance shared the same perception of injustice, as advocated by the Red Mosque 'ulama, regarding the policies of the war on terror being pursued within Pakistan. The significance of the perceived legitimacy of the cause in building popular support was also clear in the distinction these respondents drew between the jihadist and sectarian groups. The respondents explained sectarian violence as counterproductive and a sin because this resulted in the killing of fellow Muslims for following different interpretations of Islamic injunctions; they found jihad to be an honorable endeavor because here people gave up their lives for a cause. The fact that Osama bin Laden was a billionaire who left the comforts of this world to stage an ideological resistance was often quoted as an important factor shaping his popularity. One female respondent who defended jihadist groups commented, "After all why should Osama give up his comfortable life and come to live in the difficult conditions in Afghanistan if he was not genuinely committed to his stated objectives. He is a billionaire, had studied in Western universities, and could have led a comfortable life, but he did not. That shows certain character." I repeatedly saw people emphasize the role of ideological commitment of the leaders of the jihadist groups in mobilizing supporters. Said a supporter of the Red Mosque resistance: "We supported this resistance from the beginning but when the elder brother was caught escaping in the burqa, we all said that the younger brother must now resist until the end or the entire movement will become a joke. Having defended the resistance to others as ideologically motivated, the news of the elder brother escaping in the burqa was very embarrassing for us."

In these discussions with members of the general public who sympathized with the jihadist groups, similar emphasis was placed on the likely success of the strategy. Many respondents were of the view that they had initially supported Osama bin Laden because September 11 was a forceful way of bringing attention to the injustices meted out to the Muslims. These same respondents however questioned Osama bin Laden's loyalties when Al-Qaida withdrew from aggressive to defensive mode and the United States invaded Afghanistan and Iraq. In their view it was the United States, and not the Muslim world, that was proving to be the primary beneficiary of Al-Qaida's activities. It is in this sequence of reasoning that some Islamic clerics had come to view Osama as a CIA agent. Seen within their frame of reference, such conclusions do not necessarily appear to be a product of irrational beliefs as noted by Elster (2006); rather such accusations resulted from an ongoing evaluation of the benefits of the Al-Qaida's strategies for the Muslims. Similarly, the primary reason that the Red Mosque phenomenon did not win mass public sympathy until after the military operation, where the death of an 'alim and close to one hundred students created general resentment against the operation, was because even those who sympathized with the ideological position of the resistance did not see it as a viable strategy. As voiced by one sympathizer, "It was just not feasible for one madrasa to force the state to change a military government's policies."

During the period of the struggle, the ongoing debates in the media reflected constant public questioning of the motives of the 'ulama of the Red Mosque—some even accused them of being paid by the intelligence agencies to host this resistance in order to create the fear among Western countries that if they do not support General Musharraf then the country will fall to the radicals. It was only the conscious decision of the younger brother to fight to death rather than give in to the government's demands that eventually convinced the public of the movement's ideological underpinnings leading to widespread expression of public support after the operation. During the 2008 election campaign, the Red Mosque operation was an important electoral issue, and following the elections, members of the Musharraf government counted the Red Mosque operation as one of the important contributors to their embarrassing defeat.

On my follow-up visits to the Red Mosque in 2009 and 2010, I again spent time with Umme Hassan and Maulana Abdul Aziz, who by then had been released from police custody and had been allocated alternative land to build a new Jamia Hafsa. Maulana Abdul Aziz repeatedly emphasized Abdul Rasheed Ghazi's decision to die rather than compromise and the loss of his own son, Hassan, in the military operation as being instrumental in building the movement's legitimacy. The movement had retained many followers from the time of the resistance: I found many of the female students I had interviewed during the resistance in 2007 were now acting as teachers in the madrasa. By the summer of 2010, the Jamia had established over twenty-five branches across different cities on popular demand and the leadership was findings ways to respond to such demands from all over the country. Islamic bookstores were flooded with posters, books, and CDs with songs honoring the martyrs of the Red Mosque. Maulana Abdul Aziz noted, "They crushed one Jamia Hafsa but now there are calls from all corners of the country to open a hundred Jamia Hafsas. Their sacrifice removed all doubt from the public mind that we were motivated by anything else but the demand for justice." Thus, the commitment of a fighter to the stated cause is critical in giving a jihadist group popular appeal.

As for the morality of the method used to achieve the ideological ends, discussions with members of the public reveal that although it is an important criterion in determining popular support for a militant group, people's judgments on the morality of a method are quite flexible and context-specific. I found the same people who had argued against the use of force against the state, were less critical of a suicide attack on the military brigade that had carried out the Red Mosque operation, because it was seen to be a reaction to state aggression, which had resulted in the killing of innocent students. This tit-for-tat psyche was thus very important in legitimizing morally questionable acts associated with Islamic militancy in any context, be it the suicide attacks in Palestine, or the attacks in the United States. Thus, I found that once a conscious sense of grievance sets in and there is the recognition that one is pitted against a much stronger enemy, despite knowing that the resistance will not achieve the desired ends, the mere expression of resistance capable of causing suffering to the perceived aggressor acquires a certain degree of moral legitimacy among certain individuals especially if they are part of networks that actively work to heighten this sense of injustice.

Here it is important to pause for a moment and study the implications of the above discussion. If its essence is that the support for apparently irrational movements is actually based on very rational calculations, then am I proposing that all apparently violent forms of association, such as the Ku Klux Klan, have a logical appeal? The answer is negative. What I have argued here is that the actual scale of sympathy for a group or a cause is important in determining its rational appeal. This is best captured in the different levels of support enjoyed by jihadist and sectarian groups in Pakistan. I found most Muslims in Pakistan have a strong sense of sectarian affiliation, yet very few are willing to support sectarian violence because of the weak logical appeal of supporting such violence, which kills Muslims on both sides for differences in interpretation of religious precepts. Alternatively, jihadist groups are able to mobilize mass scale popular appeal due to their ability to convince segments of the population about their commitment to a just cause, namely preventing atrocities against Muslims.

## Overlap between Popular and Professional Jihad

In studying the motives and decision making of the jihadist groups, I have focused on those jihadists who actually put their lives at risk or sacrifice their material wealth to financially support these groups; however, it is also important to pay attention to the leaders of these groups. The motives of these leaders who exercise great power vis-à-vis the nation-states targeted by their groups, are not necessarily the same as those of jihadists who actually put their lives at risk in the field—an analytical distinction whose significance is also noted in Gambetta (2006). The leaders could be ideologically driven, but they could equally possibly be driven by very material incentives and could actually be working for different national or regional power, that is, they could be professionals making a business out of recruiting fighters. In the case of Pakistan, the active role of the state in creating and supporting the jihadist networks during the 1980s shows that, when a militant phenomenon acquires a great mass appeal, there is often an overlap between popular and professional jihad; the former represents the genuine public sentiments, and the latter is a calculated investment in that movement by the state or some formal organized group for some greater geopolitical or economic ends. Even if the state is not an active financier of militant groups, its sympathy is important for the working of these groups because, as noted by some respondents, even simple things like fund-raising from the general public becomes difficult for a banned organization.

According to the leader of Hizb-ul-Mujahidin, "Having official legitimacy for a platform makes it much easier to harness popular support. One needs to hold gatherings and give speeches to mobilize people and to mobilize funds. A banned organization has to organize all these activities undercover, which makes it very difficult." Thus, the relationship between the leaders of these militant organizations and the state is the result of many complex factors and cannot be fully understood without knowing the geopolitical stakes of that state, and equally important the personal interests of the ruling regimes, in supporting or checking such groups. During the time of my fieldwork, a dominant public perception was that General Musharraf actually backed the militant groups despite declaring himself an active member in the war on terror. The argument built was simple: General Musharraf's weak domestic legitimacy, which made the survival of his regime contingent on Western support, built a perverse incentive for him to support these groups. Later, the discovery of Osama bin Laden on Pakistani soil, close to the country's premier military academy, in the operation carried out by the U.S. Navy Seals, was to raise similar concerns about support for the militants within the Pakistani intelligence agencies.

## Conclusions

Based on the analysis of the motives and decision-making processes of the jihadists, I develop two important arguments. First, I argue that the pursuit of ideal rewards (even political ones) is not irrespective of the context. The jihadists do record a higher propensity for seeking ideal rewards but their decisions are not irrespective of the context. It is the context in which Muslims in many countries are pitted against forces that they cannot fight through the formal state channels that drives some of those, with a higher propensity to be drawn to political causes and who are often part of networks that actively work to harbor such sense of injustice, to join the jihad.

Second, I show that there is a need not just to better understand the working of ideal and material utility but also that actions that draw on more than one source of ideal utility demonstrate higher commitment. Thus, I found respondents were attracted to jihad because of a perceived sense of political injustice shared due to the collective Muslim identity but their religious faith helped sustain this willingness to sacrifice for an ideal end. Individuals are attracted to jihad because of political injustice but the actual will to overcome the desire to live and resist the material comforts required of a jihadist results in an internal struggle. It is in sustaining this inner struggle that I found that religious texts become important to jihad. By reassuring the potential jihadists that the outcomes of a struggle rests in God's hands, that this life is temporary, and that there is another life where they will be rewarded, religion enables them to overcome the psychological fears of taking on a powerful enemy besides helping the inner struggle to check the strong pull of material incentives and this-worldly pleasures.

Although important in sustaining jihad when purposely used to serve this end, Islamic texts do not inherently compel followers to stage armed resistance nor are they the primary source for motivating jihadists. After all, only a small fraction of the Muslims actually engages with jihadist organizations. Therefore, contexts where political causes can draw on religious sentiment are more likely to lead to the rise of strong radical groups. This highlights the need for taking the nature of rewards that humans seek seriously and studying the mechanisms guiding not only the interaction between material and ideal utility but also between different kinds of ideal rewards seriously. Research shows that normally higher material costs decrease pursuit of ideal utility (Frey 1994), however, in some cases such as jihad, the equation is reversed where ideal utility crowds out material utility. What determines these cut off points and the direction in which the utility will move thus requires serious academic analysis.

The implications of the above analysis for the study of institutions is that exclusionary institutional preference is not a result of the existing rules of the game or the strategies of the key actors representing that institution; rather, such a preference results from placement of that institution vis-à-vis other formal and informal institutions. Actors make choices not based on the incentives offered by one institution but on a mixture of incentives emerging from the prevalent social, economic, political, and religious institutions.

Through engaging with the fighters' decision-making process about whom to join and the basis of popular support for jihadist groups I have shown that the popular appeal for an informal institution depends either on the ideological appeal of what it stands for (in this case the justice of the cause) or the morality of the method and the success of the strategy. Further, I have shown that both are relative measures where the rationality of taking on a bigger enemy changes depending on the sense of persecution. Individuals can develop destructive preference when they are pushed to a point where they feel they have little to lose—in such a context they become willing to lose all if they feel that doing so will cause some harm to those limiting their choice set. The tit for tat psyche can also help raise acceptance of acts considered immoral in other circumstances; the sense of revenge can make people opt for extreme measures. Thus, what is a rational means to attain an end is contingent on understanding the context in which the decision was shaped; often what people choose is not their preferred option, but an optimal option under the given circumstances, with the result that at times preferences can shift irrespective of change in the budget set because individuals decide to take higher risk to reach their preferred option than to live by the second best option.

9

# INFORMAL INSTITUTIONS AND DEVELOPMENT

**The historic past into which the new tradition is inserted need not be lengthy, stretching back into the assumed mists of time . . . In short, they [invented traditions] are responses to novel situations which take the form of reference to old situations, or which establish their own past by quasi-obligatory repetition. It is the contrast between the constant change and innovation of the modern world and the attempt to structure at least some parts of social life within it as unchanging and invariant, that makes the "invention of tradition" so interesting for historians.**

—Eric Hobsbawm, *The Invention of Tradition* (1983: 2)

**What makes the 'ulama of the modern world worth studying is not merely that they have continued to lay claim to and self-consciously represent a millennium-old tradition of Islamic learning, however. Their larger claim on our attention lies in the ways in which they have mobilized this tradition to define issues of religious identity and authority in the public sphere and to articulate changing roles for themselves in contemporary Muslim politics. The 'ulama's tradition is not a mere inheritance from the past, even though they often argue that that is precisely what it is. It is a tradition that has had to be constantly imagined, reconstructed, argued over, defended, and modified.**

—Muhammad Qasim Zaman, *The Ulama in Contemporary Islam* (2002: 10)

In his seminal work on institutions and institutional change, North (1990) called for a further study of informal institutions. He noted that they were as important, if not more so, than formal institutions in shaping development outcomes, but remained little understood. Two decades later, an increasing number of publications verifies the importance of informal institutions in shaping social, economic, and political outcomes (Helmke and Steven 2004; Organization for Economic Cooperation and Development [OECD] 2007). However, an empirically grounded analysis identifying and explaining "the *mechanisms* through which informal institutions arise and are maintained" is still missing (Williamson 2000: 597). In this book I have sought to redress this gap. Drawing on empirical evidence on the workings of Islam, as represented through the choices and decisions of actors within the madrasas of Pakistan, I have helped us understand the working of informal institutions and have thus sought to demonstrate the strength of the NIE analytical framework (along with its limitations) in explaining a noneconomic institution. In the process, I have demonstrated the adjustments that need to be made to the core assumptions of the classical rational choice theory if this is, as argued by some of its proponents (Becker 1993; Coleman 1990), to act as a unifying framework across the social sciences. As I weave together the arguments from previous chapters, an appropriate entry point is to recall the three central puzzles regarding the behavior of the religious actor presented in the introductory chapter, raised by the armed resistance staged by the 'ulama and students at the Red Mosque in Islamabad.

First, why does a religious actor develop irrational preferences, which apparently limit his or her own well-being? The book has recounted many such instances, namely, the preference of the 'ulama of the Red Mosque for centuries-old Shari'a law over the present-day civil law designed to match the demands of modernity (chapter 8); the parental decision to send their children to a madrasa instead of secular schools or making them join the labor force (chapter 5); and many Muslim women's choice to abide by the Islamic code of conduct, which feminist thinking would suggest severely limits their well-being (chapter 6). Second, why would religious actors undertake flawed means-end calculations, for example the decision to engage in battles they are bound to lose based on religious belief? For instance, the Red Mosque 'ulama decided to take on the Pakistani state although it was clear that they had no means with which to do so. Arguably, the same perceived irrationality marks the decision of the Al-Qaida leaders to combat the United States, when they are unable to match its military strength. Third, what leads to a change in a given preference? For example, why did the 'ulama and students at the Red Mosque move from observing routine religious rituals to staging a radical resistance in the name of Islam? Why, from a position of leading the latest scientific inquiries in earlier centuries, has the Islam of today moved to being the center of attention for irrational acts of militancy? Situated within the NIE literature, these questions underline two central concerns: (1) why do rational individuals choose to restrict their choices in light of informal institutions, in this case, religious beliefs; and (2) why and how do informal institutions rise, stabilize, and change over time? This book concludes that the rationality of their individual choices becomes apparent when those choices are situated in their recent historic context.

## Religion and the Rational Actor

Behavior of a religious actor can be understood as rational when three assumptions within the classical rational choice theory are adjusted in response to the empirical evidence. First, the notion of utility must be disaggregated to account for both material and ideal utility, and to recognize that the latter comes at the cost of the former. Second, it must account for the historical and cultural specificity of preferences and acknowledge that preferences are formed under information and cognitive constraints—what Herbert Simon (1962) refers to as "bounded rationality." Third, it must acknowledge that preferences are dynamic and may change even without new additions to the existing choice set.

The Red Mosque students and the fifty jihadists I interviewed during the course of this research recorded a high disposition to fight for ideological causes; parents of madrasa-going children revealed a strong preference for gaining religious merit; and, many Muslim women find the Islamic way of life more appealing than Western feminism. All of these behaviors made me argue for the importance of recognizing the pursuit of ideal utility in shaping individual preferences. However, the data also helped me demonstrate that an appreciation for ideal utility is not developed completely irrespective of the context. Parents of madrasa students clearly valued religious rewards but at the same time the high levels of insecurity marking everyday life transactions, where weak formal state institutions have resulted in high information, enforcement, and monitoring costs, had an active role to play in developing an appreciation for the idea of God. This enabled transferring the stress of controlling the outcome of these transactions from oneself to a third party, namely God. Similarly, jihadists placed a higher preference on ideal rewards but such appreciation was not cultivated irrespective of the context. The presence of unresolved political tensions nurtured a sense of injustice that provided ideologically driven individuals the opportunity to pursue ideal rewards. Thus, though some individuals do have higher propensity for nurturing their ideal utility, an extreme preference for ideal rewards is grounded in the larger societal context.

Apart from this dynamic interplay between ideal and material utility, other factors influencing formation of a religious preference include cultural and historical influences as well as information limitations and cognitive constraints affecting individuals' interpretation of such information. However, in contrast to culturist or structuralist critiques of rational choice theory, which suggest people follow traditions out of habit, my research shows that often these historical influences exist for a rational reason, which outside observers may overlook because of an inability to relate to the historically defined value that people attribute to that particular good. Further, this research has shown that the tradition itself is often constantly changing in response to the action of the individuals at any given point in time. The importance of understanding that apparently irrational preferences can actually be very rational when studied in their context was best illustrated in the analysis of the rapid expansion of female madrasas in Pakistan since the 1980s. In a context where marriage remains the main prospect for the upward mobility of girls from middle-income families, as pursuit of higher education does not guarantee employment, the choice of parents and girls to exit the secular education system after matriculation or on receipt of a bachelor's degree to join a madrasa—which grooms girls to be good home-makers—no longer can be read as proof of individual subordination to traditional values. Rather it demonstrates the actor's strategic behavior to identify the most efficient outcome under the given circumstances.

The recognition that people in different contexts can attribute different weight to different goods in enhancing their utility, highlights the limitations of taking preferences as given—an area classical rational choice theory claims is beyond its scope. More important, it is critical for developing an understanding of means-end rationality (how best to secure desired goals), which is the primary concern of rational choice theory (Elster 1986; Gambetta 1987). As Elster (1986: 1) notes, "The theory of rational choice is a normative theory. It tells us what we ought to do in order to achieve our aims as well as possible. It does not tell us what our aims ought to be." The theory assumes that people are forward looking, and aim to strategize logically to meet their desired ends at the lowest possible cost. However, identification of the most efficient means to attain the desired ends is itself dependent on understanding the value and meaning individuals attribute to the given goods. Thus, the logic of using a madrasa education as a means to attain the end of female empowerment remains incomprehensible without understanding the context in which the failure of the formal institutions to generate opportunities within the formal economy leave marriage as the sole prospect for upward mobility for women from middle-class families.

The means-end calculations are further dictated by information limitations and cognitive constraints. The decision of the Red Mosque 'ulama to resort to an armed struggle against the state, despite lacking the means to do so, was based on their past interactions with the state. Having worked closely with the state intelligence agencies in supporting jihad in Afghanistan during the 1980s, the 'ulama miscalculated the state's reaction. Based on these prior experiences and close historic connections between the military and the religious establishment in Pakistan (Haqqani 2005), the 'ulama felt confident that the state would not match its verbal threats with severe military action. This confidence was reinforced when the state was reluctant to follow its ultimatums with any serious action in the first four months of the resistance.[1] The information drawn from their previous interactions thus had a bearing on their means-end calculations, which, to an outside observer unaware of these prior connections, were clearly irrational.

Finally, the shift in the preferences of the Red Mosque ʻulama from leading routine religious rituals to staging an armed resistance for the imposition of Shariʻa law exposes the limitations of the third important assumption of classical rational choice theory, namely that preferences are stable. Examination of the Red Mosque phenomenon revealed that often individuals adjust to second best-options in a context where the preferred option is unavailable; one important consequence of this is that such preferences remain unstable. Even if no additional options enter the choice set, individuals may shift to an alternative preference within the existing choice set because they decide it is worth risking an alternative option than to keep pursuing a second-best option. This is particularly the case when the given preference involves an inherent conflict between ideal and material utility. In such cases, factors affecting ideal utility—which may alter irrespective of material conditions rather than due to a relative change in prices—become a source of change.

The Red Mosque ʻulama wanted an imposition of Shariʻa law in Pakistan because they valued religion. However, knowing the impossibility of achieving that end, they carried on with routine religious functions, and balanced the pursuit of a religiously pious life with the comforts of material life. This equilibrium was, however, not their best choice, which in their view always rested on taking religion beyond the personal to the public sphere. After the state joined the Western war on terror, and the external environment within Pakistan became hostile toward those propagating Islam, these ʻulama felt a greater strain on their sense of moral and spiritual well-being. Their economic choices did not change but the growing strain on their sense of ideal well-being upset the balance they had configured between their material and ideal utility. The more the state pushed the war on terror strategies, the more the religiously inclined felt a compulsion to retaliate. The interviews with the ʻulama and students at the Red Mosque always suggested that shifting preferences reflected a cumulative process: "First the government started the military operation, which killed innocent people, then it started handing over individuals suspect of harboring jihadist sentiment toward the United States in return for financial compensation without giving these individuals a trial in their own country, now it has started to demolish mosques. If we don't protest now,

1. The state decision to launch the military operation was very sudden. After the operations there were many critiques that the state should have first taken intermediate steps such as cutting off the power supply and water connections, rather than following a long period of relative inaction with a full-blown military operation.

where will it stop? We don't say that every woman in Pakistan should wear burqa, but we do say that at least those who do should not be ridiculed."[2]

In most interviews in the Red Mosque, the cumulative process leading to the shift in the position of the 'ulama and the students was eventually linked to broader injustices of the society; once taking the decision to resist, they wanted to change the entire system. The Red Mosque episode thus presents a classic case to support Ostrom's (1990) emphasis on incremental and self-transforming nature of institutional change. Herein rests the explanation for why resistance was not confined to a specific demand, such as stopping the military operations in the tribal belt or reversing the policy to demolish mosques. Instead, the resistance aimed at the imposition of Shari'a because once the 'ulama and students had taken action, they wanted to aim for the optimal end, that is, to impose the law of God "because it held all equal"—a right they felt was denied under the existing legal system.

This analysis thus reveals that, preferences are not stable and especially that preferences, which affect both material and ideal utility, are constantly in flux[3]. Further, it shows that the crowding out of material and ideal utility is not a unidirectional process in which strong material incentives crowd out ideal utility, or what others have treated as other-regarding preferences (Alkire and Deneulin 2002; Frey 1994; Titmuss 1970). Rather, my data made me argue that people try to maximize both their ideal and their material utility, but if the source of ideal utility is seriously threatened, individuals can make extreme material sacrifices to preserve it despite the strong pull of material incentives in ordinary circumstances. The Red Mosque 'ulama moved from practicing daily religious rituals to staging an armed struggle because the government's countermilitancy measures cumulatively built such a strong sense of injustice among those with a strong appeal for Islam that the value they attached to their material well-being was seriously discounted. Because of these important consequences of the dynamic interaction between material and ideal utility, it is important to systematically study and model the interaction between individual cognitive reasoning and external factors. Only then it can become evident why this interaction at one point crowds out the pursuit of material rewards for attainment of ideal gains, and at another, crowds out ideological commitment for preservation of material interests. The evidence

2. Extract from an interview with Umme Hassan, the principal of Jamia Hafsa.

3. Even Gandhi (1958) notes this constant internal struggle between material temptations and the pursuit of nobler interests, and the strong pull of material passions and desires: "I have encountered many difficulties in trying to control passion as well as taste, and I cannot claim even now to have brought them under complete subjection" (29); "As we know that a man often succumbs to temptation, however, much he may resist it" (8); "Fasting, therefore, has a limited use, for a fasting man continues to be swayed by passion" (113–14).

that commitment to a given ideal strengthens if it addresses multiple sources of ideal utility, for example, the role of religious rewards in sustaining the ideologically motivated decision to fight jihad, in itself verifies the need to develop a more refined understanding of human needs because such an analysis can help identify the context where ideological commitment will become stronger.

## Informal Institutions and Development

How does disaggregating utility into ideal and material components, and acknowledging the context specificity and instability of preference, help us to understand the workings of informal institutions, such as religion, and their rise and impact on development outcomes? Analysis of madrasas shows that the last two adjustments are critical for understanding the rise of and changes in informal institutions, and recognition of the different human needs met by ideal and material rewards is an important factor accounting for distinct features of informal institutions, such as their ability to check free-riding in contexts where formal institutions fail, their greater stickiness and their ability to convert potential competition into deference for authority.

Study of the demand for madrasas made me argue that preference for the institution of religion arises because religion helps reduce the high levels of anxiety humans face when confronted with the temporary nature of life. In societies where state is unable to provide formal institutions to regulate and monitor socioeconomic and political transactions, the heightened sense of insecurity over everyday life activities (including the security of life itself) makes the idea of God even more relevant. Whether deciding on a match for one's daughter or to buy a car, formal mechanisms to assess the credentials of the other party in the bargain and to punish transgressors are absent or very weak. These transaction costs—which include the cost of information, negotiation, monitoring, coordination, and enforcement of contracts (Bardhan 1989)—make the idea of reliance on God through means such as Istikhara, which recognizes one's limited information gathering ability, and asks guidance from God, more appealing. Thus, informal institutions do at times emerge due to the genuine appeal of certain ideas, but their widespread use often depends on their practical appeal.

Further, the data led me to support the additional proposition within the NIE literature that informal institutions might not be optimal, but rather represent a second-best strategy for actors who would prefer but cannot achieve a formal institutional solution (North 1990). As seen in the case of female madrasas, though many students prioritize attainment of religious education over other options, for others it was a second-best option; some girls would have preferred to gain secular education and employment, while observing Islamic rules in personal life, if the formal institutions of the state and the market permitted that option. When secular education failed to equip these girls for positions within the economic market, religious education became a comparatively better option as it helped them to perform better the roles they are destined to play—homemakers. Thus, institutions arise because they help reduce uncertainties in human transaction. When formal institutions of the state fail to institutionalize mechanisms that can reduce this uncertainty, informal institutions become stronger. This highlights the need for understanding that choices are shaped by a combination of incentives offered by a matrix of numerous institutions.

As to why informal institutions change, this book notes the power of ideas as well as that of material incentives in provoking a shift in preference and institutional change. North (1990) views fundamental and persistence changes in relative prices, which lead parties in a transaction to perceive that they could be better off under alternative contractual and institutional arrangements, as the fundamental cause of institutional change (Bardhan 1989)—though he also argues for the power of ideas in initiating institutional change. Analysis of the choices of the working of the 'ulama of South Asia supports this view. The 'ulama in South Asian madrasas, constantly innovated, strategized, and adopted different approaches to study of religious texts to ensure their survival and that of their faith in the changing economic and political context.

This behavior, while showing the impact of relative price change on institutions, also reaffirms the close relationship between formal and informal institutions: a key source of informal institutional change is formal institutional change. To the extent that formal institutional change alters the costs and benefits of adhering to particular informal rules, it can serve as an important catalyst for informal institutional change (North 1990). However, my analysis also argues for acknowledging the power of ideas themselves in initiating institutional change more than is currently recognized in the NIE literature. When it came to changing core religious values, among the South Asian 'ulama, many resisted despite financial incentives and political persecution because of the genuine appeal of those ideas.

Institutional inertia or stability, on the other hand, occurs because of path dependence, whereby past choices condition those of the future (Pierson 2000); but here again, ideas and material interests both play a role. Deliberate (strategic) as well as genuine (historically embedded) causes of path dependence are evident. Institutional inertia can occur because of conviction in certain ideas, for example the refusal of leading 'ulama to accept state-led reforms despite financial incentives. It also exists because of skewed power dynamics in which the elite benefit from existing institutional arrangements even when they lead to socially inferior outcomes. This caused the failure of the madrasa reform programs in South Asia, as the secular elite's political interests were best protected through maintaining a cordial relationship with the religious elite; a balance that would have been disturbed if the reforms were pushed too seriously. In Bangladesh, both the secular and the religious elite could see the benefit from moving to a reformed threshold, which they did.

Path dependence can also result from a genuine inability, owing to serious resource constraints, to move to a higher equilibrium. This was visible in the inability of the 'ulama to lead a reform effort from within the madrasas to produce more competent graduates of theology, despite many 'ulama noting the need for this. Thus, as seen in the case of the evolution of the madrasas in South Asia, macro factors—such as displacement of Muslim political power in India by colonial rule—over time play a critical role in shifting institutions to a superior or inferior path. However, for analysis at any particular point in time, an understanding of the strategies of the influential players is most critical for predicting institutional change. Evolutionary forces might instigate the need for change but the exact direction it takes is determined by the ideological preferences as well as maximizing behavior of influential actors, namely the institutional elite, at that instance.

This recognition of the strategic behavior of the elite in ensuring institutional stability and change in turn highlights the importance of understanding the role of hierarchy that determines power and authority within informal institutions. Throughout this book, the gathered data led me to highlight the role of the elite in institutional evolution, change, and stability. I have also recorded that the power of the elite is not unchecked; they have to convince followers of their competence and moral commitment. This recognition checks the tendency to view informal institutions such as religion as inherently prone to abuse of power (Nussbaum 1999). The power of the elite within informal institutions such as religion is not as unchecked as is often assumed.

This leads us to the final question of importance: In what way do formal and informal institutions really differ? One way to understand the difference between the two is to assess the different basis of elite authority in formal and informal institutions. The elite within the former rely on statuary laws, financial incentives, and an organized bureaucracy to ensure public acceptance of and adherence to an institution. Alternatively, the elite of informal institutions rely on guidelines with no formal legal bearing, the provision of ideal incentives, and voluntary compliance. I have identified a correlation among the formality of the institution, the nature of the incentives it offers, and the mechanisms it develops to ensure adherence. Formal institutions develop a legal framework to check uncertainties. Two important aspects of this formality are the need to offer tangible, namely material incentives, to ensure adherence to the rules that ensure coordination among individual actors; and the need to deter noncompliance by offering equally tangible punishments, which have a direct material cost. Informal institutions also develop rules and guidelines to reduce uncertainty in the environment and to establish some level of predictability about the behavior of other actors. However, these institutions rely on nonmaterial incentives to induce followers to comply, and this compliance is often voluntary rather than based on a threat of material punishment. Here, the recognition of ideal utility in understanding the difference between formal and informal institutions becomes very clear.

The two basic characteristics of ideal utility are that it rests on a denial of material pleasures, because it exists in the realm of ideas and spirituality, and that it can be attained only by participation in activities that lead to the sacrifice of material goods and bodily comfort. The result is that although an informal institution might be deployed to ensure coordination of the delivery of a material good, it reduces the collective action dilemma arising from the unpredictability of other people's action primarily through drawing on the participants' need for ideal utility. Thus, Ostrom's (1990) villagers' ensured resolution of conflict over the use of water rights or grazing of pastures by recognizing that people do care about their reputation (inherent in the emphasis on small group size) just as micro-credit lenders in Bangladesh learned that women feel pressured to return their loans if refusal to do so will lead to them being socially ostracized (Haq 1997). Consequently, institutions that draw on ideal incentives are better at checking free-riding as attainment of these incentives rests on participation. The goal of a Marxist revolutionary to leave a legacy as a reformist can be achieved only through actual involvement in reformist movements, just as a feeling of closeness to God can be attained only by following religious precepts, which in most cases require material and bodily sacrifice (Bano forthcoming).

It is precisely this self-enforcing dimension of ideal rewards that helps address one of Bates's (1995: 44) critique of NIE theory:

> The "account" of the origins of institutions provided by new institutionalists also violates the assumption of rationality. By their reasoning, should people encounter a social dilemma, they would forge new institutions in an attempt to transcend it. But, given that the new institution would make all better off, the institution itself constitutes a public good. Would not the act of its provision also generate incentives to free ride? Any why, then, would individuals behaving rationally, be willing to pay the costs of its provision? Viewed in terms of the incentives faced by

> individuals, then, it appears that the demand for institutional solutions to collective dilemmas does not imply their supply; the solutions themselves pose collective dilemmas.

This book has shown that one way informal institutions circumvent this problem is by drawing on people's sense of ideal utility. The rewards offered by the institution are such that they can be acquired only through participation; free-riding is simply not an option.

Because informal institutions draw on ideal incentives, either exclusively or in addition to material incentives, they are therefore often more cost-effective. However, this also means that they take longer to evolve and are slower to change. Because they rely on ideal incentives, their benefits are not immediate. Consequently, the elite in informal institutions, such as the 'ulama, have to establish not just their efficiency but also a higher moral character to mobilize adherence. To build compliance to rules of an informal institution, the elite have to demonstrate first that they themselves have an appreciation for ideal rewards—an appreciation that most recognize is more difficult to develop than a taste for material goods. The reason self-sacrifice of the communist leaders was critical in mobilizing Vietnamese farmers to join in collective action (Popkin 1979) is the same as why simple living and the denial of material pursuits remains important to acquiring elite status among the 'ulama in South Asia: material sacrifice signals to followers that these leaders are driven by pursuit of ideal rewards, and therefore must genuinely believe in the ideals they espouse. Thus, the moral character of the 'ulama in building an elite stature is emphasized as they personally epitomize the appeal of the ideals and the rewards they promise.

It takes the informal elite longer to establish its authority than a state functionary or a corporate executive, as the former can demand allegiance through legal sanctions and the latter through financial incentives. However, once the hold is established, it tends to be strong because the elite in informal institutions can draw on individuals' sense of ideal as well as material well-being. For example, by offering to form credit-groups, the initiators of these groups provide not only a means to increase women's income, but also valuable friendship networks, self-recognition, and a sense of belonging (all of which are rewards of an ideal nature). Informal institutions' ability to supplement the pursuit of material goals with attainment of ideal rewards thus makes them more resilient because even when they stop serving a material objective they might still be valued because of the ideal rewards they provide. It also often makes them more cost efficient: by drawing on the individual need for ideal rewards, they reduce the financial incentives that would otherwise need to be offered to undertake the given activity thus offering financially more efficient alternatives. As Miller (1992) has shown firms that are able to include noneconomic incentives, and thereby move beyond complete reliance on financial incentives to motivate the employees, are more efficient than their competitors.

This ability to draw on ideal utility also explains the tendency of the elite within informal institutions to convert competition into deference, as was seen in case of the religious hierarchy of madrasas. This occurs because the elite of informal institutions embed their interactions with their followers not just in material transactions, but either exclusively or equally important in dense networks of relationships, whose presence in itself becomes a source of ideal utility. A better understanding of the rise of, and stability and change within informal institutions thus depends on a better understanding of the cognitive processes and external contexts that determine the interface between ideal and material utility; and equally on an understanding of how informal institutions affect socioeconomic and political outcomes. These analytical limitations have two important policy consequences. First, policies are overwhelmingly based on the introduction of economic incentives to provoke an action, neglecting the fact that people are also motivated by pursuit of ideal utility. Such policies fail to recognize, as Miller's (1992) study on impact of alternative managerial practices on efficiency of the firm shows, that the provision of supplementary nonmonetary incentives may produce better outcomes than that of material incentives alone. Second, by relying purely on financial incentives, many policies designed to enhance collective action may even reduce existing levels of participation because the material incentives introduced crowd out the ideal reasons that had previously shaped participation (Bano forthcoming; Frey 1994; Titmuss 1970).

Thus, while taking note of evolutionary forces that shape institutions, my analysis identifies strategic behavior as the main lever underlying institutional change. Evolutionary processes can create sudden opportunities or displace the existing ones, but it is the maximizing behavior of strategic actors within institutions in response to changing incentives or ideologies that shapes shifts within institutions. As a result, this book supports North's (1990) argument for drawing a distinction between institutions, which represent the rules of the game, and organizations, as players in the field. The maximizing behavior of actors within these organizations is the cause of both stability and institutional change, while the behavior of these actors is in turn influenced by incentives in the existing institutional environment. Thus, a study of the action of actors within dominant organizations in a given institutional framework enables the grounding of explanations about the macro-level working of institutions within micro-level accounts of individual actors. Focusing on the 'ulama within madrasas, which represent Islam (Hefner and Zaman 2007; Robinson 2001b), enabled an understanding of the working of Islam in South Asia, which at one time inspired rationalist scholarship and today is held responsible for irrational acts of violence. Having analyzed the factors leading to the rise and change within informal institutions and noting their unique characteristics when compared to formal institutions, it is now appropriate to move to an important concern of this book: the special importance of this approach to the study of informal institutions for developing societies.

## Informal Institutions and Development Studies

Since its introduction in 1975 (Williamson 1975), NIE and its analytical tools have made serious inroads not only in mainstream economics but also in other social sciences such as politics, economic sociology, and even anthropology (Menard and Shirley 2005). Though scattered across university departments, where its application is used to highlight the working of rural and industrial societies alike, the NIE literature across the disciplines bears an impressive cohesion. This is partly attributable to Douglass North's success, and that of Oliver Williamson, in building on work started by Coase (1937) to make theoretical predictions, many of which stand verified in very diverse empirical settings. To understand the full potential of NIE for the study of developing societies, it is useful to examine four distinct trends in the evolution of the NIE scholarship to date. Initial studies within NIE focused on developing a theory of rise of institutions that affect market behavior (Williamson 1975). The focus on the study of institutions and economic performance soon acquired a comparative dimension as the different economic paths followed across the North and South naturally lent themselves to such a comparison (North 1990; North and Thomas 1973).

The second noticeable trend within the NIE scholarship was a gradual accumulation of studied, which in the initial stage did not necessarily work explicitly in the NIE framework but contributed to the study of the role of informal institutions in checking market failures (Cohen 1981; Montiel 1993; Popkin 1979)—this to date remains a fertile area of research (OECD 2007). The third stage in the expansion of the NIE literature was marked by the accumulation of a significant number of studies deploying the NIE analytical tools to explain not only economic but also political and social outcomes in developed and developing societies. These studies lent support to the NIE claims that viewing institutions as a product of the conscious choices of individuals (albeit made under constraints) was equally important for the study of political and civic outcomes, such as the differing ability of nations to establish democracy (Collins 2002; Ellickson 1991). The recent expansion in the NIE literature, which arguably marks the fourth key trend, represents a steadily expanding call for the closer study of informal institutions, taking the analysis beyond recording their impact on socioeconomic and political development to understanding their way of operating (Greif 2006; Helmke and Levitsky 2004). However, actual contributions geared to systematically illuminate such processes are still rare (Greif 2006). This book represents one attempt to redress this gap, increasingly pinpointed within the literature; in doing so, it also helps reinforce existing claims that NIE is a particularly useful framework for the study of developing societies.

The old association between NIE and Development Economics is well known. First, Development Economics, which focuses on cases in which market failure and incomplete markets (often the result of substantive presence of transaction costs and information problems) are predominant, clearly provides hospitable territory for such institutional analysis (Bardhan 1989). Second, the NIE framework helps highlight economic significance of other forms of nonmarket institutions, which again are more prevalent in the developing world. For example, it has helped explain the establishment of credit-societies to pool savings when the capital markets are absent (Montiel 1993); and reliance on family ties and ethnic groups in absence of clear property rights (Cohen 1981). As argued by Bates (1995: 35) "Not only has the study of development thus played a seminal role in the creation of the new institutionalism. The new institutionalism now also plays—and will continue to play—a major role in the study of development."

My research has aimed to illuminate more forcefully the relevance of the NIE framework not just for Development Economics, which deals primarily with economic problems, but equally important for studying sociopolitical, religious, and/or ethnic problems within developing societies. In other words, it argues for realizing the potential contribution of the NIE framework for the broader field of development studies—which has undergone a dramatic expansion since the 1990s, and holds the promise of generating even more empirically rich and theoretical strong scholarship on developing societies in the future. The primary argument for the relevance of NIE in studying noneconomic problems in developing societies is the recognition that informal institutions become stronger in the absence of formal institutions—a common position within the NIE literature also validated in my research. This scenario is most frequently encountered in developing societies, which more often than not suffer from weak (or complete absence of) formal institutions (OECD 2007). The significance of understanding the working of informal institutions for development theory and practice was captured during a 2006 OECD conference held on this subject; participants, including development academics and experts from leading development agencies, not only noted the widespread prevalence of informal institutions in developing societies, and the opportunities and challenges they present for implementing development programs in these societies, but also cited their limited understanding of the working of these institutions. It is for filling this gap that NIE currently holds most potential.

Often development interventions designed for developing countries bear consequences for existing informal institutional arrangements—thus prompting the dilemma of who ought to assess the legitimacy of these institutions, and once the decision has been taken about their legitimacy or lack thereof, how to devise the best reform plans. Thus, if informal, clan-based networks dominate political life in Central Asian countries, thereby undermining the formal legal and electoral framework, should development programs attempt to break these networks? In Southeast Asian countries, if informal, personal relations between big business and government have been instrumental for growth, should development projects be designed to further strengthen them? If, in the Middle East and North Africa, there are restraints on the ability of Muslim women to participate in social and economic life, should development agencies support feminist NGOs to introduce new conceptions of gender-equality in these societies? Answers to these questions are problematic as they require making a judgment with regard to the efficiency of existing informal institutions, then identifying the right incentives to make the actors supporting these institutions change their behavior. Getting the answers to these questions right, as the failure of many existing development programs to reform or strengthen informal institutions shows, requires better research tools than those that are normally deployed.

In this book I have shown that attempts to reform existing informal institutions without understanding their logic not only fail to achieve reform, but they can end up having the opposite effect. An example of the former rests in the Pakistani state's inability to mobilize madrasas to accept its reforms despite offering financial incentives provided through a U.S.-assisted program. An example of the latter is evident in the increased militancy in Pakistan since the imposition of the strategies of the war on terror. Madrasa reform programs across India, Pakistan, and Bangladesh, despite attaining different levels of acceptance among the 'ulama, have failed to displace the power of orthodox 'ulama and madrasas. This is because of the reformers' faulty premise—government and development agencies included—that the choice to pursue a madrasa education is a response only to economic poverty and has no intrinsic value of its own (Nelson 2006). Consequently, reform attempts have been geared toward secularizing the madrasas rather than producing more learned 'ulama capable of reinterpreting the text. The exercise fails to replace the hold of the traditional 'ulama because the reforms fail to provide superior alternatives to meet public need for religious scholars. Likewise, the attempt to check militancy through excessive reliance on punitive measures instead of understanding the incentives that make young Muslims gravitate toward jihad has ended up breeding more violence, rather than curtailing it. Since the imposition of the war on terror policies in Pakistan, militancy has been on the rise and militant groups have resorted to ever more radical means (i.e., suicide bombing) to record their protest.

In addition, there are numerous examples in which development interventions designed to support exiting informal institutions, such as voluntary associations and civil society (Henderson 2002) can have a reverse impact due to the introduction of financial incentives without understanding their local logic. Development aid channeled through Pakistani NGOs in a bid to strengthen civil society was shown to have a reverse impact in which organizations that once thrived on a large local membership base, today have no members (Bano forthcoming). The primary reason identified for this shift was that development agencies attributed to culture the local practice, which required NGO leaders to demonstrate materially sacrificing behavior, and instead provided these leaders with comfortable salaries and posh offices to motivate them to work better. However, they failed to understand that for the public, self-sacrifice signified the commitment of NGO leaders to a cause in a context in which a weak state apparatus and corruption within formal institutions make receipts and paper-based accountability mechanisms irrelevant (Bano forthcoming). In such a context where receipts can be fudged and reports can be manipulated, material-sacrifice on the part of the NGO leaders becomes the most economical and credible mechanism for monitoring their commitment. Rather than strengthening civil society, development aid thus becomes a serious hindrance to the mobilization of collective action. By providing analytical tools to shed light on these types of consequences of existing development interventions, the NIE framework is extremely relevant to the study of social institutions in developing societies.

By starting with the assumption that individuals work toward goals that increase their utility, NIE has the potential to rid the field of development studies from crude culturist explanations that view means-end rationality as a social norm specific to modern Western societies. Such theories, Elster (1986) notes, have argued that in societies that attach less importance to instrumental efficacy actions are valued for themselves, not because of the outcomes they produce. Though apparently more respectful of local practices, as opposed to development recipes based on preferences of Western logic, such culturist accounts lead to equally detrimental consequences because they deny the societies within developing countries the power of logical reasoning (e.g., as seen in the impact of aid on NGO's ability to mobilize collective action in Pakistan). At the same time, by recognizing that individuals make choices under constraints, which are culturally and historically embedded, NIE rids development studies of equally crude economic models shaped entirely by material incentives and Western-centric cultural preferences, which fail to acknowledge that different societies can aspire for different but equally compelling conceptions of the good life.

The strength of the NIE perspective is that it develops an appreciation that, if these informal institutions exist, they do so because they either still serve a social need, which is not necessarily obvious to the outsider; because they are not the first choice but are the best choice under the circumstances; or, because they preserve the interests of the elite. North's (1990) approach to NIE does not judge whether existing institutions are optimal for society. However, it does note that they serve some purpose, for at least a particular group, and that as the product of the action of maximizing agents, they bear a certain logic. Development interventions aimed at either strengthening or replacing existing informal institutions should therefore not assume them to be the result of elite interest. Rather, it is important to understand whether the apparently archaic institution is serving some public purpose and, if it is not efficient, then to analyze the factors making individuals choose this suboptimal outcome. Such an approach is inherently better geared toward checking value-laden assessments of the efficiency of informal institutions. A researcher that starts with the intent to discover the logic that makes many Muslim women pursue apparently repressive Islamic values, while staying conscious of the power structures that could be influencing their choices, has a much higher probability of identifying the incentives that can change the behavior of these women than a researcher who starts with the assumption that ideas are valued primarily for emotive reasons and are perpetuated by vested interests of the elite. As has been established in the book, elite power even within informal institutions is not completely free from checks.

Thus, development initiatives need to understand the practical as well as the ideal appeal of existing informal institutions if any reforms attempting either to further strengthen such institutions (as in the case of the NGOs) or to replace them (as in the case of madrasa reform programs) are to be successful (Bano 2008b). It is also important to note that because development interventions are designed to induce material incentives, they often undermine the working of informal institutions, which normally rely on nonmaterial incentives (Bano forthcoming). This need to understand the rationality of the local institutions, especially in a context where those designing the interventions are foreign experts unable to relate naturally to local factors shaping people's preferences and their chosen means to attain them, brings to the forefront the methodological challenges of undertaking such research.

## Discovering the Local Logic: Methodological Concerns

Rational choice theory has long been criticized for being a product of armchair theorizing, in which theorists, armed with the assumptions of rationality, identify optimal outcomes in different theoretical puzzles (Green and Shapiro 1994). The hypotheses generated through such accounts fail to take into account how context and history affect people's preferences and their means-end calculations. As a result, a clamor of voices increasingly demands the empirical testing of rational choice hypotheses and their underlying assumptions in different contexts. Even when empirical studies have been conducted, they have been critiqued for being more eager to vindicate one universalist model or another, rather than to explain the actual outcomes (Green and Shapiro 1994). These critics argue that striving to explain observed empirical realities is preferable to fashioning theories according to the dictates of neatness. I have argued that including the voices of those whose actions are being studied is critical to discovering the rationality of informal institutions.

Although NIE has adjusted core assumptions of rational choice theory, it has been more accommodating of the latter's methodological preferences. Studies within the NIE framework, like those within rational choice theory, show little appreciation for qualitative data, especially interviews—a methodological tool that gives weight to subject's own interpretations. In addition to drawing on historical analysis—in which there is admittedly constant innovation, for instances Greif's (2006) move toward developing a case study approach to undertake a systematic analysis of institutions and examine their links with economic outcomes—NIE applications remain heavily tilted in favor of quantitative approaches,[4] including mathematical modeling and economic modeling, especially those carried out through game theory. Admittedly, these modeling exercises have a remarkable explanatory power: the former allows for the systematic checking of logical consistency and tracking of chains of cause and consequence, while the latter helps explore the rationale behind stylized facts, once they are identified. But, these studies, especially those based on economic modeling, draw on data from standardized questionnaires and surveys that confine the possible responses to a question within the frame of reference of the researcher. This leads to a process of "post-hoc theory" generation (Green and Shapiro 1994), in which correlations derived through quantitative research instruments are interpreted in terms of the importance the researcher attributes to those values rather than the value they have for the subjects under study. As seen in the case of the demand for madrasas, it is very easy to interpret survey results showing a high presence of students from low middle-income families as a consequence of economic deprivation; it is only through engaging with the voices of those making these choices and observing their actions that a researcher can appreciate the relative weight of genuine preferences for religious education

4. For a detailed discussion on the relative strengths and limitations of these methods, see Brousseau and Glachant (2008).

and economic considerations in shaping the actors' actions, which in turn affects future predictions about behavior.

Economists' concerns about the subjective nature of interview data are valid, as are their concerns about the generalizability of findings from studies relying on few interviews. However, it is equally true that large-scale surveys designed without understanding of the local value people attribute to various variables will always run the risk of omitting factors that are critical in shaping choices in a specific context. If institutions result from conscious action on the part of rational individuals, then a real appreciation of the role of these institutions requires giving some weight to individual's own reasoning about the existence and working of a given institution. Such an exercise requires in-depth engagement with the actual subjects of the study and reliance on interviews and observations. This does not imply doing away with quantitative research techniques—in fact, for certain questions such as processes shaping the interplay between ideal and material utility, the modeling of genetic and cultural evolution holds more promise than qualitative studies. However, it does imply recognizing that quantitative techniques are more appropriate for addressing certain questions than others, and in recognizing that sometimes they are better developed after the local logic underlying certain actions has been identified through qualitative research.

Only a judicious methodological mix can help development researchers appreciate the significance of an important conclusion that Bates's (1990: 34) reached: "Behavior that has been interpreted to be the result of tradition, passed on by socialization and learning, can instead be interpreted to be the result of choice, albeit choice made under constraints. Pastoralists do not resist modernization because their culture imposes constraints on them, they resist modernization because they choose to do so." NIE, by providing the analytical tools to discover this local logic, prevents the development researcher from falling into two serious pitfalls dominant in current practice of development: the tendency to deny poor communities the ability to reason; and the failure to recognize that societies can support alternative visions of development, which might run counter to Western preferences, but can be based on equally compelling moral principles.

## Appendix

# RESEARCH METHODOLOGY

This book does not present an ethnography of a single Pakistani madrasa, instead it is an ethnography of the madrasa network in the country. Four distinct research methods—in-depth interviews with relevant actors, group discussions, field-observations, and a self-administered survey with students, teachers, and heads of the madrasas—helped examine the phenomenon. Fieldwork in 110 madrasas selected through purpose sampling across eight districts of Pakistan helped cover its diversity. Primarily a qualitative study, the research methodology adopted allowed for constant re-evaluation of research techniques, during the eighteen-month field-work, in response to the findings in the field. Interviews, group discussions, and observations constituted the primary source of empirical data. A survey drawing on self-administered questionnaires to be filled by the 'ulama, teachers, and students in the selected madrasas helped investigate whether the diversity of the phenomenon was reflective of the socioeconomic variations in the Pakistani society. Research tools designed to gather data specific to a particular chapter are footnoted in the relevant chapter. This appendix outlines the overall research methodology.

Since the book set out to understand the madrasa network in Pakistan, there were two central methodological concerns: to identify the diversity of madrasas and to gain access to madrasas from each identified category. This required establishing contact with the five state-recognized madrasa regulatory bodies (wafaqs)—four belonging to the Sunni school of thought and one to the Shia—at the very start of the fieldwork. These state-recognized madrasa boards regulate the content of education taught in the madrasas belonging to their school of thought.

The first stage of the fieldwork (two months) was thus devoted to cultivating links with the senior leadership across the five wafaqs. Two rounds of visits were made to headquarters of each of the five wafaqs—the Wafaq-ul-Madaris Al-Arabia (Multan), Tanzeem-ul-Madaris Ahl-i-Sunna-wal Jamaat (Lahore), Rabata-ul-Madaris Al-Islamia (Lahore), Wafaq-ul-Madaris Al-Shia (Lahore), Wafaq-ul-Madaris Al-Salafia (Faisalabad). During these visits interviews were conducted with senior officials about the working of the wafaqs, how madrasas associate with the wafaqs, and how the five wafaqs and their associated madrasas engage with each other.

The wafaqs are also the main source of data on number of madrasas belonging to a particular school of thought in Pakistan. Wafaq membership is voluntary and consequently the unregistered madrasas are not included in the wafaq data. However, because only the wafaqs (and not the individual madrasas) have the authority to issue state-recognized madrasa degree certificates, all madrasas teaching higher levels of Islamic subjects inevitably end up registering. The Government of Pakistan also draws on the wafaq data to develop official estimates of the number of total madrasas in Pakistan and their student enrolment (GoP 2006). The data held with the five wafaqs thus became the primarily source of information to select the field sites and the madrasas at each site.

## Criteria for Selecting the Field Sites

*Geographical diversity:* Given the strong ethnic and cultural variations represented across the four provinces of Pakistan, to capture the diversity of madrasa system the sample was developed to ensure representation of all four provinces. The tribal belt of Pakistan and other federally administrated areas were not included due to their comparatively small population size. The tribal belt in particular had to be excluded due to difficulty of access.

*Concentrated areas:* The study aimed to cover areas that had a concentration of madrasas from across the five wafaqs. This allowed for covering the within-wafaq and inter-wafaq diversity among madrasas.

*Rural-urban divide:* The research aimed to ensure representation of madrasas both from urban and rural areas to compare the working of madrasas in the two settings.

## Criteria for Selecting the Madrasas

*Sectarian representation:* It was clear from the outset that since the five wafaqs represent five different schools of Islamic thought prevalent in Pakistan, it is important to ensure coverage of madrasas from all five sects.

*Scale:* During individual interviews with senior officials of the wafaqs and analysis of the madrasa registration data, it became clear that the madrasa system represents an education hierarchy: primary, secondary, senior secondary, bachelor, and master's level. A study attempting to understand the madrasa network in Pakistan thus had to ensure representation of this diversity within the madrasa hierarchy.

*Male/Female (M/F) representation:* Initial discussions and review of the madrasa registration data also highlighted the changing nature of madrasa landscape: on the average between 20 to 25 percent of the madrasa student population in each wafaq, is female (see table 6.1). It was therefore thought important to also include some female madrasas in the sample.

## Selection of Field Sites

An examination of the madrasa registration data maintained by the five wafaqs made it clear that they vary greatly in terms of total number and geographical distribution (see table 4.1). Not surprisingly, given the high population ratio of Punjab (60 percent), all wafaqs have the highest number of madrasas in this province. In other three provinces, only the Deobandi wafaq has a consistently high presence; the other four have specific pockets of concentration. For example, Jamaat-i-Islami has a strong presence in Khyber Pakhtunkhwa but has only a few madrasas in Balochistan; Ahl-i-Hadith similarly had some representation in Sindh but marginal presence in Khyber Pakhtunkhwa and Balochistan. Despite these provincial variations, all five wafaqs recorded the highest concentration of madrasas (barring few exceptions) in the capital of a given province. This fact greatly assisted with the selection of field sites.

The district level is the lowest administrative unit of governance in Pakistan for which the five wafaq maintained the data. The districts are second-order administrative divisions in Pakistan and since the 2001 Local Government Ordinance form the top tier of a three-tier system of local government. There are two lower tiers of governance below the district level: Tehsil and Union Councils. I chose to focus on the district level because most districts comprise both urban and rural areas. Focusing on the district level thus allowed for covering the rural-urban variations. At the same time, the size of a district made it logistically viable to cover the diversity.

Using this data, eight districts were identified for fieldwork (table A1). Two key criteria for this selection were high presence of madrasas and coverage of interprovincial differences. Four provincial capitals—Lahore, Karachi, Peshawar, Balochistan (see map 4.1)—recorded the maximum number of madrasas

**TABLE A1.** Number of madrasas per wafaq per district

| NO. | PROVINCE | DISTRICTS | AHL-I-HADITH | BARELVI | DEOBANDI | JAMAAT-I-ISLAMI | AHL-I-SHIA |
|---|---|---|---|---|---|---|---|
| 1 | Federal Capital | Islamabad | 2 | 60 | 107 | 14 | 7 |
| 2 | Balochistan | Quetta | 1 | 20 | 144 | 4 | 6 |
| 3 | Khyber Pakhtunkhwa | Peshawar | 7 | 22 | 90 | 17 | 4 |
| 4 | Khyber Pakhtunkhwa | Swabi | | 2 | 54 | 3 | |
| 5 | Punjab | Lahore | 25 | 306 | 220 | 15 | 12 |
| 6 | Punjab | Multan | 8 | 126 | 291 | 4 | 7 |
| 7 | Punjab | Rawalpindi | 4 | 93 | 255 | 13 | 3 |
| 8 | Sindh | Karachi | 25 | 328 | 1,084 | 103 | 9 |

*Source:* Based on data maintained by the five wafaqs at the time of my fieldwork (2008).

in a given wafaq[1] as compared to other cities in that province. In addition, Islamabad (the federal capital) and Rawalpindi (its twin city, also an important base for students traveling from Khyber Pakhtunkhwa), which are politically significant districts, recorded high representation of madrasas. These six districts covered dominant geographical and related ethnic and cultural diversity in Pakistan. However, I added two more districts to the list because they showed an exceptionally high concentration of madrasas. The district of Multan was selected to represent Southern Punjab, while Swabi district, with over 81 percent of the population living in rural areas, was selected to represent rural Khyber Pakhtunkhwa.

## Selection of Madrasas: Sect, Gender, Scale, and Rural and Urban Divide

Across these eight districts, a total of 110 madrasas were covered. These madrasas were selected based on purposive sampling technique to represent the four selection

1. There were some exceptions. In Punjab, for example, according to the data provided by the Deobandi wafaq, there is a higher number of madrasas in Multan (291) and in a few other districts such as Muzaffargarh (260) than Lahore (220), the provincial capital. However, no other wafaq had a high presence in these two districts, while they all had a visible presence in Lahore. This does raise a legitimate question: Why does a particular geographical location become an exclusive stronghold of one sect? A study aiming to understand the working of madrasa network in Pakistan, however, had to focus on those districts in a given province that showed highest presence of madrasas from all five wafaqs. The puzzle as to why some locations become stronghold of a specific sect is not entirely ignored. Rather, it is addressed at a provincial level by attempting to find answers for the exclusive domination of Deoband school of thought in Balochistan and varying strength of different wafaqs in different provinces (chapter 4).

criteria discussed above: representation of five wafaqs partially represented their ratio in the total madrasa population—Deobandi (30 M, 10 F), Barelvi (18 M, 6 F), Jamaat-i-Islami (12 M, 6 F), Ahl-i-Hadith (10 M, 4 F), and Ahl-i-Shia (10 M, 4 F); representation of different levels of madrasa hierarchy (table A3); gender representation (80 M: 30 F); and, urban/rural distribution (85 urban; 25 rural).

## Scale and Representation of Wafaqs

The proportional representation of the five sects was ensured largely through selecting the madrasas in proportion to the number of madrasas belonging to a wafaq in the given district. However, given the much smaller size of Ahl-i-Hadith and Ahl-i-Shia wafaqs, more madrasas were included than needed under proportional representation to ensure adequate understanding of their working. Thus, if in a district all five wafaqs had a very prominent presence (such as Lahore and Karachi) then higher number of madrasas was selected from each wafaq. Alternatively, in districts that showed very heavy representation of one wafaq and very small number of madrasas from others (such as in Quetta), only the large madrasas were covered from the wafaqs with lower presence.

## Representation of Different Levels

Discussions within the wafaqs helped identify four distinct levels of education to categorize the madrasas (see table 4.2). It was thought best to focus on Levels 1, 2, and 4. Level 1 and Level 4 represented two extreme ends of the madrasa system and helped study the differences in profile and aspirations of those who just come for Hifz (Level 1) and those who opt to complete the highest level of theological study, Daura-i-Hadith (Level 4). Because all madrasas offering Level 4 also normally cover all the lower levels including Level 1, the madrasas included in Level 1 are those that offer only primary level education. The justification for a focus on Level 2 as opposed to Level 3 was that the data show that after the madrasas focusing purely on Level 1 are taken out of the pool, the next main difference in the number of madrasas and students rests between Level 2 and Level 4.

It is at Level 2 that the madrasa has to demonstrate a certain level of teaching capabilities, library facilities, and other resources to establish that it can cross the senior secondary stage and can pursue teaching of higher religious texts. Data suggest that once a madrasa has achieved post-secondary level, its leadership tends to want to take it all the way to Level 4.[2] Only a few madrasas within Level 4

2. Although madrasa hierarchy represents a pyramid structure, the distribution of madrasas across Levels 2, 3, and 4 gets complicated. For instance, Rabata-ul-Madaris data show that Level 3

become capable of offering takhassus (specialization) and these become part of the elite madrasas (the most prestigious madrasas within a wafaq). Even the student data showed main variation at Level 2 and Level 4. It appears that it is at Level 2 that students need to decide whether or not they are interested in higher education. Once they decide to opt for Level 3, the preference is to go all the way to Level 4.

Initially, an attempt was made to cover all three educational levels for each of the five wafaqs in each district. However, the actual number of madrasas selected from each wafaq was based proportionally to the presence of that wafaq in a given district. Thus, if in a district all five wafaqs had a very prominent presence (e.g., Lahore and Karachi) then two to three madrasas were selected from each wafaq. On the other hand, in districts, which showed very heavy representation of one wafaq and very small number for madrasas from others (e.g., Quetta), only the most influential madrasas were covered from the wafaqs with lower presence.

In practice this implied that Level 4 madrasas had the highest concentration in the sample (65, including 18 female madrasa); Level 2 madrasas had the next highest representation (30, including 8 female madrasas); and Level 1 had the lowest representation (15, including 4 female madrasas). The focus on Level 4 and the elite madrasas is justified on the grounds that the ethnographic fieldwork and data repeatedly highlighted the role of religious leadership from these elite madrasas in the shaping of the madrasa hierarchy and influencing the public interpretation of Islam in Pakistan. Further, the fieldwork in the first two districts highlighted that the Shia wafaq unlike the Sunni wafaqs placed very little emphasis on hifz process, with the result that Level 1 madrasas within the Wafaq-ul-Madaris Al-Shia are rare. The Jamaat-i-Islami madrasas, because of being established under a more planned system of the Jamaat, similarly also had fewer Level 1 madrasas as compared to the other three Sunni wafaqs, as most madrasas were from the beginning planned to include theological subjects at least to Level 2. Thus, in studying these wafaqs, Level 1 category was not that relevant.

In selecting Level 4 madrasas, the idea was to cover the most prestigious madrasas from a given wafaq in that district. This was determined by the reputation of the head of that madrasa within the madrasa network (publications, overseas training, etc.) and the representation of the madrasa leadership on influential government committees. One of the core criteria used in the final selection was to prioritize those that offered facilities for Takhassus as within the religious community this was viewed to be the ultimate barometer of the elite credentials of a madrasa.

---

(bachelors) has fewer madrasas than Level 4. This shows that once a madrasa crosses the post-secondary stage it attempts to go all the way to master's level.

In selecting Level 2 madrasas, a deliberate effort was made to make this category more random as opposed to conscious identification of the elite madrasas within Level 4. Names of madrasas were randomly identified from the directories provided by the wafaqs and their leadership approached for participation in the study.

In selecting madrasas from Level 1, an attempt was made to select them randomly. Because many Level 1 madrasas are not even registered with the wafaqs—they do not always award degrees at the end of the hifz program and thus have weaker incentives to register—an attempt was made to randomly select a few from the madrasa directories and also to visit any Level 1 madrasa in the vicinity of a bigger madrasa being visited. Not surprisingly, access within smaller madrasas was much easier than bigger madrasas.

## Rural/Urban Representation

Close to 67 percent of the Pakistani population lives in rural areas. At the outset, this research aimed to ensure equal representation of madrasas from rural and urban areas. However, interviews with the wafaq officials and the review of the madrasa registration data revealed that it was rare to have Level 2 madrasas, and even more exceptional to have Level 4 madrasas in rural areas. In fact, one of the research findings is that a proper madrasa—a place of higher Islamic learning as opposed to a place for teaching Quranic recitation and memorization—is an urban phenomenon (see chapter 4). To understand the madrasa hierarchy it was thus important to cover the complexity of the urban madrasas. As a result, only twenty-five madrasas included in the survey were from rural area.

## Male/Female Representation

The female madrasas represent between 20 and 25 percent of the total madrasa population across the five wafaqs (table 6.1). The sample was made to reflect this ratio. Out of the 110 madrasas covered, thirty were female. The female madrasas unlike the male madrasas focus on teaching a four-year condensed course on Islamic theology instead of emphasizing memorization of the Quran or pursuing master's level degree (see chapter 6). They thus do not reflect the four-tier educational hierarchy identified for male madrasas. This facilitated the selection process. I placed emphasis on covering some of the most prominent (in terms of number and prestige) female madrasas from each school of thought in a given district: similar to the male madrasas, the elite female madrasas seemed most influential in shaping the discourse. In addition, a few smaller scale female madrasas were also included to see if there were major differences in the

**TABLE A2.** Number of selected madrasas per district

| NO. | PROVINCE | DISTRICTS | AHL-I-HADITH[1] | BARELVI | DEOBANDI | JAMAAT-I-ISLAMI | AHL-I-SHIA |
|---|---|---|---|---|---|---|---|
| 1 | Federal Capital | Islamabad | 1+ 1F | 2+ 1F | 3 + 1F | 1 +1F | 2 + 1F |
| 2 | Balochistan | Quetta | | 2 | 3 + 1F | 1F | 1 +1F |
| 3 | Khyber Pakhtunkhwa | Peshawar | 1 | 2 | 4 + 1F | 2 + 1F | 1 |
| 4 | Khyber Pakhtunkhwa | Swabi | | | 3+ 1F | 1 | |
| 5 | Punjab | Lahore | 1+1F | 3+ 1F | 5+1F | 2+1F | 1+1F |
| 6 | Punjab | Multan | 2+1F | 3 + 1F | 3+ 2F | 1+ 1F | 2+ 1F |
| 7 | Punjab | Rawalpindi | 2+1F | 3 + 2F | 3+ 2F | 2 | 1 |
| 8 | Sindh | Karachi | 3 | 3 +1F | 6+ 1F | 2+ 1F | 2 |
| Total | | | 10+ 4F | 18 + 6F | 30+ 10F | 12+6F | 10+ 4F |

*Source:* Based on the fieldwork (2006–2008).

[1] The Wafaq-ul-Madaris Al-Salafia is based in Jamia Salafia in Faisalabad, which is the tenth Ahl-i-Hadith madrasa included in the survey.

socioeconomic background of the students in the bigger and smaller madrasas, and if the students had different motives for joining (see table A2).

Thus, the actual sample of madrasas does not claim a random selection. Instead, it is a purposive sample carefully selected, using the wafaq data, and qualitative research techniques to capture the variation of madrasas in Pakistan using clearly defined selection criteria.

## Fieldwork Inside Madrasas

To facilitate access to 110 madrasas, I secured a letter of support from each of the five wafaqs after some trust had been built with the wafaq leadership. However, there was no compulsion for any madrasa to participate in the research: the madrasas have no formal obligation to respond to any such requests supported by the wafaq leadership. The main purpose of the support letter was for it to act as an introduction. In total, only four madrasas (1 Deobandi, 1 Barelvi, and 2 Ahl-i-Hadith) refused to take part in the research. During the visits to madrasas, I interviewed the Mohtamim (principal of the madrasa) and teachers. Within male madrasas, the 'ulama preferred arranging group interviews with the students instead of organizing individual interviews; within female madrasas, I was completely free to mingle with the students, observe lessons, and join the students for evening and after-dinner informal conversations.

The quantitative data of this study mainly draws on a self-administered questionnaire designed to cover seven core issues: socioeconomic background of the students, identification of intrahousehold decision-making process leading to enrollment of a child in a madrasa, the motives guiding the preference for madrasa education, parental influence in shaping the decision to join a madrasa, the number and profiles of the siblings of these students, the criteria shaping a student's decision to move from one madrasa to another, and the students' future plans. In addition, a brief questionnaire was designed for the head of the madrasa, including questions about history of the madrasa (who started it, when, and why), profile of the current head of the madrasa (educational qualifications, publications, representation on government committees), and basic facts about the madrasa (such as annual expenditure, sources of income, student and teacher number).

I prepared a similar questionnaire for the teachers covering their educational backgrounds and qualifications. 150 student questionnaires were distributed in each one of the Level 4 madrasas, 100 in Level 2, and 50 in Level 1. The questionnaires were divided between the final year students of theology in that madrasa and those engaged in the hifz process. I used to leave the questionnaires with the madrasa management after my field visits and they were collected later by the field assistants. The findings from this survey were primarily used to support the qualitative data to identify factors that shape the demand for madrasa education presented in chapter five.

## Fieldwork Outside Madrasas

On average I spent a month in each of the eight districts, interviewing individuals who donate to a madrasa and parents of the madrasa-going children. I did not match the donors or the parents to the selected madrasa. I made a two-to-three weeks long follow-up visit to each of these eight districts in the last five months of the fieldwork. When in a district, I also attempted to identify people supporting jihadist organizations, willing to speak about the subject.

# References


Abbas, H. 2005. *Pakistan's Drift into Extremism: Allah, the Army, and America's War on Terror.* Armonk, NY: M.E. Sharpe.

Agai, B. 2007. Islam and Education in Secular Turkey: State Policies and the Emergence of Fethullah Gulen Group. In *Schooling Islam: The Culture and Politics of Modern Muslim Education*, eds. R. W. Hefner and M. Q. Zaman. Princeton: Princeton University Press.

Ahmed, A. S. 1997. *Jinnah, Pakistan and Islamic Identity: The Search for Saladin.* New York: Routledge.

Akerlof, G. A., and R. E. Kranton. 2010. *Identity Economics: How Our Identities Shape Our Work, Wages, and Well-Being.* Oxford: Princeton University Press.

Akhtar, S. 1993. *Terror in Indian Held Kashmir: Massive Violation of Human Rights.* Islamabad: Institute of Regional Studies.

Alchian, A. 1950. Uncertainty, Evolution and Economic Theory. *Journal of Political Economy* 50 (June): 211–221.

Alchian, A., and H. Demsetz. 1972. Production, Information Costs, and Economic Organization. *American Economic Review* 62:777–795.

Ali, N. 1963. *Musalaman-i-Hind-ki Tareekha Ta'leem.* Karachi: Suleman Academy.

Ali, S. M. 1973. *After the Dark Night: Problems of Sheikh Mujibur Rahman.* Delhi: Thomson Press.

Ali, T. 1970. *Pakistan: Military Rule or People's Power?* London: Trinity Press.

Alkire, S., and S. Deneulin. 2002. Individual Motivation, Its Nature, Determinants, and Consequences for Within-Group Behaviour. In *Group Behaviour and Development: Is the Market Destroying Cooperation?* ed. J. Heyer, F. Stewart, and S. Throps. Oxford: Oxford University Press.

Al-Mohsinat Trust. 2007 (January). *Al-Mohsinat Newsletter.* Karachi: Al-Mohsinat Trust.

Alt, J. E., and K. A. Shepsle, eds. 1990. *Perspectives on Positive Political Economy.* Cambridge: Cambridge University Press.

Andrabi, T., J. Das, A. I. Khwaja, and T. Zajonc. 2005. Religious School Enrollment in Pakistan: A Look at the Data. World Bank Working Paper Series 3521.

Andrabi, T., J. Das, and A. I. Khwaja. 2006. A Dime a Day: The Possibilities and Limits of Private Schooling in Pakistan. World Bank Policy Research Working Paper no. 4066.

Andrabi, T., J. Das, A. I. Khwaja, T. Vishwanath, and T. Zajonc, and the LEAPS Team. 2008. *Pakistan: Learning and Educational Achievements in Punjab Schools (LEAPS)—Insights to Inform the Education Policy Debate.* Islamabad: World Bank. http://go.worldbank.org/YUFOT05SA0.

Arthur, W. B. 1989. Competing Technologies, Increasing Returns, and Lock-In by Historical Events. *Economic Journal* 97: 642–665.

———. 1990. Positive Feedback in the Economy. *Scientific American* 262: 92–99.

Asadullah, M. N., and N. Chaudhury. 2006. Religious Schools, Social Values, and Economic Attitudes: Evidence from Bangladesh. *QEH Working Paper Series* no. 139.

Asian Development Bank. 2008. Asian Development Bank and Pakistan: 2008—A Fact Sheet. www.adb.org/Documents/Fact_Sheets/PAK.pdf

Aydar, H. 2006. Istikhara and Dreams: An Attempt to Predict the Future through Dreams. Paper presented at the 23rd Annual Conference of the International Association for the Study of Dreams.
Azzam, M. 1996. Inequality in Quran on Divorce and Inheritance: Gender and Politics of Religion in the Middle East. In *Feminism and Islam: Legal and Literary Perspectives,* ed. M. Yamani. Berkshire: Ithaca Press.
Azzi, C., and R. Ehrenberg, 1975. Household Allocation of Time and Church Attendance. *Journal of Political Economy* 83 (February): 27–56.
Baber, H. E. 2007. Adaptive Preference. *Social Theory and Practice* 33(1): 105–126.
Bahl, A. 2007. *From Jinnah to Jihad: Pakistan's Kashmir Quest and the Limits of Realism.* New Delhi: Atlantic Publishers and Distributors.
Bano, M. 2007a. Beyond Politics: Reality of a Deobandi Madrasah in Pakistan. *Journal of Islamic Studies* 18(1): 43–68.
———. 2007b. *Contesting Ideologies and Struggle for Authority: State-Madrasa Engagement in Pakistan.* Working Paper, DIFD Religions and Development Research Programme, University of Birmingham.
———. 2008a. *Allowing for Diversity: State-Madrasa Relations in Bangladesh.* Working Paper, DIFD Religions and Development Research Programme, University of Birmingham.
———. 2008b. Dangerous Correlations: Aid's Impact on NGOs' Performance and Ability to Mobilize Members in Pakistan. *World Development* 36(11): 2297–2313.
———. forthcoming. *Breakdown in Pakistan: How Aid Is Eroding Institutions for Collective Action.* Stanford: Stanford University Press.
Bardhan, P. 1989. The New Institutional Economics and Development Theory: A Brief Critical Assessment. *World Development* 17(9): 1389–1395.
Barlas, A. 1995. *Democracy, Nationalism and Communalism: The Colonial Legacy in South Asia.* Boulder, CO and Oxford: Westview Press.
Bates, R. H. 1988. *Towards a Political Economy of Development: A Rational Choice Perspective.* Berkeley: University of California Press.
———. 1990. Macro Political Economy in the Field of Development. In *Perspectives on Positive Political Economy,* ed. J. E. Alt and K. A. Shepsle. Cambridge: Cambridge University Press.
———. 1995. Social Dilemmas and Rational Individuals: An Assessment of the New Institutionalism. In *The New Institutional Economics and Third World Development,* ed. J. Harriss, J. Hunter, and C. M. Lewis. New York: Routledge.
Becker, G. S. 1993. Nobel Lecture: The Economic Way of Looking at Behaviour. *Journal of Political Economy* 101(3): 385–409.
———. 1996. *Accounting for Tastes.* Cambridge: Harvard University Press.
Behera, A. D. 2001. The Supporting Structures for Pakistan's Proxy War in Jammu & Kashmir. *Strategic Analysis* 25(3): 393–410.
Bentham, J. 1982. An Introduction to the Principles of Morals and Legislation. In *Utilitarianism, On Liberty, Essay on Bentham, John Stuart Mill,* ed. M. Warnock. Glasgow: William Collins & Sons.
Berger, P., ed. 1999. *The Desecularization of the World: Resurgent Religion and World Politics,* Grand Rapids, MI: Eerdmans.
———. 2001. Reflections on the Sociology of Religion Today. *Sociology of Religion* 62(4): 443–454.
Bliss, C. 1993. Lifestyle and the Standard of Living. In *The Quality of Life,* ed. M. Nussbaum and A. Sen. Oxford: Clarendon Press.
Bowles, S. 2004. *Microeconomics: Behavior, Institutions and Evolution.* Princeton: Princeton University Press.

Boyd, R., and P. J. Richerson. 1985. *Culture and the Evolutionary Process.* Chicago: University of Chicago Press.
Brousseau, E., and J. M. Glachant, eds. 2008. *New Institutional Economics: A Guide Book.* Cambridge: Cambridge University Press.
Bruce, S. 1999. *Choice and Religion: A Critique of Rational Choice Theory.* Oxford: Oxford University Press.
———. 2000. *Fundamentalism.* Cambridge: Polity.
Buckley, M. E. A., and R. Fawn. 2003. *Global Responses to Terrorism: 9/11, Afghanistan, and Beyond.* New York: Routledge.
Casanova, J. 1994. *Public Religions in the Modern World.* Chicago: University of Chicago Press.
Chamberlain, M. 1994. *Knowledge and Social Practice in Medieval Damascus, 1190–1350.* Cambridge: Cambridge University Press.
Chong, D. 1991. *Collective Action and the Civil Rights Movement.* Chicago: University of Chicago Press.
———. 1996. Rational Choice Theory's Mysterious Rivals. In *The Rational Choice Controversy: Economic Models of Politics Reconsidered,* ed. J. Friedman. New Haven: Yale University Press.
Clements, F. 2003. *Conflict in Afghanistan: A Historical Encyclopaedia.* Santa Barbara, CA: ABC-CLIO.
Coase, R. H. 1937. The Nature of the Firm. *Economica* 4: 386–405.
———. 1960.The Problem of Social Cost. *Journal of Law and Economics* 3:1–44.
Cobban, A. B. 1988. *The Medieval English Universities: Oxford and Cambridge to c.1500.* Aldershot, UK: Scolar Press.
Cohen, A. 1981. *Custom and Politics in Urban Africa.* Berkeley: University of California Press.
Cohen, C., and D. Chollet. 2007. When $10 Billion Is Not Enough: Rethinking U.S. Strategy towards Pakistan. *Washington Quarterly* 30(2): 7–19.
Cohen, S. P. 2003. The Jihadist Threat to Pakistan. *Washington Quarterly* 26(3): 7–25.
Cohn, B. S. 1996. *Colonialism and Its Forms of Knowledge: The British in India.* Princeton: Princeton University Press.
Coleman, J. 1990. *Foundations of Social Theory.* Cambridge: Harvard University Press.
Collier, P., and A. Hoeffler. 2000 (May). *Greed and Grievance in Civil War.* World Bank Working Paper No. 2355. Washington D.C.
Collins, K. 2002. Clans, Pacts and Politics in Central Asia. *Journal of Democracy* 13(3): 137–152.
Connors, J. 1996. The Women's Convention in the Muslim World. In *Feminism and Islam: Legal and Literary Perspectives,* ed. M. Yamani. Berkshire: Ithaca Press.
Cornell, V. J., ed. 2007. *Voices of Islam: Voices of Tradition.* Westport, CT: Praeger.
Cockcroft, A. et al. 2009. Challenging the Myths about Madaris in Pakistan: A National Household Survey of Enrolment and Reasons for Choosing Religious Schools. *International Journal of Educational Development* 29(4): 342–349.
Donnan, H., ed. 2002. *Interpreting Islam.* Thousand Oaks, CA: Sage.
Dorronsoro, G. 2002. Pakistan and the Taliban: State Policy, Religious Networks and Political Connections. In *Pakistan: Nationalism without a Nation?* ed. C. Jaffrelot. London: Zed Books.
Doumani, B., ed. 2006. *Academic Freedom after September 11.* New York: Zone Books.
Durkheim, E. 1915. *The Elementary Forms of the Religious Life.* London: George Allen & Unwin.
Edwardes, M. 1971. *Nehru: A Political Biography.* London: Allen Lane.
Eickelman, D. F., and J. Piscatori. 1996. *Muslim Politics.* Princeton: Princeton University Press.

El Guidi, F. 1999. *Veil: Modernity, Privacy and Resistance.* Oxford: Berg.
Ellickson, R. C. 1991. *Order without Law: How Neighbors Settle Disputes.* Cambridge: Cambridge University Press.
Elster, J. 1983. *Sour Grapes: Studies in the Subversion of Rationality.* Cambridge: Cambridge University Press.
———. 1985. Rationality, Morality, and Collective Action. *Ethics* 96:136–155.
———. 1986. Introduction. In *Rational Choice,* ed. J. Elster. Oxford: Basil Blackwell.
———. 2006. Motivations and Beliefs in Suicide Missions. In *Making Sense of Suicide Missions,* ed. D. Gambetta. Oxford: Oxford University Press.
Engineer, A. A. 1998. *Dossier 20: Indian Islam and Reform Movements in Post-Independence India.* Mumbai: Centre for Study of Society and Secularism.
Ensminger. J. 1992. *Making a Market: The Institutional Transformation of an African Society.* Cambridge: Cambridge University Press.
Esposito, J. L. 1992. *The Islamic Threat: Myth or Reality.* New York: Oxford University Press.
———. 1999. *The Oxford History of Islam.* New York: Oxford University Press.
Euben, R. 1999. *Enemy in the Mirror: Islamic Fundamentalism and the Limits of Modern Rationalism—A Work of Comparative Political Theory.* Princeton: Princeton University Press.
Evans, H. 1988. Bangladesh: South Asia's Unknown Quantity. *Asian Affairs* 19(3): 306–317.
Fair, C. C. 2008. *The Madrassah Challenge: Militancy and Religious Education in Pakistan.* Washington, DC: U.S. Institute of Peace Press.
Fehr, E., and Schmidt, M. 1999. The Theory of Fairness, Competition, and Cooperation. *Quarterly Journal of Economics* 114(3): 817–868.
Frey, B. S. 1994. How Intrinsic Motivation Is Crowded Out and In. *Rationality and Society* 6(3): 334–352.
———. 1997. *Not Just for Money: An Economic Theory of Personal Motivation.* Aldershot, UK: Edward Elgar.
Frey, B. S., and F. Oberholzer-Gee. 1997. The Cost of Price Incentives: An Empirical Analysis of Motivation Crowding Out. *American Economic Review* 87(4): 746–755.
Friedman, J., ed.1996. *The Rational Choice Controversy: Economic Models of Politics Reconsidered.* New Haven: Yale University Press.
Furseth, I., and P. Repstad. 2006. *An Introduction to the Sociology of Religion: Classical and Contemporary Perspectives.* Aldershot, UK: Ashgate.
Gambetta, D. 1987. *Were They Pushed or Did They Jump? Individual Decision Mechanisms in Education.* Cambridge: Cambridge University Press.
———. 2006. Can We Make Sense of Suicide Missions? In *Making Sense of Suicide Missions,* ed. D. Gambetta. Oxford: Oxford University Press.
Gambetta, D., and S. Hertog. 2006. *Engineers of Jihad.* Department of Sociology: 2007–10 Working Paper, University of Oxford.
Gandhi, M. 1958. *All Men Are Brothers: Life and Thoughts of Mahatma Gandhi as Told in His Own Words.* Geneva: UNESCO.
Ganguly, S. 1986. *The Origins of War in South Asia: Indo-Pakistan Conflicts since 1947.* Boulder, CO: Westview Press.
———. 2006. The Rise of Islamist Militancy in Bangladesh. Special Report, U.S. Institute of Peace.
Gellner, D. 1982. Max Weber, Capitalism and the Religion of India. *Sociology* 16(4): 526–543.

Glock, C. Y. 1964. The Role of Deprivation in the Origin and Evolution of Religious Groups. In *Religion and Social Conflict,* ed. R. Lee and M. Marty. New York: Oxford University Press.

Goldthorpe, J. H. 1998. Rational Action Theory for Sociology. *British Journal of Sociology* 49(2): 167–192.

Goode, W. J. 1978. *The Celebration of Heroes: Prestige as a Social Control System.* Berkeley: University of California Press.

Goodin, R. E., ed. 1996. *The Theory of Institutional Design.* Cambridge: Cambridge University Press.

Gordon, M. S. 2002. *Understanding Islam: Origins, Beliefs, Practices, Holy Texts, Sacred Places.* New York: Oxford University Press.

Government of Pakistan [GOP]. 2006. *Report on Deeni Madaris of Pakistan: Base-Line Information 2003–2004 & 2004–2005.* Islamabad: Academy of Educational Planning and Management, Ministry of Education.

Granovetter, M. 1973. The Strength of Weak Ties. *American Journal of Sociology* 78(6): 1360–1380.

———. 1985. Economic Action and Social Structure: The Problem of Embeddedness. *American Journal of Sociology* 91(3):481–510.

Grare, F. 2006a. *Pakistan: The Myth of an Islamist Peril.* Carnegie Endowment for International Peace Policy Brief 45.

———. 2006b. *Pakistan-Afghanistan Relations in the Post-9/11 Era.* South Asia Project, Carnegie Endowment for International Peace.

Green, D. P., and I. Shapiro. 1994. *Pathologies of Rational Choice Theory: A Critique of Applications in Political Science.* New Haven: Yale University Press.

Green, V. H. H. 1974. *A History of Oxford University.* London: B. T. Batsford.

Greif, A. 2006. *Institutions and the Path to the Modern Economy: Lessons from Medieval Trade.* Cambridge: Cambridge University Press.

Hackett, M. B. 1984. The University as a Corporate Body. In *The History of the University of Oxford,* ed. J. I. Catto. Vol. 1. Oxford: Clarendon Press.

Haq, M. 1997. *Human Development in South Asia 1997.* Karachi: Oxford University Press.

Haqqani, H. 2003. Pakistan's Endgame in Kashmir. *India Review* 2(3): 34–54.

———. 2005. *Pakistan: Between Mosque and Military.* Lahore: Vanguard Books.

Hardin, G. 1968. The Tragedy of Commons. *Science* 162: 1243–1248.

Hardin, R. 1982. *Collective Action.* Baltimore: Johns Hopkins University Press.

Harford, T. 2008. *The Logic of Life: Uncovering the New Economics of Everything.* London: Little, Brown.

Harsanyi, J. C. 1982. Mortality and the Theory of Rational Behaviour. In *Utilitarianism and Beyond,* ed. A. Sen and B. Williams. Cambridge: Cambridge University Press.

Hassan, R. 1987. Religion, Society, and the State in Pakistan: Pirs and Politics. *Asian Survey* 27(5): 552–565.

Hechter, M. 1987. *Principles of Group Solidarity.* Berkeley: University of California Press.

Hefner, R. W., and M. Q. Zaman, eds. 2007. *Schooling Islam: The Culture and Politics of Modern Muslim Education.* Princeton: Princeton University Press.

Helmke, G., and S. Levitsky. 2004. Informal Institutions and Comparative Politics: A Research Agenda. *Perspectives on Politics* 2(4): 725–740.

Henderson, S. L. 2002. Selling Civil Society, Western Aid and the Nongovernmental Organization Sector in Russia. *Comparative Political Studies* 35(2): 139–167.

Hilali, A. Z. 2005. *US-Pakistan Relationship: Soviet Invasion of Afghanistan.* Aldershot, UK: Ashgate.

Hirschman, A. O. 1985. Against Parsimony: Three Easy Ways of Complicating Some Categories of Economic Discourse. *Economics and Philosophy* 1: 7–21.

Hobsbawm, E., ed. 1996. Introduction: Invented Traditions. In *The Invention of Tradition,* ed. R. Hobsbawm and T. Ranger. Cambridge: Cambridge University Press.

Hoffman-Ladd, V. 1987. Polemics on the Modesty and Segregation of Women in Contemporary Egypt. *International Journal of Middle Eastern Studies* 19: 23–50.

Hope, M., and J. Young. 1994. Islam and Ecology. *Cross Currents* 44(2): 180–193.

Huque, A. S., and M. Y. Akhter. 1987. The Ubiquity of Islam: Religion and Society in Bangladesh. *Pacific Affairs* 60(2): 200–225.

Hussain, R. 2005. *Pakistan and the Emergence of Islamic Militancy in Afghanistan.* Aldershot, UK: Ashgate.

Hussain, Z. 2007. *Frontline Pakistan: The Struggle with Militant Islam.* New York: Columbia University Press.

Iannacone, L. R. 1992. Sacrifice and Stigma: Reducing Free-Riding in Cults, Communes and Other Collectives. *Journal of Political Economy* 100(2): 271–292.

———. 1995. Risk, Rationality, and Religious Portfolio. *Economic Inquiry* 33: 285–295.

Iqbal, M. 2009. *The Reconstruction of Religious Thought in Islam.* London: Dodo Press.

Interface. 2007. Fears of Break-Up of Wafaq-ul-Madaris. August 5. www.interface.edu.pk/students/Aug/Wafaq-ul-Madaris.asp.

International Crisis Group (ICG). 2002. Pakistan: Madrasas, Extremism, and the Military. ICG Asia Report 36, Islamabad/Brussels.

Jaffrelot, C., ed. 2002. *Pakistan: Nationalism without a Nation?* London: Zed Books.

Jalandari, M. H. 2006. Deeni Madaris Aur 'Asari Takazaat: Aaik Haqeeqat Pasandana Jaiza. *Wafaq-ul-Madaris Al-Arabia Pakistan Monthly* no. 9.

James, M., and P. Lyon. 1993. *Pakistan Chronicle.* London: Hurst.

Kaplan, M. A. 1976. Means/Ends Rationality. *Ethics* 87(1): 61–65.

Karmi, G. 1996. Women, Islam and Patriarchalism. In *Feminism and Islam: Legal and Literary Perspectives,* ed. M. Yamani. Berkshire: Ithaca Press.

Kepel, G. 2006. *Jihad: The Trail of Political Islam.* Trans. A. F. Roberts. London: I.B. Tauris.

Khaldun, Ibn. 1967. *The Muqaddimah: An Introduction to History.* Trans. Franz Rosenthal; abridged and edited by N.J. Dawood. Princeton: Princeton University Press.

Knight, J. 1992. *Institutions and Social Conflict.* Cambridge: Cambridge University Press.

Kochhar, R. 1999. Science and Domination: India Before and After. *Current Science* 76(4): 596–601.

Krebs, D. 1982. Psychological Approaches to Altruism: An Evaluation in Ethics. *Ethics* 92: 447–458.

Kreps, D. M. 1997. The Interaction between Norms and Economic Incentives: Intrinsic Motivation and Extrinsic Incentives. *American Economic Review* 87(2): 359–364.

Kukreja, V. 2003. *Contemporary Pakistan: Political Processes, Conflicts, and Crises.* New Delhi: Sage.

Krueger, A. B. 2007. *What Makes a Terrorist: Economics and the Roots of Terrorism.* Princeton: Princeton University Press.

Lapidus, I. 1997. Islamic Revival and Modernity: The Contemporary Movements and Historical Paradigms. *Journal of Economic and Social History of the Orient* 40(4): 444–460.

Lawrence, C. H. 1984. The University in State and Church. In *The History of the University of Oxford,* ed. J. I. Catto. Vol. 1. Oxford: Clarendon Press.
Leaman, O. 1999. *A Brief Introduction to Islamic Philosophy.* Cambridge: Polity Press.
Leff, G. 1968. *Paris and Oxford Universities in the Thirteenth and Fourteenth Centuries.* New York: John Wiley & Sons.
Lepper, M. R., and D. Greene, eds. 1978. *The Hidden Costs of Reward: New Perspectives on the Psychology of Human Motivation.* Hillsdale, NJ: Erlbaum.
Lewis, B. 2002. *What Went Wrong? Western Impact and Middle Eastern Response.* Oxford: Oxford University Press.
Libecap, G. D. 1989. *Contracting for Property Rights.* Cambridge: Cambridge University Press.
Liebowitz, S. J., and S. E. Margolis. 1995. Path Dependence, Lock-In, and History. *Journal of Law, Economics and Organization* 1: 205–226.
Lindbeck, A. 1997. Incentives and Social Norms in Household Behavior. *American Economic Review* 87(2): 370–377.
MacIntyre, A. 1988. *Whose Justice? Which Rationality?* Notre Dame: University of Notre Dame Press.
MacLeod, A. E. 1991. *Accommodating Protest: Working Women, the New Veiling and Change in Cairo.* New York: Columbia University Press.
Mahmood, S. 2005. *Politics of Piety: The Islamic Revival and the Feminist Subject.* Princeton: Princeton University Press.
Makdisi, G. 1981. *The Rise of Colleges: Institutions of Learning in Islam and the West.* Edinburgh: Edinburgh University Press.
Malik, J. 1996. *Colonialization of Islam: Dissolution of Traditional Institutions in Pakistan.* Lahore: Vanguard.
———. 1997. Dynamics among Traditional Religious Scholars and their Institutions in Contemporary South Asia. *Muslim World* 87(3–4): 199–220.
Mann, E. A. 1989. Religion, Money and Status: Competition for Resources at the Shrine of Shah Jamal, Aligarh. In *Muslim Shrines in India: Their Character, History and Significance,* ed. C. W. Troll. New Delhi: Oxford University Press.
Margolis, H. 1982. *Selfishness, Altruism, and Rationality: A Theory of Social Choice.* Cambridge: Cambridge University Press.
Markey, D. S. 2008. *Securing Pakistan's Tribal Belt.* Washington D.C.: Council on Foreign Relations Press.
Martin, G. 2006. *Understanding Terrorism: Challenges, Perspectives, and Issues.* Thousand Oaks, CA: SAGE.
Marx, K., and F. Engels. 1964. *On Religion.* New York: Schocken Books.
Meher, J. 2004. *America's Afghanistan War: The Success That Failed.* New Delhi: Gyan Books.
Menard, C., and M. M. Shirley, eds. 2005. *The Handbook of New Institutional Economics.* Netherland: Springer.
Metcalf, B. 1978. The Madrasa at Deoband: A Model for Religious Education in India. *Modern Asian Studies* 12: 111–134.
———. 1982. *Islamic Revival in British India: Deoband, 1986–1900.* Princeton: Princeton University Press.
Mill, J. S. 1982. Utilitarianism. An Introduction to the Principles of Morals and Legislation. In *Utilitarianism, On Liberty, Essay on Bentham, John Stuart Mill,* ed. M. Warnock. Glasgow: William Collins & Sons.
Miller, G. J. 1992. *Managerial Dilemmas: The Political Economy of Hierarchy.* Cambridge: Cambridge University Press.
Minault, G. 1998. *Secluded Scholars: Women's Education and Muslim Social Reform in Colonial India.* New Delhi: Oxford University Press.

Ministry of Education (MOE). 2006. *National Education Census*. Government of Pakistan. Islamabad: Academy of Educational Planning and Management.
Misra, A. 2003. Rise of Religious Parties in Pakistan: Causes and Prospects. *Strategic Analysis* 27(2): 186–215.
Montiel, P. 1993. *Informal Financial Markets in Developing Countries*. Oxford: Blackwell.
Morris, B. 1987. *Anthropological Studies of Religion: An Introductory Text*. Cambridge: Cambridge University Press.
Mumtaz, K., and F. Shaheed, eds. 1987. *Women of Pakistan: Two Steps Forward, One Step Back?* London: Zed Books.
Nair, P. 2009. The State and Madrasas in India. Working Paper, DFID Religions and Development Research Programme, University of Birmingham.
Nasr, S. V. R. 2000. The Rise of Sunni Militancy in Pakistan: The Changing Role of Islamism and the Ulama in Society and Politics. *Modern Asian Studies* 34(1): 139–180.
———. 2002. Islam, the State and the Rise of Sectarian Militancy in Pakistan. In *Pakistan: Nationalism without a Nation?* ed. C. Jaffrelot. London: Zed Books.
Nasulgc, C. F., and S. M. O'Briant. 2002. Foreign Student Enrollment Up, but Paperwork Delays Lengthen. Press Release, National Association of State Universities and Land-Grant Colleges.
Nelson, M. J. 2006. Muslims, Markets and the Meaning of a "Good" Education in Pakistan. *Asian Survey* 46(5): 699–720.
Nizami, F. A. 1983. Madrasahs, Scholars and Saints: Muslim Response to the British Presence in Delhi and Upper Doab, 1803–1857. PhD diss., University of Oxford.
Noman, O. 1990. *Pakistan: A Political and Economic History since 1947*. London: Kegan Paul.
Noor, F. A. 2008. The Uncertain Fate of Southeast Asian Students in the Madrasas of Pakistan. In *The Madrasa in Asia: Political Activism and Transnational Linkages*, eds. Y. Sikand and M. van Bruinessen. Amsterdam: Amsterdam University Press.
North, D. C. 1981. *Structure and Change in Economic History*. New York: Norton.
———. 1985. Transaction Costs in History. *Journal of European Economic History* 6: 703–716.
———. 1990. *Institutions, Institutional Change and Economic Performance*. Cambridge: Cambridge University Press.
———. 1995. The New Institutional Economics and Third World Development. In *The New Institutional Economics and Third World Development*, ed. J. Harriss, J. Hunter, and C. M. Lewis. London and New York: Routledge.
———. 2005. *Understanding the Process of Economic Change*. Princeton: Princeton University Press.
North, D. C., and R. P. Thomas. 1973. *The Rise of the Western World: A New Economic History*. Cambridge: Cambridge University Press.
Norris, P., and R. Inglehart. 2004. *Sacred and Secular: Religion and Politics Worldwide*. Cambridge: Cambridge University Press
Nussbaum, M. C. 1999. *Sex and Social Justice*. Oxford: Oxford University Press.
———. 2001. Symposium on Amartya Sen's Philosophy: 5 Adaptive Preferences and Women's Options. *Economics and Philosophy* 17(1): 67–88.
Organization for Economic Cooperation and Development (OECD). 2007. *Informal Institutions: How Social Norms Help or Hinder Development*. Paris: OECD.
Olson, M. 1971. *The Logic of Collective Action: Public Goods, and the Theory of Groups*. Cambridge: Harvard University Press.
Ostrom, E. 1990. *Governing the Commons: The Evolution of Institutions for Collective Action*. Cambridge: Cambridge University Press.

———. 2003. How Types of Goods and Property Rights Jointly Affect Collective Action. *Journal of Theoretical Politics* 15(3): 239–270.

———. 2005. Doing Institutional Analysis: Digging Deeper than Markets and Hierarchies. In *The Handbook of New Institutional Economics,* eds. C. Menard and M. M. Shirley. Berlin: Springer.

Pakistan Madrasa Education Board (PMEB). 2002. *First Annual Report: August 2001–September 2002.* Islamabad: Government of Pakistan.

Parsons, T. 1937. *The Structure of Social Action.* Glencoe, IL: Free Press.

Pierson, P. 2000. Increasing Returns, Path Dependence, and the Study of Politics. *American Political Science Review* 94(2): 251–267.

Piscatori, J. 1988. *Islam in a World of Nation-States.* Cambridge: Cambridge University Press.

Platteau, J. P. 2008. The Causes of Institutional Inefficiency: A Development Perspective. In *New Institutional Economics: A Guidebook,* ed. E. Brousseau and J. M. Glachant. Cambridge: Cambridge University Press.

Plett, B. 2006. *Madrasas Nothing to Do with 7/7* http://news.bbc.co.uk/1/hi/world/south_asia/5148502.stm.

Popkin, S. L. 1979. *The Rational Peasant.* Berkeley: University of California Press.

Prest, J. 1993. *The Illustrated History of Oxford University.* Oxford: Oxford University Press.

Rabasa, A. et al. 2004. *The Muslim World after 9/11.* Pittsburgh: RAND Corporation.

Rais, R. B., ed. 1997. *State, Society, and Democratic Change in Pakistan.* Karachi: Oxford University Press.

Rao, C. N. R. 2008. Science and Technology Policies: The Case of India. *Technology in Society* 30 (3–4): 242–247.

Rashid, A. 1998. Pakistan and the Taliban. In *Fundamentalism Reborn? Afghanistan and the Taliban,* ed. W. Maley. London: Hurst.

———. 2001. *Taliban: Islam, Oil and the New Great Game in Central Asia.* London: I.B. Tauris.

Ricolfi, L. 2006. Palestinians, 1981–2003. In *Making Sense of Suicide Missions,* ed. D. Gambetta. Oxford: Oxford University Press.

Robinson, F. 1997. Ottomans-Safavids-Mughals: Shared Knowledge and Connective Systems. *Journal of Islamic Studies* 8(2): 151–184.

———. 2000. *Islam and Muslim History in South Asia.* New Delhi: Oxford University Press.

———. 2001a. Islam and the West: Clash of Civilisations? *Asian Affairs* 33(3): 307–320.

———. 2001b. *The 'Ulama of Farangi Mahall and Islamic Change in South Asia.* London: Hurst.

———. 2007a. Islamic Reform and Modernity in South Asia. *Modern Asian Studies* 41(5): 1–23.

———. 2007b. *Islam, South Asia, and the West.* New Delhi: Oxford University Press.

Ronald, A. S. 2001. *Women in Islam: The Western Experience.* London: Routledge.

Roy, O. 1994. *The Failure of Political Islam.* London: I.B. Tauris.

———. 2002. The Taliban: A Strategic Tool for Pakistan. In *Pakistan: Nationalism without a Nation?* ed. C. Jaffrelot. London: Zed Books.

Sachar, R. 2006. *Prime Minister's High Level Committee, on Social, Economic and Educational Status of the Muslim Community of India.* Delhi: Government of India.

Sager, P. 2005. *Oxford and Cambridge: An Uncommon History.* London: Thames and Hudson.

Saliba, G. 1994. *A History of Arabic Astronomy: Planetary Theories during the Golden Age of Islam.* New York: New York University Press.

———. 2007. *Islamic Science and the Making of the European Renaissance.* Cambridge: MIT Press.
Schofield, N. 1985. Anarchy, Altruism, and Cooperation: A Review. *Social Choice and Welfare* 2: 207–219.
Schofield, V. 2003. *Kashmir in Conflict: India, Pakistan and the Unending War.* London: I.B. Tauris.
Scitovsky, T. 1976. *The Joyless Economy.* New York: Oxford University Press.
Seal, A. 1968. *The Emergence of Indian Nationalism: Competition and Collaboration in the Later Nineteenth Century.* Cambridge: Cambridge University Press.
Sen, A. 1977. Rational Fools: A Critique of the Behavioral Foundations of Economic Theory. *Philosophy and Public Affairs* 6(4): 317–344.
———. 1995. Gender Inequality and Theories of Justice. In *Women, Culture, and Development,* eds. M. Nussbaum and J. Glover. Oxford: Clarendon Press.
———. 2002. *Rationality and Freedom.* Cambridge: Harvard University Press.
———. 2006. *Identity and Violence: The Illusion of Destiny.* London: Allen Lane.
Sewell, W. H. 1996. Three Temporalities: Towards an Eventful Sociology. In *The Historic Turn in the Human Sciences,* ed. T. J. McDonald. Ann Arbor: University of Michigan Press.
Shafiq, M. M., and A. H. Sinno. 2010. Education, Income and Support for Bombings: Evidence from Six Muslim Countries. *Journal of Conflict Resolution* 54(1): 146–178.
Shafqat, S. 2002. From Official Islam to Islamism: The Rise of Dawat-ul-Irshad and Lashkar-e-Taiba. In *Pakistan: Nationalism without a Nation?,* ed. C. Jaffrelot London: Zed Books.
Shaheed, F. 2009. Gender, Religion and the Quest for Justice in Pakistan. Final Research Report prepared for the project on Religion, Politics and Gender Equality, United Nations Research Institute for Social Development.
Sherani, A. R. 1991. Ulema and Pir in the Politics of Pakistan. In *Economy and Culture in Pakistan: Migrants and Cities in a Muslim Society,* eds. H. Donnan and P. Werbner. Basingstoke: Macmillan.
Shibli, M. 2009. Kashmir: Islam, Identity and Insurgency (with case study: Hizbul Mujahideen). *Kashmir Affairs.* http://www.spearheadresearch.org/pages/documents/Islam,identity_and_insurgency.pdf
Sikand, Y. 2002. *Reforming the Indian Madrasas: Contemporary Muslim Voices.* New Delhi: Genuine Publications.
Simmel, G. 1959. *Sociology of Religion.* New York: Wisdom.
Simon, H. A. 1962. The Architecture of Complexity. *Proceedings of the American Philosophical Society* 106(6): 467–482.
Singer, P. W. 2001. Pakistan's Madrasahs: Ensuring a System of Education not Jihad. Brookings Institute, Analysis Paper no. 4.
Sinha, J. N. 1991. Science and the Indian National Congress. In *Science and Empire: Essays in Indian Context, 1700–1947,* ed. D. Kumar. Delhi: Anamika Prakashan.
Smith, A. 1976. *The Theory of Moral Sentiments.* Oxford: Oxford University Press.
Smith, J. I., and Y. Y. Haddad. 2002. *The Islamic Understanding of Death and Resurrection.* Oxford: Oxford University Press.
Sober, E., and D. S. Wilson. 1998. *Unto Others: The Evolution and Psychology of Unselfish Behavior.* Cambridge: Harvard University Press.
Solow, R. 1990. *The Labour Market as a Social Institution.* Cambridge: Basil Blackwell.
Sorokin, P. 1957. *Social and Cultural Dynamics: A Study of Change in Major Systems of Art, Truth, Ethics, Law and Social Relationships.* London: Peter Owen.

Southern, R. W. 1984. From Schools to University. In *The History of the University of Oxford,* ed, J. I. Catto. Vol. 1. Oxford: Clarendon Press.
Stark, R., and W. S. Bainbridge. 1985. *The Future of Religion.* Berkeley: University of California Press.
Stark, R., and R. Finke. 2000. *Acts of Faith: Explaining the Human Side of Religion.* Berkeley: University of California Press.
Stern, J. 2000. Pakistan's Jihad Culture. *Foreign Affairs* 79(6): 115–126.
Stolz, J. 2006. Salvation Goods and Religious Markets: Integrating Rational Choice and Weberian Perspectives. *Social Compass* 53(10): 13–32.
Talbot, I. 1998. *Pakistan: A Modern History.* London: Hurst.
———. 2000. *India and Pakistan.* London: Arnold.
Tapper, T., and D. Palfreyman. 2000. *Oxford and the Decline of the Collegiate Tradition.* London: Wobrun Press.
Tapper, T., and B. Salter. 1992. *Oxford and Cambridge and the Changing Idea of the University: The Challenge to Donnish Domination.* Buckingham: SRHE and Open University Press.
Tessler, M., and D. H. Robbins. 2007. What Leads Some Ordinary Arab Men and Women to Approve of Terrorist Acts against the United States. *Journal of Conflict Resolution* 51(2): 305–328.
Tibi. B. 1998. *The Challenge of Fundamentalism: Political Islam and the New World Disorder.* Berkeley: University of California Press.
Titmuss, R. M. 1970. *The Gift Relationship: From Human Blood to Social Policy.* London: Allen and Unwin.
UNICEF. 2008. Education Statistics: Sweden. Division of Policy and Practice: Statistics and Monitoring Section. http://www.childinfo.org/files/IND_Sweden.pdf.
UNESCO. 2008. *Overcoming Inequality: Why Governance Matters.* Paris: UNESCO.
Usmani, M. T. 2004. *Naqoosh-e-Raftagan.* Karachi: Maktaba Maruf-ul-Quran.
Varisco, D. M. 2005. *Islam Obscured: The Rhetoric of Anthropological Representation.* New York: Palgrave Macmillan.
Wade, R. 1998. *Village Republics: Economics Conditions for Collective Action in South Asia.* Cambridge: Cambridge University Press.
Wafaq-ul-Madaris. 2006. *Wafaq-ul-Madaris Al-Arabia Tarjaman.* Monthly Newsletter no. 9.
Waseem, M. 1994. *Politics and the State in Pakistan.* Islamabad: National Institute of Historical and Cultural Research.
Weaver, M. A. 2002. *Pakistan: In the Shadow of Jihad and Afghanistan.* New York: Farrar, Straus and Giroux.
Weber, M. 1946. *From Max Weber: Essays in Sociology,* eds. H. H. Gerth and C. W. Mills. Oxford: Oxford University Press.
———. 1993. *The Sociology of Religion.* Boston: Beacon Press.
Wickham, C. R. 2002. *Mobilizing Islam: Religion, Activism and Political Change in Egypt.* New York: Columbia University Press.
Williamson, O. E. 1975. *Markets and Hierarchies: Analysis and Antitrust Implications.* New York: Free Press.
———. 1985. *The Economic Institutions of Capitalism.* New York: Free Press.
———. 2000. The New Institutional Economics: Taking Stock, Looking Ahead. *Journal of Economic Literature* 38(3): 595–613.
Wilson, B. 1982. *Religion in Sociological Perspective.* Oxford: Oxford University Press.
Wolpert, S. A. 1989. *Jinnah of Pakistan.* Karachi: Oxford University Press.
World Bank. 2002. *Pakistan Poverty Assessment—Poverty in Pakistan: Vulnerabilities, Social Gaps, and Rural Dynamics.* Islamabad: World Bank.

———. 2007a. Edstats: Summary Education Profile Pakistan. http://devdata.worldbank.org/edstats/SummaryEducationProfiles/CountryData/GetShowData.asp?sCtry=PAK.

———. 2007b. Pakistan Data Profile. http://devdata.worldbank.org/external/CPProfile.asp?PTYPE=CP&CCODE=PAK.

Wright, D. 1987. Islam and Bangladeshi Polity. *Journal of South Asian Studies* 10(2): 15–27.

Yadav, Y. 1999. Electoral Politics in the Time of Change: India's Third Electoral System, 1989–99. *Economic and Political Weekly* 34 (August 21–28): 2393–2399.

Young, H. P. 2001. *Individual Strategy and Social Structure: An Evolutionary Theory of Institutions.* Princeton: Princeton University Press.

Young, L., ed. 1997. *Rational Choice Theory and Religion: Summary and Assessment.* New York: Routledge.

Zaidi, A. S. 1999. *Issues in Pakistan's Economy.* Karachi: Oxford University Press.

———. 2003. *Continuity and Change: Socio-Political and Institutional Dynamics in Pakistan.* Karachi: City Press.

Zakaria, F. 2001. The Politics of Rage: Why Do They Hate Us? *Newsweek* (October 15).

Zaman, M. Q. 1999. Religious Education and Rhetoric of Reform: The Madrasa in British India and Pakistan. *Comparative Studies in Society and History* 41(2): 294–323.

———. 2002. *The Ulama in Contemporary Islam: Custodians of Change.* Princeton: Princeton University Press.

———. 2007. Tradition and Authority in Deobandi Madrasas of South Asia. In *Schooling Islam: The Culture and Politics of Modern Muslim Education,* ed. R. W. Hefner and M. Q. Zaman. Princeton: Princeton University Press.

Zuhur, S. 1992. *Revealing Reveiling: Islamist Gender Ideology in Contemporary Egypt.* Albany: State University of New York Press.

# Index

Note: Page numbers followed by *m* or *t* indicate maps or tables.